Leavis and Lonergan

Leavis and Lonergan

Literary Criticism and Philosophy

Joseph Fitzpatrick

Hamilton Books
Lanham • Boulder • New York • Toronto • London

Published by Hamilton Books
An imprint of The Rowman & Littlefield Publishing Group, Inc.
4501 Forbes Boulevard, Suite 200, Lanham, Maryland 20706
Hamilton Books Acquisitions Department (301) 459-3366

6 Tinworth Street, London SE11 5AL, United Kingdom

Copyright © 2021 by The Rowman & Littlefield Publishing Group, Inc.

All rights reserved. No part of this book may be produced in any form or by any electronic means, including information storage and retrieval systems,without written permission from the publisher, except by a reviewer who may quote passages in a review.

British Library Cataloguing in Publication Information Available

Library of Congress Control Number Available

ISBN: 978-0-7618-7137-8 (pbk.: alk paper)
ISBN: 978-0-7618-7138-5 (electronic)

∞™ The paper used in this publication meets the minimum requirements of American National Standard for Information Sciences Permanence of Paper for Printed Library Materials, ANSI/NISO Z39.48-1992.

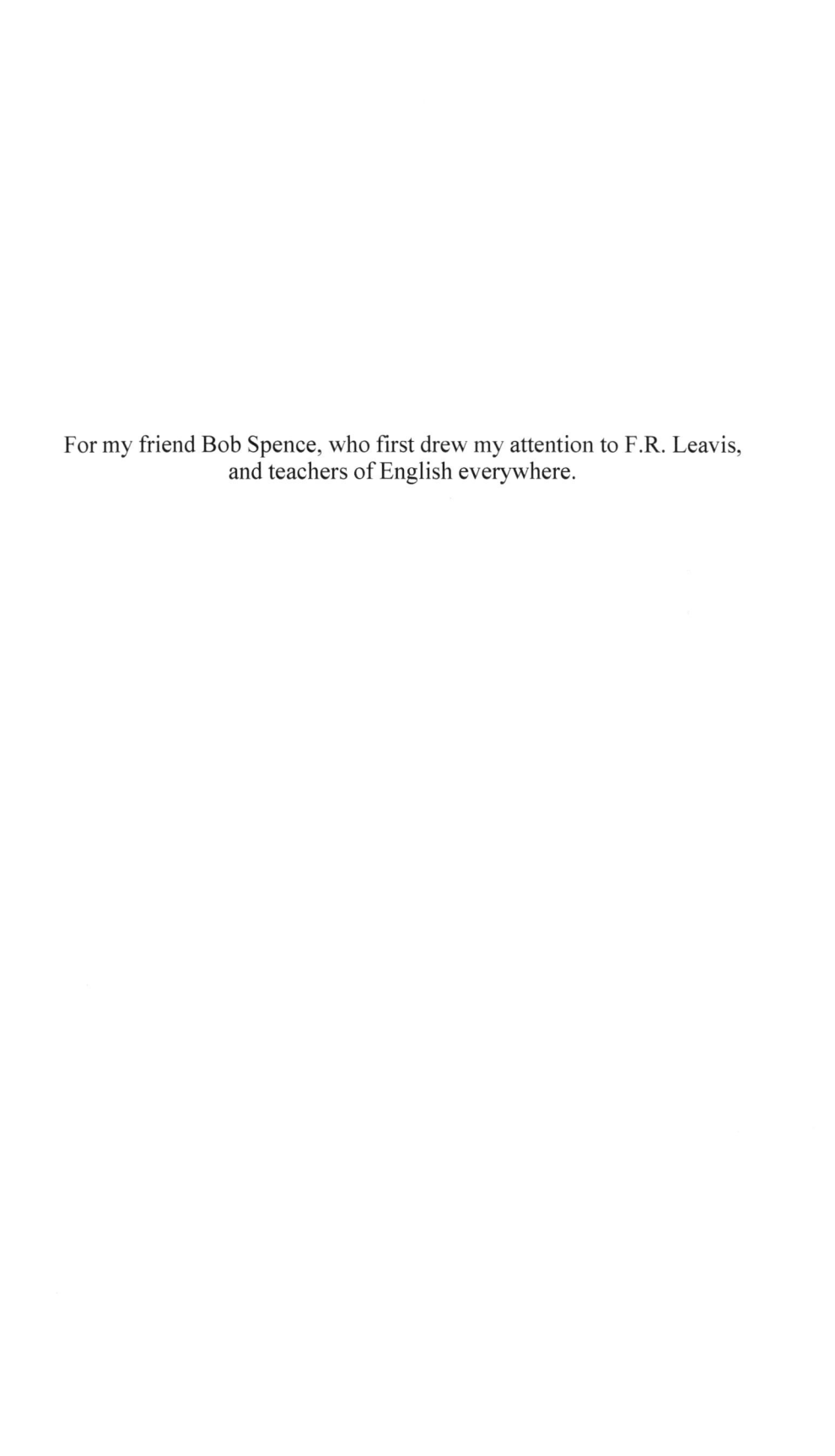

For my friend Bob Spence, who first drew my attention to F.R. Leavis, and teachers of English everywhere.

Contents

Acknowledgments		ix
Introduction		1
1	What Lonergan is About	7
2	Leavis and Lonergan	39
3	Poetry: Lonergan, Leavis and Langer	67
4	The Arnoldian Influence	99
5	Reading as Understanding	137
6	Hemingway's Naturalism	157
7	Conversion in *Anna Karenina*	175
Conclusion		191
Bibliography		203
Index		207
About the Author		209

Acknowledgments

I have received the support of a number of people while preparing this book for publication. I would like to record my thanks for the generous support of Professor Patrick Byrne and Kerry Cronin at the Lonergan Centre in Boston College. I am also grateful for the wise advice and helpful questions and suggestions made by two scholars who are specialists in English literature, Doctor Colin Wood and emeritus Professor Michael Bell, along with philosopher William Charlton, who were kind enough to read drafts of my work. I also owe a debt of gratitude to Dr. Robin Leavis who warmed to my project and gave me permission to quote from the writings of his father, F.R. Leavis. Thanks also go to the publishers of the books by Lonergan quoted in the text. I would like to extend thanks to the editors of *New Blackfriars* and *Method: Journal of Lonergan Studies*, for their permission to reuse material that originally appeared in their journals in article form. A special thanks is owed to former HMI colleagues, Colin Roberts and the late Alf Monk, who studied under Leavis at Downing College and provided invaluable insights into Leavis's teaching styles and methods. I have also enjoyed working with Brooke Bures and Della Vache of Hamilton Books who were unfailingly efficient and helpful. Finally and most importantly, I must thank my wife Eileen for the extraordinary patience she has shown over recent months and her great generosity of spirit in the loving support she has consistently provided.

Introduction

This is a book about mutuality and complementarity. On the one hand, there is the English literary critic, FR Leavis. For most of his long academic career he looked to philosophy in the hope of finding support for his critical approach to literary texts, but, given the dominance of Logical Positivism in British philosophy, for most of that time he failed to find the support he sought. On the other hand, there is the Canadian Jesuit philosopher-theologian, Bernard Lonergan, whose philosophy of Critical Realism, I shall argue, provides exactly the kind of support Leavis was looking for. What is more, Lonergan's scholarly aim was to find a method of investigation for the discipline of theology which would also, he claimed, serve as a method of investigation for all of the humane disciplines that sought to bring the best of the past into a living and significant relationship with the present and the future—such as literary criticism as conceived by Leavis. That is essentially what this book is about.

Along the way I argue that the scholarly writings of these two twentieth century men of genius have things of importance to say to us today not only in their respective fields of philosophy and literary criticism but things concerning the quality and health of contemporary culture. This is because the affinity between Lonergan and Leavis I discern is not only intellectual but also relates to their moral outlook. My argument, in summary, is

- that Lonergan's epistemology underwrites Leavis's approach to literary criticism
- that it endorses Leavis's contention that English Literature is a valid university discipline

- that Lonergan's exploration of interiority and his analysis of the relationship between subjectivity and objectivity provide valuable support for Leavis's claims for the moral benefits of studying English literature
- that Leavis's method or practice as a literary critic, which he developed independently of Lonergan, exemplifies Lonergan's epistemology as applied to literature and, in this way, illustrates its versatility and fruitfulness
- and that Lonergan and Leavis are at one in providing convincing philosophical arguments against Cartesian dualism and the dominant positivist philosophies of their times.

The pairing of the literary critic, Frank Raymond Leavis, with the philosopher-theologian, Bernard Lonergan, might strike some as surprising and, indeed, odd. Temperamentally the two could hardly have been more different. Although a brilliant critic, Leavis, the English academic, was something of a fire-brand, a prickly character, openly critical of many fellow critics and academics; when people talk about him it is often to recall the rude comments he made at the expense of others (although it ought to be added here that his pupils often cite his unfailing kindness and support, and his publisher and others speak of "the personal kindness and consideration" Leavis showed them at all times[1]). Lonergan, the Canadian Jesuit priest, by contrast, had a calming presence; he has been described as a "perfect gentleman," simple and humorous in manner and outlook. It is pertinent to add here that the community of scholars and teachers, mainly Jesuit priests, who staffed the institutions he worked in were very different in ambition and outlook from those who worked in the English School at Cambridge in Leavis's day, with its hot-house atmosphere and academic rivalries.[2] In fairness, it might be added that Cambridge was probably a more exciting place to study than the Jesuit institutions.

Lonergan could, it is true, be devastating and pugnacious in argument and at times gave the impression of being watchful about new ideas or proposals—at least, until he had tried them out and seen how they fitted into his overall outlook. It is, initially, in respect of their overall outlook that we begin to see the resemblances in the thinking of this unlikely pair. Each of them was gripped by a profound moral seriousness resulting in a deep concern about the health of contemporary civilization and the forces that threatened the moral wellbeing of people today, and each proposed approaches and strategies that could be brought to bear on the dehumanising influences abroad in our culture. And while neither deserted their chosen academic field—the literary critical or the philosophical-theological—when their respective methods of inquiry are closely scrutinised a remarkable intellectual affinity between the two begins to emerge. It is this intellectual affinity and shared moral outlook that I attempt to explore and expound in the three opening chapters; I then move on to other interests which, though different and distinct in their own right, relate to and throw further light on some of the issues raised in these three opening chapters. Taken together, the various chapters are an attempt to show how the cross-fertilisation of philosophy and literary criticism is to the benefit of both disciplines, something Leavis began to advocate in his later writings.

I am unable to account fully for the intellectual affinity I discern between Lonergan and Leavis. In their extensive written output neither of them ever refers to the writings of the other; it is possible that neither knew of the existence of the other, although there is a better chance that Lonergan had at least heard of Leavis, who for various reasons was the better known of the two in English-language academia during their lifetimes. However, in his own writing about poetry and literary art, Lonergan, as we shall see, was content to endorse the position put forward by the American neo-Kantian philosopher, Susanne K. Langer. I argue that, although this was understandable, it was in fact mistaken since this position, being Kantian, fails to match key features of Lonergan's Critical Realism.

As for the intellectual affinity between Lonergan and Leavis, a number of clues suggest themselves as to how and why it might have come about. To begin with, they were close to each other in age: Leavis's dates are 1895–1978 and Lonergan's are 1904–1984. And one of the chapters in this book attempts to trace the intellectual and moral debt each owes to the Victorian poet, critic and social commentator, Matthew Arnold. It is my intention in the chapter on Arnold to provide an historical background that will, to some extent at least, enrich and deepen our appreciation and understanding of both Leavis and Lonergan; it would not be too much to claim that Arnold provided both of our authors with an agenda, a basic orientation. If anyone had suggested to Leavis that his closest intellectual "look-alike" would turn out to be a Canadian Jesuit philosopher-theologian, he would probably have been incredulous; but if they had added that the bridge between them could be Matthew Arnold he might have begun to admit this as a possibility.

However, I suspect that the intellectual roots of both go further than Arnold. We know that Leavis was well read in philosophy and, while he was deeply hostile to the positivism that dominated British philosophy in the late 1930s through to the 60s, he welcomed the arrival in later life of philosophical approaches that began once more to place a greater emphasis on the role played by the inquiring subject in epistemology. My suspicion is that he saw in this a return to the philosophical reflections to be found among British philosophers in the era before the rise of positivism. He was certainly of an age to be influenced by these earlier thinkers. And although Lonergan was born and raised in Canada, at age 22 he was sent by his superiors to study philosophy at Heythrop College, at that time a Jesuit study house close to Oxford; and there Lonergan may well have come in contact with the writings of those British thinkers who lived and wrote in the pre-positivist era. Certainly, as well as Arnold, Newman's *Grammar of Assent* (1870), J.A. Stewart's *Plato's Doctrine of Ideas* (1909) and H. W. B. Joseph's *An Introduction to Logic* (1916) are known to have been strongly influential, and there may well have been others. Later English influences include R.G. Collingwood on history and Herbert Butterfield on the origins of modern science, and he also makes references to the writings of Christopher Dawson and Arnold Toynbee. Matthew Arnold, Newman and most of these twentieth century authors mentioned above were familiar to Leavis, their names are mentioned in *Scrutiny*, and some contributed to the journal. Although Lonergan's doctoral thesis was on aspects of the thought of Thomas Aquinas, who was probably the greatest influence on his thinking, the influence of these other English authors, dating from the late nineteenth century and first half of the twentieth century, should not be underestimated. He was heard to say in later life how grateful he was to have studied philosophy at Heythrop at that time (1926–30) and expressed admiration for what he called "the English way."[3]

There are several other areas of similarity between Lonergan and Leavis. First, each developed through their teaching roles and their prolific writings a solid body of followers or "disciples," many of whom went on to teaching roles of their own throughout the English-speaking world; and, in the case of Lonergan, beyond that. Second, despite being out of step with some of the dominant intellectual movements of their time, each manifests a profound self-confidence that they hold positions that are intellectually convincing, robust and, indeed, correct. Leavis, who was conscious of being a pioneer in the field of literary criticism, was quite confident that his critical method provided an intellectual rigour that had been lacking among the dilettante critics, such as members of the "Bloomsbury Group," who operated before the arrival of what he termed "Cambridge English." And Lonergan was able to exploit the versatility of his originating theory of cognition in various ways, such as in his reading of the history of philosophy,[4] with a boldness that hints at his genius. This inner self-confidence probably explains both the attraction to others of our two authors and also some of the antipathy that has gone their way; it probably goes a long way to explaining Leavis's impatience with those less inclined to accept his brand of moral seriousness as well as his and Lonergan's espousal of self-transcendence as *the criterion* of intellectual and moral authenticity; this is the criterion that stands at the centre or what Leavis calls "the common pursuit of true judgment"[5] that is, at the same time, a feature constitutive of human personality. And third, each was the recipient of public honours, Leavis being appointed a Companion of Honour in 1978, the year he died, and Lonergan being awarded Companion of the Order of Canada in 1970.

It is because of the emphasis Lonergan places on the inquiring subject that I chose to include in this book the chapter on "Reading as Understanding" because, apart from illustrating in another context the versatility of Lonergan's "transcendental method," it explores in greater detail than the other chapters the precise manoeuvres performed by readers and inquirers in their efforts to access and grasp the meaning on the printed page before them; these are not unlike the manoeuvres performed by scientific inquirers, or even by people of common sense as they go about their daily business; in this way it helps us to understand the role of the subject or inquirer in coming to know something. It has been said that Lonergan's master work, *Insight*[6], might more accurately have been entitled *Inquiry*[7], since it explores the questions, anticipations and self-corrections of inquirers and readers when they set about interrogating the data they have chosen to investigate. And as we shall see, the role of the reader when taking "possession" of a poem is also a subject examined in some detail by Leavis. Finally, I have included the last two chapters because, having argued in favour of the cross-fertilisation of philosophy and literary criticism, I felt it incumbent upon me to attempt to illustrate the benefits that literary criticism can derive from references to such disciplines as philosophy and theology, something that Leavis practised and advocated. Furthermore, I hope to have illustrated in the Hemingway chapter how an understanding of a variety of inter-related philosophical positions can be of assistance in gaining an in-depth grasp of a creative artist's fundamental outlook on life.

I chose to focus on Hemingway and Tolstoy in these two chapters because they project two starkly contrasting outlooks on life. By engaging in a close reading of each of these novelists, I hope to illustrate how such an approach builds up to and underpins an evaluative judgment on the moral maturity of the views being artistically realised and presented to us; as such, they reveal, I hope, the validity of the Leavisian criterion of "life" when judgment is passed on a work of literary art, and how, for Leavis, art and life are inseparable. As it is, the theme of authentic conversion explored in the last chapter loops back to the same theme as it appears in the earlier chapters on Lonergan and Leavis, and in this way helps to bind the book into a coherent unit. Suffice it to say at this point that human authenticity is central to the thinking of both Lonergan and Leavis.

It is, perhaps, fitting that Leavis should be found to share a depth of moral concern and an intellectual outlook similar to that of a distinguished Jesuit scholar, since he was known to remark, rather impishly, that Catholics took to him because he had "promoted" one of their number; he was referring to his frequently expressed admiration for the writings of the Jesuit priest-poet, Gerard Manley Hopkins.[8] Expressing his admiration for Leavis as a critic and teacher, the Catholic monk and theologian, Dom Sebastian Moore, who studied under Leavis at Downing College, observes that Leavis was the "only critic of note to discover that an obscure Victorian Jesuit had, in his attempt to spell out his dialogue with the infinite, achieved that combination of emotional honesty with technical sophistication that is the mark of high poetry. Who else paid attention to Hopkins in the early thirties?"[9] Moore expresses his gratitude that he had the good luck to encounter Leavis: he opens his essay by saying, "It is a rare and awesome thing to have had one's life touched by a genius. The chances against it are astronomical. Yet this luck, or grace, has been mine."[10] In the same essay he goes on to say, "There has been one other such teacher in my life: the Canadian Jesuit Bernard Lonergan. I have long felt that there must be a profound connection between these two crucial influences."[11] I shared this perception of Moore's many years before I came across his memoir of Leavis, and in this book I attempt to explore the "profound connection" between these two remarkable scholars and teachers; this will inevitably lead me to say something about the differences between them.

NOTES

1. Ian Parsons, "On being F. R. Leavis's publisher" in *The Leavises: Recollections and Impressions*, edited by Denys Thompson (Cambridge: Cambridge University Press, 1984), p. 85. I have found the contributions to this volume by former students, colleagues and friends of Leavis and the Leavises, highly informative in regard to both the human qualities of the couple and the critical methods and judgments of Leavis himself.

2. Parsons, *The Leavises*. In the same volume, see the sharply observed account of the English School at this time in Muriel Bradbrook's essay, "Nor Shall My Sword," p. 29–43.

3. *Collection, Papers by Bernard Lonergan* (London: Darton, Longman and Todd, 1967), edited and introduced by Frederick E. Crowe SJ, p. ix.

4. For a brief sketch of this, see chapter 7 of my book, *Philosophical Encounters: Lonergan and the Analytical Tradition* (Toronto: University of Toronto Press, 2005); I offer some examples of Lonergan's position on this in Chapter One.

5. The phrase is borrowed from T. S. Eliot's *The Function of Criticism* and forms the title of one of Leavis's most admired books, *The Common Pursuit* (London: Chatto and Windus, 1952, The Hogarth Press, 1984).

6. B. J. F. Lonergan SJ, *Insight: A Study of Human Understanding* (London: Longmans, Green and Co, 1957).

7. By Professor Charles Byrne of Boston College in a series of televised lectures on Lonergan's *Insight* that can be accessed at bclonergan.org/insight.

8. Of Hopkins' comment that "The effect of studying masterpieces is to make me admire and do otherwise," Leavis says, "He was a man of rare character as well as intelligence . . . — Self-sureness of that kind (it was justified) is genius." See the chapter on Hopkins in F. R. Leavis, *New Bearings in English Poetry* (London: Chatto and Windus, 1932, Pelican Books edition, 1982), p. 124. Leavis concludes this chapter by observing that "He (Hopkins) is likely to prove, for our time and the future, the only influential poet of the Victorian age, and he seems to me the greatest."

9. Sebastian Moore, "F. R. Leavis: a memoir" in *The Leavises: Recollections and Impressions*, edited by Denys Thompson (Cambridge: Cambridge University Press, 1984), p. 61–2.

10. Moore, *The Leavises*, p. 60.

11. Moore, *The Leavises*, p. 68.

Chapter One

What Lonergan is About

PART ONE: LONERGAN'S AMBITION

As a young Jesuit of about 34 years of age, Bernard Lonergan declared his ambition to be nothing less than the 'total transformation' of Roman Catholic philosophy and theology. No modest ambition. But I think it is important to grasp that Lonergan's ambition was primarily a theological one; and the main ingredient for the proposed transformation of Roman Catholic theology he had in mind was to help theologians grasp the *historical dimension* of their discipline. The 'method' he proposed for theology was devised as a means to that end, namely to assist theologians in their task of exploring and understanding what occurred or was said in the past in order to bring it into a living and significant relationship with the present and the future. To prepare such a method, he realized, would require an accurate account of epistemology and what it is to come to know something. To fashion a method of inquiry to guide the discipline of theology was a task requiring considerable philosophical preparation, the construction of philosophical tools that could then be applied to theology. *Insight* (1957), with all its philosophical riches, was preparatory to *Method in Theology* (1972). It is worth pointing out at the start that Lonergan believed his philosophical writings acquired their strength and usefulness on the basis of their generality, in so far as they were capable of being translated into a wide variety of concrete situations; at all times, he strived to work at the transcultural level.

Insight and *Method in Theology* are undoubtedly the best known works of Bernard Lonergan written originally in English. (In order to indicate the reach and breadth of Lonergan's thinking, I should perhaps add here that his extensive theological writings on the Incarnation, Christology and the Trinity were written first in Latin, and that he also wrote and lectured on such subjects as macroeconomics, Phenomenology and the foundations of mathematics.) *Insight* is Lonergan's detailed treatment of cognition, epistemology and metaphysics, which also manages to deal with several kinds of bias, human progress and decline, and how decline should be countered. *Method in Theology* deals mainly with the eight functional specialities which he deems to constitute theology, but which he also puts forward as the basis for any humane discipline that attempts to bring the past into a living relationship with the present and the future. In this opening chapter I want to give the reader a broad brush introduction to Lonergan's theory of cognition, in the first place, and then to show how he exploits this both in his understanding of the history of philosophy and also in working out a method for theology and the other humane disciplines, such as the study of English literature. In this way this opening chapter should serve as a preparation for what I have to say when I come to comparing Lonergan with Leavis and to exploring the remarkable overlap in their central concerns along with their methodological affinities.

In *Insight*, Lonergan claims to have unearthed the invariant pattern of human cognition and sets about demonstrating this in the context of mathematical, scientific and common sense knowing. His technique is to examine how we come to understand and to know in highly respected disciplines such as science and mathematics. Beginning with instances of human knowledge, he then shifts the focus from the object of this or that inquiry to the conscious operations of the knowing subject and the dynamic structure that relates these operations to each other. The operations, he argues, comprise three essential stages: experience, understanding and judgment. By experience here Lonergan means primarily sensory experience, our every-day seeing, hearing, touching, tasting and smelling. These, he argues, provide what he calls the data, the given. But Lonergan does not follow the empiricists in suggesting that these sensory operations provide our ideas; rather he says that it is the human subject or agent by means of her understanding who provides ideas—or rather grasps ideas since ideas are not confined to the mind but also help to constitute reality.[1] Sensation is nothing like understanding but is simply the *first stage* in the structured process of coming to know something; sensory data do not themselves provide ideas and ideas are not internalised sensations or sensory impressions. What the data of sense can do is stimulate inquiry by the subject and with inquiry we move on to a new, *second stage*, or level of consciousness, the intellectual level. We begin to ask questions such as What is that? Why does it happen? How often does it happen? These are questions searching for understanding. If we are successful we come up with an answer to these questions—we explain the data by means of interpretation or explanation; we come up with an idea, we enter the realm of meaning. But understanding on its own does not constitute knowledge; understanding has to be verified in order to constitute knowledge, it has to be shown to be true. Understanding is confronted with the further question: Is that so? Is it probable? In the ideal detective story the explanation provided has to pull all the data together by accounting for each element of the data—the footprints, the fingerprints, various timings and locations, the method and manner of the murder, the motivation of the murderer, and so forth. Once it has done so, we can safely move to judgment, the *third stage* or level of consciousness, and make the knowledge claim that 'X is the culprit.' We are now done with hesitation and take a stand on what we claim to be so; we claim that our understanding is true. And it is through the truth that we come to know reality; the verified is the real, the real is the verified.

It would be misleading to suggest or imply that in all cases of coming to know something we start, as it were, from scratch. In more cases than not, our knowledge claims are built on, or are developments of, knowledge we have previously acquired; but even in cases where we build our new knowledge on previous knowledge, the pattern of knowing remains constant. Successful knowledge stimulates further successful knowledge, just as unsuccessful knowledge or mistaken understanding tends to breed further errors and intellectual blunders. In the next section of this chapter we shall see how Wittgenstein, Lonergan and Leavis are at one in repudiating the epistemological errors flowing from Cartesian mind-body dualism

I have attempted to illustrate the threefold structure of knowledge by reference to the pattern of a detective story, but this threefold pattern is invariant in human knowing. It corresponds to the method employed by the scientist who gathers the data, interrogates them, comes up with a hypothesis in order to explain the data and then carries out carefully constructed experiments in order to test the validity of the explanation. Verification and its opposite, falsification, are integral to Lonergan's model of how human beings come to know. The three operations he uncovers in scientific, mathematical and common sense knowing constitute the common pattern of all human knowing in all fields of empirical inquiry, whatever their particular modes of procedure may be. It is this *a priori* structure that makes knowledge possible; it is a normative pattern because to claim that any one stage could legitimately be ignored is to commit intellectual suicide. Coherence is the essential normative ingredient: the explanation proposed must itself be coherent and it must also cohere with or fit the data. A hypothesis that leaves some elements of the data unexplained is to that extent weakened and may eventually have to be discarded. Knowledge claims or judgments have to be adjusted to the strength of the evidence that supports them—and the data, the given, are the evidence. The question arises: how do I know that this model of knowledge is valid or correct? The answer must be that the inquirer or knower must discover it for herself by catching on to the operations she performs whenever she comes to know something. We are dealing here with the procedures of the human mind which all of us perform. That is the claim. All of us have to discover for ourselves if the claim is valid.

To do that we have, as I say, to catch on to what we are doing when we come to know something. And that means that we have to attend to the data of our own consciousness. For the operations we perform in coming to know something are conscious operations. They are not unconscious operations such as the beating of my heart or the neurological occurrences in my brain. And because they are conscious we can note them, track them and work out their pattern and the relations between them. That is the invitation that Lonergan extends to the reader in his book, *Insight*. He invites her to attend to the data of consciousness, to note the operations she goes through when finding something out. For example, I hear a sharp noise in the room next door and wonder what could have caused it. A number of hypotheses or guesses come to mind: perhaps the gas fire has exploded, perhaps my small son has hit something with a hammer or some other implement, perhaps the window has been blown open, or something might have fallen from the shelf. All sorts of possibilities come to mind, some of them worrying. I hurry next door and find that the window has come off its catch and is being blown about by the wind. I check to see that the gas fire is intact and my son is peacefully asleep in bed and nothing appears to have fallen from the shelf. I relax: the least dangerous of my hypotheses has been verified, others have been eliminated. I now know what happened. This simple example illustrates the pattern of cognition: an auditory cue in a domestic context; various explanatory hypotheses; one of these is verified and others are eliminated. It is a very simple example but the pattern of operations is exactly the same as that performed by the scientist when conducting a complicated investigation. Readers are invited to attend to their own conscious operations when coming to know something. Lonergan is able to construct a coherent cognitional theory by means of the distinction he makes between the data of sense and the data of consciousness.

Lonergan's cognitional theory, which underpins his epistemology, rests on a totally harmonious and necessary reciprocity between the positive and the normative aspects of knowledge. Without the positive—if the three operations were not carried out—then knowing would not take place. But mere performance of these three operations does not ensure that knowledge will result; on the other hand any knowledge claim that fails to follow these three operations will be defective. Without this normative aspect, knowing would not be correct and judgments would not be considered valid.

It is unlikely that Lonergan would have been able to accomplish his work on cognitional theory without his prior research into the thinking of Aquinas (and Aristotle). In the company of other distinguished scholars, Lonergan rescued Aquinas from those who portrayed him as a conceptualist. Lonergan argued with cogency that Aquinas was an intellectualist.[2] The difference between conceptualists and intellectualists is that conceptualists consider that concepts precede understanding while intellectualists consider that understanding precedes concepts. Lonergan's espousal of the intellectualist position was to have profound and lasting consequences for his thinking on theological method. For the conceptualist position is rather stiff and mechanical claiming, as it suggests, that we simply process the world through our *a priori* or acquired concepts. The intellectualist position, by contrast, is pliant, flexible, creative and full of uncertainty. Concepts can be fashioned only if there occurs the intellectual breakthrough—insight—and this cannot be had to order. But when it does occur it transforms how we see things; the veil falls from our eyes; at the intellectual level we experience a smaller or greater conversion. The intellectualist position places a very strong emphasis on the subject and the subject's role in coming to know, in particular what Lonergan terms the subject's capacity for self-transcendence. By this term Lonergan refers to the ability of the subject to put aside her own personal preferences, satisfactions and biases and submit to the evidence, the data. It is by means of such self-transcendence that objectivity is achieved with the result that what is affirmed in judgment is so independently of the subject: it is not the wish or will or the say-so of the inquiring subject that determines the truth, but the coherence or match of the proposed explanation with the data, the evidence. Lonergan's is a realist philosophy but the real is known through the truth and the acquisition of the truth depends on the ability of the inquiring subject to transcend all selfish or false motives.

In this way the intellectualist position is highly moral. The move from ignorance to answer is not mechanical but creative and is often arduous and disagreeable. It requires hard work, steady application, learning from others, and, as said already, it entails proportioning our judgments to the scope of the data and the depth of our understanding. The moral dimension in knowing is important. If the pattern of knowledge forms a triad of experience, understanding and judgment, the moral dimension, and the general area of values, represents a *fourth stage* or level of consciousness on top of the previous three. And so we come to what Lonergan terms 'transcendental method'—a fourfold structure comprising experience, understanding, judgment and (fourthly) valuing, deciding and acting. This is termed 'transcendental' because it is the common core and ground of all successful and responsible empirical inquiry and subsequent action in any civilisation, culture or context. We ask questions of our experience, come to an understanding, test our understanding to see if it is true or probable, then base our decisions and actions on what we know to be the facts of the matter. Omission of any one stage results in errors and blunders. The structure is unified and dynamic because, under pressure of the human desire to know or to reach a decision, each level or stage summons forth the next and each stage builds on what went before. The questions that lead to understanding—what is that? why does it happen? etc. ?—and the questions that lead to judgment—is that so? is it probable?—are propelled by the desire to know. The questions, What is to be done? Is that right?—are propelled by the desire for the good, for right action. When applied in the fields of scholarship and science transcendental method corresponds to a recurrent pattern of operations yielding cumulative and progressive results. Applied over time it builds up the various areas of knowledge represented by the many intellectual disciplines to be found in the school or university curriculum.

Transcendental method also yields insight into the structure of human consciousness and, for this reason, the structure of human personality since human beings are define by their consciousness. The four operations we perform as human beings represent four levels or stages of consciousness: the empirical level of experience, the intellectual level, the reasonable or rational level and the moral or existential level. With each stage we move more deeply into our personal consciousness as with each step we are called on to exercise our freedom more fully. At the empirical level, we are simply aware of our surroundings, what we hear and see, and so forth, or of the movements we make; we also experience heat and cold and the like. We move to the intellectual level when we begin to ask questions and the search for answers to these questions challenges us to be honest and to base our answers on the data of experience; simply spinning hypotheses out of thin air will not do. We achieve fulfilment at this level when we come to an understanding or a hypothesis that explains the data. We move to the rational level when we make a judgment or when we form a knowledge claim; with judgment we are done with hesitation and take a stand on what is so; we make a commitment. We affirm that our understanding, or one of our hypotheses, is true. We move from the rational to the moral or evaluative level when we exercise our freedom self-consciously by deciding on a course of action; at this level, consciousness becomes fully self-conscious, becomes conscience. At this fourth level we are not simply making a claim about some external matter but we are making ourselves by our decisions and actions; at this level we do not merely take a stand on what is or is not the case but we determine what we stand for; that is why this level can also be seen as the existential level. It is in this way and for these reasons that transcendental method can be seen to be a framework that explains how human consciousness is organised, a framework that provides an insight into the structure of human personality. The word 'framework' can be misleading, suggesting something static and unchanging; but in fact it is a framework for creativity and originality, since the notion of human freedom stands at its heart; it is a framework that allows for human growth and development or for the deterioration and even corruption of our human personality.

I hope it is clear by now that this is not a framework that we choose or adopt freely; it is a framework that defines us and establishes us as human.

For this reason Lonergan proposes what he terms the four transcendental imperatives: Be Attentive (at the empirical level); Be Intelligent (at the intellectual level); Be Reasonable (at the level of judgment); and Be Responsible (at the fourth level of evaluation and moral choice). But beware: we do not always work in this systematic order and it is very possible that the later stages hold sway over the earlier—for example, we may wish to embark on a course of action and this fact might lead us to gather the relevant data together before coming to an understanding and judgment as to the facts of the matter. In this sense, it is a highly flexible framework.

PART TWO: A HISTORICAL PERSPECTIVE

Descartes, Wittgenstein, Lonergan and Leavis

It might help us gain a deeper insight into Lonergan's position and a greater appreciation of his achievement if we examine how his position deals with some of the problems that have beset modern attempts in the Western philosophical tradition to solve what has been called 'the problem of knowledge.' These problems, by and large, go back to Descartes and his fateful division of the universe into two broad but opposing substances, namely the *res cogitans* (the thinking thing) and the *res extensa* (the extended thing). The *res extensa* refers to the world of bodies, physical things that can be measured mathematically, and the *res cogitans* refers to the human mind. Positing two completely disparate entities, spatiality and consciousness, Descartes assigns the body to the first and mind or soul to the other. Mind-body dualism is the result and, in this way, Western philosophy was primed and prepared to follow the routes such dualism would allow.

The picture is complicated by the fact that Descartes sought to counter the pervasive scepticism of his age by making the fact of doubt itself the starting point for his philosophy. To doubt is to think and to think is to exist: '*cogito ergo sum.*' A mathematician who delighted in the certainty yielded by mathematical reasoning, Descartes believed that he had found such certainty also in the simple proposition, 'I think therefore I am'; this was an empirical proposition that was simply indubitable. What is arresting about this proposition is that it grounds knowledge of existence on knowledge of the operations of the mind: it implies the priority of mental knowledge over knowledge of the world. According to Descartes, we know the contents of the mind, ideas,— which include sensations as well as thoughts and beliefs—with greater certainty than we know the physical universe which these ideas are said to represent. However, Descartes believed that the simple empirical proposition, *cogito ergo sum*, shared the certainty provided by what he deemed to be the basic operation of mathematics, namely 'intuition.' It is important to grasp the characteristics of Cartesian intuition. Though infallible, it is not discursive but single and momentary, 'simply vision.' In this way Descartes sets in motion the understanding of intellect as analogous to sensation, and specifically to an act of vision—what has been termed the 'ocular metaphor' for the understanding of knowledge has been quietly introduced (or re-introduced) into Western philosophy. It was this understanding of intellect and understanding that gave rise to the central problem that was to afflict Western epistemology for the succeeding centuries. Since all that the mind perceives are private to it, how can we know that such privately entertained ideas truly correspond to the world of bodies 'out there'? That is the central problem that besets most subsequent treatments of 'the problem of knowledge': the result is *veil of ideas' scepticism* since, if all that the mind has immediate access to are its ideas, there is no way of getting round this veil of ideas to the reality that is supposed to be 'out there,' spread out in space and time. We can only ever access the supposed world of bodies mediately, via the ideas in the mind, and there is no way of knowing if these ideas truly represent reality: we are, if you like, trapped in our minds. The model of knowledge projected by Descartes gave rise to all sorts of assumptions that have been entertained by the majority of subsequent philosophical positions: the notion that reality is, as Lonergan puts it, 'already-out-there-now' and that objectivity is reaching out to this reality with our senses.

The understanding of 'ideas' put forward by Descartes differs decisively from that entertained by Aristotle and Aquinas as well as Lonergan. For Descartes and the British empiricists of the seventeenth and eighteenth century ideas were strictly mental; they dwelt in the 'inner space' of the mind. But this understanding of ideas is a consequence of Descartes's division of the universe into the *res extensa* and the *res cogitans*: if bodies inhabit the external world of space then ideas are considered to inhabit the mind, they are strictly mental entities. But Aristotle, Aquinas and Lonergan do not confine ideas to the mind, believing that the world of bodies is also made up of ideas or 'forms.' An entity like a house, for example, is made up of a range of materials such as bricks, wood, glass, tiles, metal, and so forth; these constitute what Aristotle would call the 'matter' of the house. But by themselves they do not make a house. For that there is required the 'form' or design or idea that makes them into a house. A house is a single substance or thing despite being made of a variety of materials; and it is the form that causes these materials to be a single entity, identified as a house. Matter and form are not two substances but together they combine to make a single substance. Every material entity that exists consists of matter and form and the form is the cause, the formal cause, of the entity being what it is.[3] When I grasp the meaning of a building or of a lion or of a mountain, I am grasping the form or idea that makes this thing the thing it is. Understanding occurs when I grasp the idea or meaning in things and understanding is true when the idea I grasp is *identical with the idea* that makes these the things they are. The understanding of substance as composed of matter and form overcomes the habit that developed after Descartes of considering the mind and its ideas to be 'in here' and reality to be 'out there.'

One consequence of Cartesian dualism is that language, understood as that which expresses the ideas we have in our minds, is, like our ideas, primarily a private matter and only derivatively public. This was the understanding of language that Wittgenstein had entertained when writing his first famous philosophical work, the *Tractatus Logico-Philosophicus*;[4] and it was when he reacted against this notion in his later work, *Philosophical Investigations*,[5] that Wittgenstein could be seen to be reacting against the tradition that had dominated Western philosophy since Descartes, and taking a stance against the notion of language, of meaning, of understanding and knowing that this tradition had propagated and sustained. While Lonergan, unlike Wittgenstein, has much to say about human consciousness, he does not consider consciousness to stand apart from language. He says, 'conscious intentionality develops in and is moulded by its mother tongue. . . . Not only does language mould developing consciousness but it structures the world about the subject. Spatial adverbs and adjectives relate places to the place of the speaker. The tenses of verbs relate times to his present. Moods correspond to his intention to wish, or exhort, or command, or declare. . . .'[6] A similar point, in his own inimitable style, is made by Leavis who clearly thought long and hard about language and human consciousness: 'The language one speaks, which seems so inwardly, intimately and personally *of* one's individual being, was not created by oneself, though one plays incidentally one's part in keeping it alive and continually renewed. One doesn't, on the other hand, resort to it "out there" for communication as if it were an instrument lying ready to be used. . . . But it is "there," inescapably, in all thought, and in such a way that the forms, idioms, and conventions of what is recognized as thinking make, and *could* make, no provision for dealing with it explicitly. It is antecedent to consciousness and formulation, which have supervened upon it. In fact, the uniqueness of the unique relation is such that 'relation,' a word one has to use, seems to lack felicity and is perhaps misleading.'[7]

The conception of the mind that Wittgenstein is attacking in *Philosophical Investigations* is of the mind as some isolated, disembodied entity standing behind the body and looking out at the world. Against this understanding of the self, Wittgenstein insists on our bodiliness. It is the body's basic needs, appetites and instincts—our need for food, drink and shelter, for example— and the *communal* economies and institutions (including language) these give rise to that provide the common core and wide variety of 'forms of life' within which individuals operate and order their lives. It is for this reason that Wittgenstein writes, 'The human body is the best picture of the human soul' (P.I., pt 2, 178). Feelings should not be interpreted as *lying behind* someone's physical expression but are actually *revealed* by her physical expression.

Wittgenstein's basic position is that the language we use is first and foremost an established public possession that is then acquired by the individual; he asserts the priority of the communal to the individual, of the public to the private. His objection to the notion that language is primarily private and only derivatively public is that a purely private language could not be rule-governed and hence would lack the agreed criteria required for a proposition to be considered correct or incorrect.[8] The object of Wittgenstein's principal attack is the notion that language is primarily private and only derivatively public. The object of Lonergan's principal attack is the notion that knowing is like looking—the 'ocular metaphor' entertained by Descartes. His argument against this is not unlike Wittgenstein's attack on private language, since Lonergan contends that the model of 'knowing as looking' leads to an incapacity to verify any proposition. For verification in such a model of knowing would require checking that what is claimed to be so truly corresponds with what in fact is so; and this would require, in turn, something like a superlook, capable of looking at both the looking and the looked at to see if they match, and such a superlook is simply not available or possible. In short, such a model of knowing is mired in the privacy of sensation and incapable of furnishing criteria or procedures for the verification of its knowledge claims.

Wittgenstein responded to Cartesian and post-Cartesian philosophy by taking his stance on language—on language as it is used 'in the language-game which is its original home. What we do is to bring words back from their metaphysical to their everyday use.' (P.I., 116) Lonergan's approach is to say that knowing is already going on—in mathematics, science, and common sense—and to suggest that we carry out an empirical investigation of what is going on in these areas of knowledge. It is not philosophy's task to provide foundations for the knowledge claims made in mathematics, science or other fields of inquiry; the methods employed in these disciplines are in perfectly good working order as they stand. The philosopher should attend to these methods and find their common core, the meta-method of operations that underpins them. Like Wittgenstein, Lonergan believes that philosophers should attend to what is already going on. Far from endorsing the Cartesian notion of 'the ghost in the machine,' the isolated disembodied mind—the *res cogitans*—looking at the world 'out there' in space and time, Lonergan conceives of knowledge as rooted in sensory experience. According to him, the cognitive subject is a body hooked through the senses to the strip of space-time she occupies; we are umbilically tied to the world of sensory experience and there is no way we can break loose and become detached. Without our bodies we could not know anything or communicate anything. As he writes, 'Human communication is not the work of a soul hidden in some unlocated recess of a body and emitting signals in some Morse code. . . . The bodily presence of another is the presence of the incarnate spirit of the other; and that incarnate spirit reveals itself to me by every shift of the eyes, countenance, color, lips, voice . . . such revelation is not an object to be apprehended. Rather it works immediately upon my subjectivity, to make me share the other's seriousness or vivacity.'[9] F. R. Leavis shares this insistence on human bodiliness, praising Polanyi's epistemology for holding that '"mind" is "there" only in individual minds, and that an individual mind is always a person's, and a person has a body and a history. His mind is the mind of his body, and his body is the body of his mind. The dualism that has defeated so many epistemologies is eliminated here.'[10] Although Leavis portrayed himself as an 'Anti-philosopher,' his ability to see through Cartesian dualism and the many mistaken philosophical movements it gave birth to suggests that he was less philosophically innocent than he made out. It is not surprising that he told the publisher, Michael Black, that a philosophical friend of Sir Karl Popper had sent him his book 'by way of justifying the bracketing of me with *him.*'[11]

The extent of the agreement that exists between Lonergan and Leavis on epistemological issues can be gathered from Lonergan's affirmation that the individual ego, 'I,' or person is socially rooted and unintelligible outside the context of the relationships in which she is situated:

> From the 'we' of the parents comes the symbiosis of mother and child. From the symbiosis of mother and child comes the 'we' of the family. Within the 'we' of the family emerges the 'I' of the child. In other words the person is not the primordial fact. What is primordial is community.[12]

Finally, the social and historical dimensions of understanding and knowledge are evident in the importance Lonergan attaches to belief. Almost all of us, and some more than others, move on occasion from ignorance to answer by our own efforts, so to speak; we achieve what Lonergan calls 'immanently generated knowledge' by attending to the evidence and basing a judgment on the evidence. But such occasions are the exception rather than the rule. More common is knowledge based on belief, on 'taking someone's word for it'; and even the knowledge we achieve by ourselves is meshed with all sorts of commonly held presuppositions. So much for the solitary inquirer working on her own.

At one time it was believed or presumed that Lonergan's epistemology, based as it is on mental acts or operations, was vulnerable to Wittgenstein's criticism of the notion of a private language. This is not surprising in view of what Wittgenstein has to say about mental operations, understanding and meaning in *Philosophical Investigations*, where he simply assumes that reference to mental operations, understanding or 'meaning in the head' reveals the mindset that gives rise to the notion that language is primarily private and only derivatively public. Indeed, one famous Wittgensteinian is reported as saying that Lonergan's work, *Insight*, simply 'provides fodder for Wittgensteinian analysis.' This point of view was also expressed by Lonergan's fellow Jesuit, Professor Edward MacKinnon, which Lonergan quotes at length in *Method*:

> Since the publication of Wittgenstein's *Philosophical Investigations* (MacKinnon writes) there has been a growing consensus that the meaningfulness of language is essentially public and only derivatively private. Unless this were so language could not serve as a vehicle for intersubjective communication. The meaning of a term, accordingly, is explained chiefly by clarifying its use, or the family of usages associated with it. . . .
>
> A consequence of this position. . . . Is that the meaning of a word is not explicable by reference or reduction to private mental acts. The usual scholastic doctrine (is that) . . . meanings are primarily in concepts, private mental acts or states, and then derivatively in language which expresses such a concept. Within this view of language, transcendence does not present too formidable a linguistic problem. A word, such as 'God' can mean a transcendent being, if that is what one intends in using the word. Comforting as such a simple solution might be, it, unfortunately, will not work.[13]

Lonergan responds to this view at some length and here I shall confine myself to a few essential points. He says he has 'no doubt that the ordinary meaningfulness of ordinary language is essentially public and only derivatively private. For language is ordinary if it is in common use. It is in common use, not because some isolated individual happens to have decided what it is to mean, but because all the individuals in the relevant group understand what it means. . . . Children and foreigners . . . learn the language by learning how it ordinarily is used, so that their private knowledge of ordinary usage is derived from the common usage that essentially is public.' He then goes on to say that

> what is true of the ordinary meaningfulness of ordinary language is not true of the original meaningfulness of any language, ordinary, literary, or technical. For all language develops and, at any time, any language consists of the sedimentation of the developments that have occurred and have not become obsolete. Now developments consist in discovering new uses for existing words, in inventing new words, and in diffusing the discoveries and inventions. All three are a matter of expressed mental acts. The discovery of a new usage is a mental act expressed by the new usage. The invention of a new word is a mental act expressed by the new word. The communication of the discoveries and inventions can be done technically by introducing definitions or spontaneously as when *A* utters his new verbal constellation, *B* responds, *A* grasps in *B*'s response how successful he was in communicating his meaning and, in the measure he failed, he seeks and tries out further discoveries and

inventions. Through a process of trial and error a new usage takes shape, and, if there occurs a sufficiently broad diffusion of the new usage, then a new ordinary usage is established . . .[14]

This passage from Lonergan's *Method* reminds me of what Leavis says when explaining how the literary critic spontaneously seeks to gain a true and full reading of a poem:

> It is in the study of literature . . . that one comes to recognise the nature and priority of the third realm (as, unphilosophically, no doubt, I put it, talking with my pupils), the realm of that which is neither merely private and personal nor public in the sense that it can be brought into the laboratory or pointed to. You cannot point to the poem; it is 'there' only in the re-creative response of individual minds to the black marks on the page. But—a necessary faith—it is something in which minds can meet. . . . A judgment is personal or it is nothing; you cannot take over someone else's. The implicit form of a judgment is: This is so, isn't it? The question is an appeal for confirmation that the thing *is* so; implicitly that, though expecting, characteristically, an answer in the form, 'yes, but'—' the 'but' standing for qualifications, reserves, corrections. Here we have a diagram of the collaborative-creative process in which the poem comes to be established as something 'out there,' of common access in what is in some sense a public world.[15]

This account echoes Lonergan's description of how the meaning of a new word or term, grasped by individual minds, gradually becomes public and is no longer private. Leavis's reference to the third realm as 'something in which minds can meet' is felicitous. The key point to grasp here is that while sensation is private and incommunicable as a sensation (no one but 'I' can feel my pain or taste my tastes etc.), meaning can be communicated and shared. This occurs when the inquirer moves beyond sensations and the data of sense and grasps a meaning in what is being investigated. This meaning can be shared with others and, as Lonergan says, if sufficiently diffused a new established meaning can be made public by means of speech or writing. Wittgenstein is widely credited as the one who in the twentieth century overthrew Descartes's seventeenth century philosophy of mind by showing how even when we are thinking our most private thoughts we are employing the medium of language which cannot be severed from its public and bodily expression.[16] In this section I hope to have shown how Lonergan also overthrew the Cartesian philosophy of mind while taking a different approach from Wittgenstein; but even more remarkably, I hope to have shown how the 'unphilosophical' Leavis, by attending to how we respond to a poem, achieved the same result.

I trust I have said enough in this section to show that Lonergan and Wittgenstein are united in rejecting the Enlightenment notion of the inquirer as a disembodied individual consciousness confronting the world and attempting to understand it by some form of picturing or pointing. Such a conception of the self and of reality gives rise to all sorts of dislocations—between thought and language, mind and body, self and others, meaning and behaviour—that Wittgenstein exposes brilliantly. It is, I hope, by now clear that Lonergan repudiates these dislocations with the same force as Wittgenstein. Both philosophers are united in rejecting these aspects of the Western philosophical tradition. Kenny has said that Wittgenstein has undermined the assumptions of post-Cartesian philosophy and that 'if Wittgenstein was right, philosophy has been on a wrong track since Descartes.'[17] Lonergan goes even further in his diagnosis of the durability of the ocular myth and the confrontational view of knowing it has supported. He writes, 'Five hundred years separate Hegel from Scotus. . . . That notable interval of time was largely devoted to working out in a variety of manners the possibilities of the assumption that knowing consists in taking a look.'[18]

No one could gainsay the massive impact of Wittgenstein on modern English language philosophy. But there is one important aspect in which it can be shown that Lonergan's approach to philosophy is superior to the kind of linguistic analysis favoured by Wittgenstein. The whole thrust of Wittgenstein's argument in *Philosophical Investigations* and in his later work, *On Certainty*,[19] presumes that the network of word meanings in any language-game is settled and established so that the meaning of any term or word or sentence in that game can be determined by reference to established practice. It is a technique designed to uphold and maintain the linguistic *status quo*. What it cannot do is explain how language develops and changes. While there are undoubtedly many factors that contribute to linguistic change, one prominent factor is conceptual or intellectual change. Once we had no vocabulary for describing and explaining microbes, genes or viruses, but today we do, and with further scientific advancement new terms and new vocabularies will be generated. Language changes *pari passu* with changes and developments in understanding, and the meaning of words is empty without originating acts of understanding. Lonergan's account of knowing explains one important way by which linguistic change comes about.

Lonergan, Hume and Leavis

In this section I shall, first, compare Lonergan's understanding of consciousness with that of David Hume before going on to indicate how he solves Hume's 'is-ought' problem—the problem identified by Hume concerning the relationship between judgements of fact, on the one hand, and moral and value judgments, on the other, which has some grave consequences for any discipline claiming that value judgments can be cognitively valid.

Lonergan draws a distinction between experience as sense and experience as consciousness. It is because of this distinction that he is able to develop his theory of cognition, for this theory is not based on our experience of sensory data—the objects of our seeing, hearing, touching, tasting or smelling—but on the data of consciousness—what we experience or are aware of as we come to know something or to form a value judgment. The data of consciousness provide the grounds for Lonergan's analysis of knowing and deciding along with his claim that the notion of transcendental method provides an insight into the structure of human personality. When Hume considers the question of personal identity, he raises doubts concerning the existence of the self:

> For my part, when I enter most intimately into what I call myself, I always stumble on some particular perception or other, of heat or cold, light or shade, love or hatred, pain or pleasure. I never catch myself at any time without a perception, and never can observe anything but the perception. When my perceptions are removed for any time, as by sound sleep; so long am I insensible of myself, and may truly be said not to exist. The mind (he concludes) is nothing but a bundle or collection of different perceptions, which succeed each other with an inconceivable rapidity, and are in a perpetual flux and movement.[20]

Throughout his cogent analysis Hume takes consciousness to be perception and perception to be equivalent to knowledge. In answering Hume, Lonergan would be in agreement with him if consciousness simply equated with perception. For 'if consciousness is knowledge of an object, it can have no constitutive effect upon an object; it can only reveal its object as it was in its proper reality prior to the occurrence of the cognitive act or function named consciousness.'[21] Lonergan continues:

> If without consciousness John has no other psychological unity beyond the unity found in the objects of his knowledge, then by consciousness John is merely manifested as having no psychological unity beyond the unity found in the objects of his knowledge.

This far Lonergan is in agreement with Hume. But he then goes on to drive home the consequences that follow from an identification of consciousness with perception:

> Again, if without consciousness John cannot possibly be the conscious subject of physical pain, then by consciousness John is merely manifested as being incapable of suffering. Similarly, if without consciousness John cannot be the consciously responsible principle of his own intelligent, rational, free, or responsible acts, then by consciousness as knowledge of an object John merely knows himself as neither consciously intelligent, nor consciously rational, nor consciously free, nor consciously responsible.

The notion that consciousness is nothing more than perception, Lonergan argues, 'overlooks the fact that consciousness is not merely cognitive but also constitutive. It overlooks as well the subtler fact that consciousness is cognitive, not of what exists without consciousness, but of what is constituted by consciousness.' The point to grasp here is that such is human consciousness that *what is known is known to be known*. Were it not, Hume could not begin to talk about perceptions, since unless consciousness not only allows me to perceive but allows me further to be aware of myself as a perceiver, it would not be possible for me to know that I had perceptions. Human consciousness is, if you like, raised to the power of two: it is because I am present to myself that anything else can be present to me; when I am not present to myself, nothing else can be present to me. It is by attending to this presence-to-myself that Lonergan seeks to fashion a theory of cognition. It is the awareness that accompanies sensing, understanding, judging and evaluating that supplies the data on which such a theory can be based.

Further light might be shone on Lonergan's basic position if we consider the Lonerganian response to another 'problem' raised by Hume. Hume writes:

> In every system of morality, which I have hitherto met with, I have always remark'd, that the author proceeds for some time in the ordinary way of reasoning, and establishes the being of God, or makes observations concerning human affairs; when of a sudden I am surpriz'd to find, that instead of the usual copulations of propositions, *is* and *is not*, I meet with no proposition that is not connected with an *ought*, or an *ought not*. This change is imperceptible, but is, however, of the last consequence. For as this *ought*, or *ought not*, expresses some new relation or affirmation 'tis necessary that it shou'd be observ'd and explain'd; and at the same time that a reason should be given for what seems altogether inconceivable, how this new relation can be a deduction from others, which are entirely different from it.[22]

As a statement of the restrictions imposed by logic, Hume's comments here are unassailable, for in logic we can only take from our premises what is already there, and there is no way in which *ought* is implied by or entailed in *is*. What is, however, open to question is Hume's assumption that the relationship obtaining between *is* propositions and *ought* propositions is or is intended to be one of logical deduction. When Lonergan maps out human intentional consciousness, dividing it into four levels or stages, he argues that we enter each new level by means of questions: we pass through the question-gate, we might say, in order to enter each higher level. So questions for understanding—such as 'what is that?' or 'why does that happen?' or 'what does this mean?'—lead from the empirical level, the level of sense, to the intellectual level; questions for judgment—such as 'is that true?' or 'is that probable?'—lead from the intellectual level to the rational level, the level of affirmation or negation; and questions for evaluation, or moral judgment—such as 'is that right?' or 'ought this to be so?' or 'what is to be done about that?'—lead us from judgments about facts to discriminating judgments about options, decisions and actions. These four sets of questions are intentional in the sense that they seek or intend answers; they are also questions that human beings ask and have asked spontaneously and irresistibly down through the ages and in all cultures and civilisations, and as such they represent the structure and dynamism of the human personality. What Hume proposes in the passage quoted above turns out to be a pseudo-problem, but one that gave rise to a great deal of heated speculation by empiricist philosophers in the twentieth century, who were inclined to view moral judgments and value judgments in general as no more than statements of emotional preference, statements that lacked any cognitive status. As the logician Rudolph Carnap expressed it: 'The suppositious sentences of metaphysics, of the philosophy of values, of ethics . . . are pseudo-sentences, they have no logical content, but are only expressions of feelings, which in their turn stimulate feelings or volitional tendencies on the part of the hearer.'[23]

The other notable feature of the four stages of intentional consciousness manifested by these four types of questions is how each level or stage builds on the former—the term used by Lonergan is that each new stage 'sublates' the former. The first three stages—experience, understanding and judgment—are the steps that lead up to judgments of fact, to knowledge claims. The fourth stage builds on that since judgments of value or judgments about what is morally right or wrong rely on and must be guided by accurate information of a factual nature; to offer evaluative or moral judgments without attending to the facts of the matter is to be inauthentic and is likely to end in blunders. It is this element of sublation that guarantees that moral judgments and judgments of value have genuine cognitive content. The importance of this for literary criticism need hardly be stressed; for if value judgments were deemed to have no cognitive status then clearly the educational claims made for literary criticism would be worthless. As Barry Cullen has argued, 'it was apparent to him (Leavis) that if literature was not to be vindicated as a form of knowledge with its own kind of objectivity then, in the contemporary world, it would cease to matter. . . . If however it was to be defended as a form of knowledge—and Leavis was not prepared to see it as anything less—then by what methodology was it to be so justified?'[24] It is my contention in these pages that the methodology represented by Lonergan's 'transcendental method' provides Leavis with the philosophical support that is desired and needed for literary criticism to be valued as an intellectual discipline worthy of respect and one that can claim genuine and unique educational merits.

A Wittgensteinian response to Hume's arguments against the existence of the self would most likely take the form of pointing to the many references in this argument to 'myself' and the many uses of the first person singular, 'I,' which would suggest that in his argument Hume is presuming the existence of that whose existence he is calling into question. Lonergan achieves similar results by his detailed analysis of human consciousness. But his analysis has the advantage of demonstrating how judgments of fact and of value are arrived at and it also affirms and upholds the objectivity of both types of judgment, and this is surely of great importance when the academic status of literary criticism is in question. Moreover, Lonergan's notion of transcendental method provides the basis for a conception of the human person that avoids Cartesian mind-body dualism. Lonergan posits an integrative view of the human person. The laws of physics, chemistry, biology and neurology are not negated in any way, but they do open up to ever higher integrations. Just as the laws of physics and chemistry are not negated in plants but encompassed within the higher integration of botany, so in human beings lower levels are integrated into the higher levels of the conscious operations of human thinking, deciding and acting. And through the activation of these conscious operations women and men not only make the world around them but also make themselves.

Lonergan, Kant and Leavis

Lonergan is a technical thinker and in an early essay, first published in 1943, he considers the form of logical inference, the way in which we move from a set of premises to a conclusion.[25] He begins by reducing the various forms of inference found in scholastic philosophy to one basic form of inference, which he calls 'the simple hypothetical argument.' This takes the form 'If A, then B. But A. Therefore, B.' Lonergan describes the process of thought involved in the simple hypothetical argument as 'connotational,' meaning that the conclusion follows from the very form of the argument and not from what he calls 'denotational coincidence,' the phrase he uses to indicate the way in which 'some' or 'one' are implied in 'all.' He says, 'The same point may be put differently by asking the logician, If when you say that all organisms are mortal you do not mean to speak of "all organisms" but of the nature of "organism," then why on earth do you say "all organisms"? To that query I have never heard a sensible answer . . .' Against the view that logical implication is demonstrated by the implication of 'some' or 'one' in 'all,' a form of implication he considers to depend on the contingent fact of how things are in the world—'denotational coincidence'—Lonergan posits a form of implication that arises from the connotational relations of the terms. These relations are of a condition—'If A'—and a conditioned—'then B.' The condition is the antecedent, the conditioned the consequent. It is the fulfilment of the condition, stated in the minor premise, that licenses the conclusion to be drawn by force of logical necessity. Lonergan refers to the fulfilment of the conditions as creating 'a virtually unconditioned,' a conditioned whose conditions have been fulfilled; it is the 'virtually unconditioned,' a condition that has been fulfilled, that generates the logical necessity leading to the conclusion. Such a conclusion follows by virtue of the form of argument alone and in no way depends on the world being the way it is, empirically speaking. This is a point on which Lonergan is in agreement with Wittgenstein who, in rejecting Bertrand Russell's quantitative understanding of entailment—the entailment of 'some' or 'one' in 'all'—stated, 'The general validity of logic might be called essential, in contrast with the *accidental* general validity of such propositions as "All men are mortal."' (*Tractatus,* 6.1232).[26] But my reason for referring here to the notion of logical inference is to demonstrate a point underlying Lonergan's disagreement with Kant.

Kant considered the mind to have two complementary faculties, the sensibility and the understanding. The sensibility is receptive, receiving the input of the senses, and the understanding is creative, that which makes the objects of sensible intuition into objects of thought. 'Without sensibility no object would be given to us, without understanding no object would be thought. Thoughts without content are empty, intuitions without concepts are blind. . . . The understanding can intuit nothing, the senses can think nothing. Only through their union can knowledge arise.'[27] Kant claims that our sensible intuitions are due to what he calls things-in-themselves, but we can have no knowledge of these; he refers to them as noumena, which he distinguishes from phenomena, the objects we do have knowledge of by virtue of the experiences provided by the faculty of sensibility being brought under the concepts and categories provided by the faculty of understanding. For Kant the 'manifold' of sensation—the things in themselves that affect our senses—are unified and ordered by means of the categories of the understanding, which operate *a priori*. For Kant knowledge consists of a composition of intuition—sensory impressions—and thought—this latter being what the faculty of knowledge 'supplies from itself'; there can be no knowledge that is not a composition of and by these two operations. Kant says that all knowledge begins with the senses, proceeds from the senses to the understanding, and ends in reason. Kant explains the role of reason by referring to the different forms of logical inference, the categorical, the hypothetical and the disjunctive. Reason belongs to the faculty of understanding and, like understanding, reason operates through *a priori* concepts. Having called the concepts of the understanding 'categories,' Kant refers to the concepts of reason as 'Ideas.' In order to make a knowledge claim, Kant maintains, reason seeks the unconditioned.

Lonergan's central criticism of Kant's philosophy concerns the role of the unconditioned in the achievement of knowledge. For Kant, the unconditioned is a regulative idea lying beyond experience and the phenomenal world, the world we access through our understanding. Its function is to systematize and unify human rationality, bidding us seek ever greater syntheses of phenomena. As merely a regulative idea it is not constitutive of the real, nor could it be. For Lonergan, by contrast, the unconditioned is required for verification to take place; and since the verified is the real, the unconditioned is constitutive of the real. The unconditioned is attained when a direct act of understanding is reflectively understood as a conditioned whose conditions have been fulfilled; that is, the unconditioned is known when reflective understanding grasps that the data (or some of the data) 'fit' direct understanding. This 'fit' is not privileged in any way but has to be checked and established as being the case. But once this 'fit' is verified the inquirer can legitimately proceed to make a judgment about what is, a knowledge claim. In judgment the data of sense and the intelligible grasped by understanding are affirmed and posited as a unity. The unconditioned is the real and the real is the unconditioned. The split between sense and understanding, the dualism of sense and understanding, is overcome in judgment. The merely regulative role of the unconditioned in Kant's theory of knowledge means that it cannot function in this way. It should be noted that in critical realism the shift from understanding to judgment comes about by force of logical necessity: by insisting on conditionality, Lonergan makes it clear that once the conditions are fulfilled the conditioned must logically be affirmed as being the case—If A, then B; but A; so, B.

The reason Lonergan makes much of this is because it indicates Kant's failure to reconcile two forms of realism to be found in his philosophy, the realism of (Humean) empiricism and the realism of (Cartesian) rationalism. The first is the realism of animal extroversion, the notion that we access reality through our senses. The second is the realism of rational affirmation, the notion that we infer the existence of objects—including of self—from our inner mental experiences.[28] Kant's synthesis of the empiricist and rationalist strands in his philosophy fails to produce an effective bridge between sensibility and understanding. The gulf between the unknowable noumenal world and the knowable phenomenal world means that the synthesis of understanding and sensibility cannot deliver the 'really real'; all we can have knowledge of are phenomena, or appearances.

Finally, we might note that Kant was awakened from his dogmatic slumbers by his encounter with the philosophy of David Hume and the impact of Hume on Kant's philosophy is not hard to discern. For Hume the world is a manifold of sensations, the mind a bundle of impressions. The question arises as to why we do not experience the world as a chaos or disjointed flux. The reason we experience the world as ordered and predictable, Hume maintains, is because of the power of the association of ideas which gives rise to beliefs and habits that guide the imagination to impose a unity and pattern on the manifold of sensory impressions. According to Hume, the association of ideas provides the 'cement' that binds the world into a unity in place of the discarded notion of 'substance.' In a somewhat analogous fashion, Kant maintains that the 'given' manifold of sensitive intuitions received by the faculty of the sensibility is ordered and unified by the synthesizing powers of the *a priori* categories provided by the faculty of understanding and judgment. The influence of Hume can also be seen in Kant's combination of the operations of understanding and reason, not with the *data* of sense, but with the *sensitive intuitions* of phenomena.[29] By referring to 'sensitive intuitions,' Kant in effect incorporates Hume's perceptionism into his account of knowledge: the German word translated as 'intuition'—*Anschauung*—is not a special kind of knowledge but is simply the same as the ordinary English verb 'to see.'[30] Lonergan, by contrast, distinguishes sharply between sensation, understanding and judgment, and considers the move from understanding to judgment to be legitimate only if *a comparison* of the data of sense with the proposed understanding produces a convincing or probable match—that is to say, only if the conditions attached to any hypothesis or proposed understanding are fulfilled. It is the possibility of making such a comparison that makes Lonergan's epistemology 'critical': an explanation of the data that fails to account for, or cohere with, the data cannot legitimately be affirmed as true; that is the reason Lonergan refers to his philosophy as 'Critical Realism.' By making the understanding (*Verstand*) the faculty of judgment, by failing to distinguish between the two operations of understanding and judgment, Kant makes such a comparison both unnecessary and impossible. Lonergan seeks to correct both empiricism and idealism by drawing attention to what each leaves out: empiricism leaves out understanding as an operation distinct from sensation, and idealism leaves out judgment as an operation distinct from understanding. For this reason Lonergan repudiates the claim that critical realism is a halfway house between empiricism and idealism but rather considers idealism to be the halfway house between empiricism and critical realism. The relevance of these comments to the aesthetic theories of Lonergan and Leavis should become apparent when I turn to the difference between the Leavisian approach to literary criticism and that of the neo-Kantian philosopher, Susanne Langer.

In the period after Kant, the two strands of his philosophy—the empiricist and the rationalist—tended to float free of one another, and philosophy bifurcated into positivism and pragmatism, on the one hand, and idealism and immanentism, on the other.[31] As they moved further apart, each became more and more entrenched in its own exclusivity, with positivism and pragmatism affirming the triumph of the physical and natural sciences, while idealism took up the notion of thought thinking itself in human history. And so we end up with what Lonergan refers to as the 'naturalism' of much English-language philosophy, which prizes mathematical and scientific knowledge, and the 'historicism' of the German philosophical tradition, which prizes meaning. Analytic philosophy has been drawn to the former, while the German philosophical tradition has dwelt on the latter.

This bifurcation of philosophy takes us to the heart of one of Leavis's central preoccupations: the quality of modern 'technologico-Benthamite' civilization, in which the great danger, he believes, is the loss by the industrialised 'masses' of the humane and humanising values that had characterised older and more 'organic' communal life in England. At the intellectual level, this divide between these two types of civilization—for to a large extent he deals in 'ideal types'—is figured by Leavis as being supported, respectively, by positivist philosophy, on the side of modern mechanised civilization, and, on the side of the endangered humane values, by human studies and, in particular, literary criticism. Leavis's passion was driven by the deeply felt need to ensure that what was best in the tradition, humanly speaking, was brought into a living and civilizing relationship with the present and the future. It was this deeply felt need that coloured his attitude to philosophy, since so much of English-language philosophy in his life-time was of a positivist character.

In light of this, it is not surprising that literary critics have often felt under-valued or even rejected by analytic philosophy and drawn to the methods of investigation prized and esteemed by continental philosophy. The reasons for this are well expressed in David Holbrook's chapter in *The Leavises: Recollections and Impressions*, where he writes:

> One of our major tasks (of saving and safeguarding the humanities) is to restore to the quest the search for insight into the subjective realm, that half of reality which has been seriously neglected since the triumph of the scientific revolution in the seventeenth century, and the predominance of the 'objective' ideal, which can only find as real the outer (and dead) things. Only then can we overcome the alienation which men feel, as they now seem to be in a universe (that delineated by Newtonian physics and Cartesian science) in which man's culture and achievements have no place, and in which no meaning is possible, because everything is only matter in motion operating by chance and necessity, in which "everything exists and nothing has value."[32]

By means of his exploration of human intentional consciousness and his reconciliation of subjectivity with objectivity, I contend, Bernard Lonergan provides a bridge between analytic and continental philosophy, not by attempting to reduce one to the other but by completing what each is inclined to exclude or leave out. Lonergan refrains from setting the humanities against the natural sciences, one school of philosophy against another; rather he seeks to bridge the gulf between them by testing each against his 'transcendental method.' Transcendental method is thoroughly comprehensive and capable of being integrated with the methodology of science, of mathematics, of history, of hermeneutics[33] and of literary criticism. To avoid the danger of sounding just too pat and over-confident at this point, I should add that Lonergan does not think of transcendental method as mechanical—as if to say that if you follow the method all will be well. No mechanical method, independent of the subject, relieves her of the responsibility of judging; no human authenticity can be automatic. The actuation of transcendental method is always dependent on the subject's free decision and, as such, to be authentic it must itself conform to the transcendental imperative, 'Be responsible.'[34]

PART THREE: METHOD IN THEOLOGY AND THE HUMANE DISCIPLINES

Transcendental method is the key to Lonergan's division of theology and the humane disciplines into eight functional specialities: this division is simply the fourfold division of transcendental method—experience, understanding, judgment and decision—multiplied by two. There is, first, theology in its positive phase: research, interpretation, history and dialectic. As a discipline with claims to intellectual respectability this positive phase of theology is indispensable. It is the guarantee that empirical scholarship plays an essential role in theology. Each of the first three functional specialities employs empirical methods of investigation, seeking to establish conclusions as verified hypotheses. Not only does each of these functional specialities apply empirical methods but the manner in which the specialities relate to each other represents the methodology of empirical inquiry on a larger scale. With research we seek, primarily, to establish what the data are. With interpretation we seek, primarily, to understand the data. With history we seek, primarily, to establish the facts, what actually was said and what actually took place along with the intentions and meaning of human words and actions. The fourth stage, dialectic, completes the process: conflicting positions and conclusions are lined up together with the methodologies by which they were established, they are probed and examined, and those found wanting in respect of the norms of empirical inquiry are eliminated. Lonergan sees this first phase as one devoted to appropriating the religious tradition, of mediating the past, and this is a thoroughly empirical endeavour. As such it can be done by anyone, believer or non-believer.

But dialectic, the fourth stage of the positive phase of theology, brings the individual to a decision, a challenge, a crisis. And this gives rise to a second fourfold division of theology, this time in its normative phase. Because theology is scholarship designed for men and women and not for robots, the human subject is faced with the challenge of taking a stand on what has been established in the positive phase. The second fourfold division of theology into conversion, doctrines, systematics and communications corresponds to the four stages of transcendental method, this time running in reverse order from values to knowledge, from knowledge to understanding, from understanding to providing the data for others. As such, conversion is foundational—along with the four functional specialities that mediate the tradition—for the last three functional specialities. It provides the faith context in which one decides to give intellectual assent to certain beliefs and teachings (doctrines). It provides the faith context in which one maps out the relations of the various doctrines to each other (systematics). And it provides the dynamism for creating the community in which new religious adherents will be nurtured and developed (communications). This second, normative, division of theology will be determined by the presence or absence of religious conversion, by which Lonergan means the state of being in love with God, of responding to God's free gift of his love.

Most of us have a positive and normative side to our thinking and living. We read newspapers, books and articles, absorb a great many facts and statistics, listen to the pronouncements of politicians, moralists, journalists, scientists and other intellectual pundits and experts of various kinds. If we read and listen honestly we do so with an open mind, willing to change our minds in the light of new thinking, new interpretations, new evidence. If we are truly engaged we read and attend critically, attempting to assess with precision the truth or validity of the conclusions or recommendations put forward. Among other things, we test what we learn against what we already understand, know or believe to be the facts of the matter and what we perceive to be the honesty and acumen of the writer or speaker. But most of all, in the field of policy, we judge what we hear or read guided by our prevailing values. From this process we build up our own personal store of opinions, judgments and beliefs, we establish norms to guide our behaviour, and so forth. In other words, we establish the normative side of our lives, we take part in the process of forming our personalities and outlook on life. The shift from the positive to the normative side of our thinking is perfectly natural and totally necessary if we are to become integrated human beings, if we are to have beliefs and opinions of our own, if we are to form something resembling a coherent world-view, if we are to build up community and hand on understanding and discipline to our children.

The interplay between the positive and normative sides of our lives may help the reader to catch on to what Lonergan is about when discussing the methodology of theology and the other humane disciplines. The pivotal point in the shift from positive to normative in the context of our lives is the area of values. In a similar way values are pivotal in the shift from the positive to the normative phase in theology. But prior to values and determining what they will be is authentic conversion to God. Conversion is, of course, a well established religious ground for action with an excellent pedigree in both Old and New Testaments. Lonergan sees authentic conversion as being in complete harmony with the positive, empirical tasks of theology and indeed as being their culmination and goal.

For to be carried out according to the norms of transcendental method the positive tasks require the investigator to free herself of bias and place the value of achieving the truth above any merely personal satisfaction. This requires both cognitive and moral self-transcendence. By committing themselves to God, Lonergan argues, people achieve the pinnacle of self-transcendence since conversion is the enemy of bias, the natural ally of righteousness in both conduct and understanding. This is so because Lonergan considers the valid philosophical argument for God's existence to rest on human beings' intellectual and moral nature: God is the source of the universe's intelligibility and the ground of its moral order. There is a fulfilling reciprocity between humans in all our intellectual questioning and questing, our moral struggling and striving, and God in his gift of love to humanity. Through conversion the human capacity for self-transcendence meets fulfilment in being in love without conditions or reservations. So it is that authentic conversion provides the pivot from the positive to the normative phase in theology. There is nothing false or forced in the relationship between the two phases. Authentic conversion does not interfere with the freedom of the researcher to research, of the interpreter to interpret, of the historian to pin down exactly what went on. Rather conversion upholds the search for truth in every field of inquiry. The positive and the normative phases of theology, though distinct, complete each other. It is for this reason that some of Lonergan's followers have suggested a fifth level of consciousness, the level of religious conversion; this goes along with a fifth transcendental imperative: Be in Love.

PART FOUR: SOME PRACTICAL CONSEQUENCES

There is a pleasing intellectual elegance in the theological method Lonergan proposes: the fourfold division of transcendental method as manifested in both its positive and normative phases yields an eightfold division of the work that is theology. The one phase finds its completion in the other. But as in the case of scientific laws, intellectual elegance can be matched by great practical gains if and when the method is applied. What, we might ask, might these gains be? Well, straight off we can say that the method has the potential to bring clarity where before there was confusion, to place theology alongside other human studies, and to provide a basis for ecumenical encounter both within the Christian religion and between Christianity and other world faiths.

Clarity can be imposed on confusion because the method makes it possible to say what theology is and who is doing theology. Is the systematic theologian the one who is really doing theology or is the biblical exegete, perhaps, the truer theologian? What about the popular preacher or those who devote themselves to tracing sources, editing texts and so forth? The division of theology and other human studies into eight functional specialities brings order to the field of endeavour. It indicates the value and indispensability of each function and relates each function to the others. Precisely because it encompasses the whole of theology, because it is completely comprehensive in its sweep, Lonergan's eightfold division provides a vantage point which allows the parts to be related to the whole. Such a vantage point brings clarity. It allows the researcher, the interpreter and historian, for example, to get on with their work unimpeded by considerations of doctrinal orthodoxy or heterodoxy. In so doing, it confers on theology the status of an honest intellectual discipline. But care must be taken here: Lonergan is not attempting to confine the theologian to one particular functional speciality, as if one theologian ought to be nothing but an historian, for example, or another nothing but a researcher. When he talks about functional specialities he is thinking more about the *specific tasks* that any theologian or scholar might perform; it is quite possible for any scholar to undertake work in a number of functional specialities; it is the tasks that are specialist and not necessarily the individual scholar.

At the same time, theology is, through its normative work, a palpable force in the present. It is not a museum piece or curiosity, but something that speaks to us of reality, a source of vision and values. The normative phase of any humane discipline brings the discipline into a significant relationship with the present—a point, we shall see, of crucial importance in Leavis's understanding of the role of literary criticism.

Lonergan's eightfold division is of a high level of generality. It can be applied not only to theology but to all human studies that invite the student to appropriate the past in order to take a stand on the present and the future. Such an approach has provided educationalists with a rationale for the study of history and the classics as well as English literature. In each case the past is studied because it has something of importance to say to us in the present. Reading the great poetry of the past 'moralizes' us, as Matthew Arnold put it. F. R. Leavis truly hoped that frequent encounter with serious literature would so work on our sensibility and intelligence that we would undergo something akin to moral conversion. From time to time there are disputes in the educational profession about the kind of history that ought to be taught in British schools, with particular reference to the attention that should be devoted to 'British heritage.' Lonergan's method indicates how an answer to such a question could be found. There is nothing wrong with teaching children about their national heritage, indeed it should be encouraged, but historians should be free to establish what the facts truly are and students should be acquainted with the processes by which historical facts are established. Both positive and normative sides of the subject can be emphasized; exclusion of either side would be a distortion. Confusion of one side with the other would be the worst distortion of all; for example, the subordination of empirical inquiry to the desire to foster a fanatical patriotism, as occurred in Nazi Germany, is clearly dishonest and undesirable. And finally, because it does justice to other human studies besides theology, Lonergan's method helps to place theology among the intellectual disciplines pursued in school and higher education. Theology is not alone in investigating the past in order to bring it into a living relationship with the present and future.

The eightfold division can also provide a basis for fruitful ecumenical dialogue. Precisely because of its high level of generality, which follows from its correspondence with transcendental method, Lonergan's theological method provides us with an instrument with which we can measure the various Christian traditions, as they have come down to us shaped by history, scarred by the battles of the past. There is nothing novel in saying that each of the traditions has its own basic orientation, biases and hang ups. They have, all of them, been through a lot. The method proposed for theology should help us to see the strengths and weaknesses of the various traditions in a clearer light than would otherwise be possible. It should help us to see where they fall short, where a particular emphasis, because it has been exaggerated, has led to a distortion of the message of Jesus. It might even help fundamentalists, who tend to be wedded to the normative, doctrinal phase of theology but to eschew the positive phase with horror, to become reconciled with agnostic scientific investigators, who can see the point of research, interpretation and historical inquiry but view theology's normative phase with suspicion. The theological method Lonergan proposes could perform a similar service for the wider ecumenism, in promoting balanced and fruitful dialogue between the various world faiths. Because it is grounded in transcendental method it transcends cultural divisions and provides central human norms of honesty and authenticity by which such dialogue could be guided.

PART FIVE: THE NECESSITY OF CHANGE

These are some of the practical gains we might look to theological method to deliver. But besides these gains, Lonergan's *Method in Theology* is written by a member of the Roman Catholic community who has something of value to say to his fellow members. He has an eye open to the hang ups and misleading preoccupations of the Catholic tradition, or so it seems to me. While *Method* is concerned largely with the eight functional specialities that constitute theology, there is another strong theme that runs through the work like a motif. *That theme is the necessity of change.* I recall attending one of

Lonergan's seminars on the texts of St Thomas Aquinas, when at one point he declared (in Latin, the medium of education at the Gregorian University at the time), 'St Thomas was not stupid. He changed his mind.' The significance of this incident dawned on me forcefully later on, when I came to recognise the influence exerted on Lonergan by Matthew Arnold, which I shall expand upon in a later chapter. For one thing Arnold wished to cultivate through education was openness and flexibility of mind, the characteristics of the ancient Athenians, the secret of their success.

Now 'openness and flexibility of mind' have not exactly been outstanding Catholic characteristics in recent centuries. The Catholic Church has been characterised by its fixed and unmoving positions in matters theological. There is indeed a suggestion that the Church is imprisoned behind a carapace of past decrees and affirmations from which it cannot break free. Lonergan was no liberal Protestant but he wished to liberate Catholicism from the straight-jacket in which certain false attitudes and assumptions had placed her. In *Method in Theology* he sets about laying the axe to the roots of these attitudes and assumptions. These roots are what he terms 'the classicist conception of culture,' the Aristotelian conception of science and the logico-deductive model of establishing theological conclusions. I shall conclude this opening chapter by suggesting briefly the nature of each.

The classicist conception of culture is of a single, unique culture open only to the initiated, from which the vulgar, the barbarians, the others are excluded. Within the classicist notion of culture theology is viewed as a permanent achievement, something fixed and immutable, in which there is no room for change of any consequence. Opposed to the classicist notion of culture is the empirical notion of culture by which culture is conceived as the set of meanings and values that inform a way of life; as such, cultures change, develop, impact on each other. Hence Lonergan's repetition in the 1960s and 70s that what Catholics were experiencing was not a crisis of faith but a crisis of culture. Catholics were having to adjust to the notion of change. I hope to develop in the next chapter how Lonergan's understanding of the classicist notion of culture resonates with certain comments of Leavis on the study of literature.

The Aristotelian notion of science is of true, certain knowledge of causal necessity. But modern science is not true, is not strictly speaking knowledge, and is not concerned with Aristotle's four causes (efficient, final, formal and material), or with necessity. Modern science speaks instead of hypotheses, the best scientific opinion of the day, of verifiable possibility, and it addresses itself to contingent facts. Scientific theories are permanently open to revision, they can be and are superseded by new theories that offer a more fruitful and powerful account of the data. The problem is that in the past Catholic theology has been conceived as analogous to science understood in its Aristotelian sense. Now Lonergan is no relativist; he believes in the permanence of truth. But he distinguishes between permanence and immutability and argues for the permanence of truth on the basis of the open-ended structure of transcendental method that yields cumulative and progressive results.

A third factor that stands behind the Catholic aversion to change has been the habit among certain Catholic theologians of arriving at conclusions by often dubious short-cut methods of deductive reasoning. Examples of this kind of argument are the following: 'The bible says X; but the bible is the inspired word of God; therefore X is true'; or, 'The Church has taught X; the Church was founded by God; therefore X is true.' This obsession with logical deduction as the standard mode of theological argument has tended to demote genuine scholarly exploration and discursive reasoning; it tends to short-circuit historical inquiry into how ideas have developed and how certain doctrines came to be established; it gives rise to the false notion that theological development could be fully explained by claiming that it was achieved by making 'explicit' what had been 'implicitly revealed.'[35] Development in these terms becomes simply a matter of unpacking what is already logically contained in scripture and tradition; it is the natural ally of the classicist notion of culture.

I explained earlier that Lonergan is an intellectualist. As such he does not regard knowledge as a branch of logic, as some epistemologists have done, but rather assigns logic an essential but subordinate role within the move from ignorance to knowledge in the course of empirical reasoning. For the intellectualist what is prized above all, what brings about progress in empirical inquiry, is insight, the understanding of the data. And for insight to occur there is required imagination, openness of mind, the ability to envisage several possibilities. Development of understanding consists of a series of verified imaginative leaps. Conceived in this way, theology is an ongoing process developed by means of collaborative creativity and open-ended dialogue. And because there occur among peoples of different times and in different places many varieties of common sense and various differentiations of consciousness, theological development takes place by making Christian revelation intelligible in terms of these variations.

From what I have been able to offer in this sketch of Lonergan's thinking I hope it has emerged that Lonergan's position is intellectually robust as well as daring. It bears the stamp of the Catholic trust in the compatibility of reason and faith, of science and religion, of the God of philosophy with the God of revelation, while at the same time the foundational role allocated to conversion accords with one of Protestantism's basic religious insights. Lonergan's method bids fair to assist the ecumenical process and the radical reconstruction of Christian theology over the next fifty years or so. And its strong insistence on the indispensability for theological inquiry of objective research and scientific rigour should provide a much needed bulwark against the religious fundamentalism which holds such sway in the world today

NOTES

1. For example, a hospital is not a meaningless building but a building that embodies an *idea* (or a particular plan related to a specific purpose.) Where sensation grasps the sensible, the data, understanding grasps the intelligible, the idea. True understanding occurs when the idea grasped by the subject is identical with the idea that is to be found in a particular set of data. By means of this understanding of understanding, Lonergan's epistemology avoids the hoary problem of 'veil of ideas' scepticism (that all we have direct knowledge of are the ideas in our minds) which haunts traditional empiricism.

2. Bernard Lonergan, *Verbum: Word and Idea in Aquinas* (London:Darton, Longman and Todd, 1968), edited by David B. Burrell C. S. C. The chapters of this book first appeared as articles in the Jesuit journal, *Theological Studies*, between 1946 and 1949.

3. For Lonergan's historical investigation of this point as expounded by Aristotle and Aquinas, see *Verbum:Word and Idea in Aquinas*, p. 24–5.

4. L. Wittgenstein, *Tractatus Logico-Philosophicus* (1922), trans D. F. Pears and B. F. McGuinness (London: Routledge, 1974).

5. *Philosophical Investigations*(1953), trans. G. E. M. Anscombe (Oxford: Basil Blackwell, 1953).

6. Lonergan, *Method*, p. 71.

7. Leavis, *The Living Principle*, p. 185.

8. *Philosophical Investigations*, 258.

9. Lonergan, *Collection*, p. 264.

10. Leavis, *The Living Principle*, p. 39.

11. P. 95.

12. Lonergan, *Philosophy of God and Theology*, (London: Darton, Longman and Todd, 1973), p. 59.

13. Lonergan, *Method in Theology* (London: Darton, Longman and Todd, 1972), p. 254–55.

14. Ibid., p. 255–56.

15. This account occurs in several places in Leavis's writing but this neat summary is given in F. R. Leavis, *The Two Cultures?* edited by Stefan Collini (Cambridge: Cambridge University Press, 2013), p. 74–75.

16. See the article on Descartes by Anthony Kenny in *The Oxford Illustrated History of Philosophy* (London: QPD, 1994), ed. Anthony Kenny, p. 113.

17. Anthony Kenny, *Aquinas* (Oxford: Oxford University Press, 1980), p. 28.

18. Lonergan, *Insight*, p. 362.

19. L. Wittgenstein, *On Certainty*, trans. D. Paul and G. E. M. Anscombe (Oxford: Basil Blackwell, 1979). For a more extended comparison of Lonergan's and Wittgenstein's philosophies, see chapter six of my book, *Philosophical Encounters: Lonergan and the Analytical Tradition*.

20. *Treatise*, 251–52.

21. This and the subsequent quotations are from *Collection*, p. 176–77.

22. D. Hume, *Treatise of Human Nature*, ed. L. A. Selby-Bigge (London: Clarendon Press, 1888), p. 467–70.

23. Quoted in *Kant* by S. Korner (London: Pelican Books, 1955), p. 15.

24. Barry Cullen in 'The Impersonal Objective' in *F. R. Leavis*, ed. Ian MacKillop and Richard Storer (London: Continuum, 2005), p. 172.

25. 'The Form of Inference' in *Collection: Papers by Bernard Lonergan*, ed. F. E. Crowe (London: Darton, Longman and Todd, 1967).

26. My italics.

27. Immanuel Kant, *Critique of Pure Reason*, B 75; the B indicates that the quotation is from the second edition of the *Critique*.

28. Lonergan, *Insight*, p. 414–15.
29. Lonergan, *Method*, p. 264.
30. This valuable point is made by Giovanni Sala in 'Kant's Theory of Knowledge," *Lonergan Workshop 16*, edited by Fred Lawrence (Boston: Boston College, 2000), p. 206.
31. Lonergan, *Method*, p. 264; also, *Insight*, p 412–415.
32. David Holbrook, 'F. R. Leavis and the sources of hope," in *The Leavises: Recollections and Impressions*, ed. Denys Thompson, (Cambridge University Press, 1984), p. 156–7.
33. See the many references to hermeneutics in *Method in Theology*.
34. See Lonergan, *A Third Collection*, ed. F. E. Crowe, (London: Geoffrey Chapman, 1985) p. 152–53.
35. On this, see *Method in Theology*, p. 270.

Chapter Two

Leavis and Lonergan

INTRODUCTION

An elderly don who had worked for many years in the English School at Cambridge once remarked to me, "You must understand that Leavis is not just a person; Leavis is a *force*." And indeed the impact made by F. R. Leavis, ably supported by his wife, Q. D. Leavis, on English intellectual and cultural life was at one time remarkable; whether it is as strong today is doubtful and I hope to show that this is a loss to British cultural life. Leavis's influence was exerted through his editorship of the literary journal, *Scrutiny,* throughout the two decades of its existence (1932 to 1953) and through the large body of his literary critical writings which spanned almost half a century. It also derived from the strategic position commanded by Cambridge University during his life. Though Leavis's relations with the establishment at Cambridge and in the English School (and indeed with the values of metropolitan literary society emanating from the so-called "quality British press") were far from happy, his position as founder and director of the Centre of English Studies at Downing College (in 1932; he became a university lecturer only in 1936) enabled him to inspire a large number of undergraduates with his own ideals and critical methods. In turn, many of the undergraduates were to become influential authors, editors, journalists, theatrical producers, university lecturers and professors; many more became teachers in order to teach English in the service of the cause for which he had taught it to them.

But the reference to Leavis as a *force*, while suggesting the range of his influence, was also intended to draw attention to the power and vigour of his personality and the strength of the passion that drove him. Though his thinking is unusually subtle and wide ranging, moving from a microcosmic concern with a given literary text to a macrocosmic treatment of the quality of civilization (and insisting on the organic connection between micro and macro), his mind and tongue are also sharp and incisive. He knows who and what the enemy are and he hits hard. While he presents his own position and the cause for which he stands with an extraordinary persuasive insistence, treating the reader as an intelligent and informed participant in an on-going discussion, his attacks on those he considers his opponents startle at times by their sheer brutality—a fact that earned him many enemies or opponents and at times sadly soured his relationships with those who had previously admired him or worked with him. Sarcastic puns and jibes, devastating *argumenta ad hominem*, curt asides are all used to reduce his opponents (as opposed to those he considers his collaborators) to objects of scorn and derision. The reasons for the malicious element in Leavis's style, especially when lecturing, are probably rather complex,[1] but inevitably added to the controversy that surrounded him when alive and which continues to surround his name and reputation today, a controversy widely reflected in the huge wave of obituary notices and reminiscences that followed his death in April 1978 at the age of 82.

Leavis's passionate advocacy of the benefits of studying English literature can be explained in part by his experience as a conscientious-objecting, non-combatant stretcher bearer in the First World War. This left its mark on him and is said to have interfered with his sleep in later life; he often expressed his horror at seeing waves of young men being mown down by enemy machine guns. This experience stands behind his profound belief that education had a *moral role* to play as well as an intellectual one, and his fierce dedication to the education of his students' "sensibilities." It is probably impossible to appreciate the moral force of Leavis's writings, his concern for the tone and quality of contemporary culture, without taking account of the psychological impact of his early brutal encounter with the consequences of modern mechanised warfare.

Bernard Lonergan is not a controversial figure in the way that Leavis was. His writing style, like his mind, is broad and ample, methodical, uncluttered, persistent, a combination of precision and concision. His tone is rarely polemical; most commonly he expounds with clarity and force; at times he is magisterial and there are occasional rhetorical flourishes. However, his tendency to argue in a cumulative fashion, listing and numbering points for or against a particular position, can at times tax, not to say weary, the reader. (At one point in chapter 19 of his book *Insight*, Lonergan writes "In the twenty-fifth place" before going on, three paragraphs later, to "Finally"![2]) But most of the time, when dealing with living opponents, he combines a certain ruthlessness in argument with consideration for his opponents' feelings. Nor was Lonergan situated within the complex web of a nation's cultural life and tradition in a way that Leavis was. This is partly due to the difference between the North American hemisphere and England (which Leavis referred to as "a tight little island" in contrast to America). It also relates to the fact that Lonergan did not work and teach at a recognised centre of culture and influence, at least within the Anglo-Saxon perspective. He taught and worked mainly in relatively obscure academic institutions in his native Canada and in Rome, and many of his writings were in the decidedly minority language of Latin. That despite these handicaps his influence has been wide ranging, particularly in Catholic and/or theological circles, and continues to grow is owing to the respect—*awe* in some cases would be the more appropriate word—his thinking has succeeded in commanding. Suffice it to say that such is the range and sweep of his thinking that there is hardly a branch of learning or an intellectual discipline that his methodological investigations can fail to touch and illuminate.[3]

By contrast, Leavis's intellectual interests are focused almost exclusively on England, English culture and the English literary tradition. Though widely read and conversant with several foreign languages, his academic preoccupation is with English, his points of reference are Arnold, Eliot (George and T. S.), Lawrence, James, Hopkins, Conrad, Wordsworth, Shakespeare, Donne, Blake etc. and—rather late in the day, Dickens—as well as other contemporary critics. The use he makes of the philosophy of Michael Polanyi in his later writings, while indicating the breadth of his reading, serves his purpose as a literary critic, and I would suggest that the attraction Polanyi held for him was due in no small measure to the fact that, unlike many English-language philosophers of the period, Polanyi paid attention to the role of the subject in coming to know. On the whole, however, if not positively hostile to philosophy, Leavis is resistant to it and to the philosophical temperament, fearing, as he expressed it, the "consequences of queering one discipline with the habits of another." Despite these marked contrasts between the literary critic Leavis, and the highly systematic and philosophical Lonergan, who deliberately works at the transcultural level, I shall attempt to indicate broad areas of overlap in their respective thinking, which indicate a profound similarity of concern and outlook; in another chapter I shall trace in greater detail some of these similarities to the influence exerted on both Lonergan and Leavis by the writings of Matthew Arnold.

With luck the talents and preoccupations of the one—Leavis and Lonergan—will illuminate those of the other. Lonergan's philosophical reflections should lend weight to Leavis's comments on the critical method he advocates when reading a poem, and Leavis's critical method should exemplify the value of Lonergan's epistemology, or "transcendental method," when applied to literary studies. Like Polanyi, Lonergan explores at length the role of the subject in acquiring knowledge and, if anything, places an even stronger emphasis than Polanyi on moral self-transcendence and responsible commitment; but *unlike Polanyi*, he explores and makes explicit what the latter terms the "tacit dimension" in knowing, which Polanyi considers incapable of being made explicit, and in this way he avoids Polanyi's failure to make his philosophy "critical"; it is this failure of Polanyi's that leads Polanyi to propose the *merely fiduciary basis of all explicit knowledge*.[4] The weakness in Polanyi's theory of knowledge, as I see it, is the distinction he makes between "What we can know and prove" and "What we know and *cannot* prove" and his contention that the former is founded on the latter. It is as if the impressive edifice of explicit knowledge was founded on a swamp. This is not a view that Leavis's writings suggest he could have supported with consistency. Leavis's writings and robust critical judgments lead one to believe that he would have agreed with Lonergan's contention that human beings are perfectly capable of making true and objective knowledge claims based on evidence; in claiming that "objectivity (in knowing) is merely the consequence of authentic subjectivity,"[5] Lonergan avoids subjectivism since by "authentic subjectivity" he refers to the subject's impartiality or willingness to submit to the evidence. It is the features shared by Lonergan's epistemology and by Leavis's critical method, as well as the depth of their respective moral outlooks, that cause me to believe that Bernard Lonergan is a closer philosophical ally of Leavis than Michael Polanyi.

PART ONE: DECLINE AND THE ENGLISH SCHOOL, BIASES AND COSMOPOLIS

"It is a commonplace today that culture is at a crisis. It is a commonplace more widely accepted than understood: at any rate, realization of what the crisis portends does not seem to be common." Thus Leavis writes in the third page of *Mass Civilization and Minority Culture*[6] (published in 1930). Together with *Fiction and the Reading Public* (the doctoral thesis of Leavis's wife, Queenie, published in 1932) and *Culture and the Environment* (co-authored with Denys Thompson and published in 1933), this short work sets out the Leavisian understanding of the material conditions that have produced a crisis in contemporary culture. The root cause of the crisis, according to Leavis, is "the machine" and the mechanisation of the processes of production. Referring to *Middletown* ("a remarkable work of anthropology"), he says:

> We see in detail how the automobile (to take one instance) has, in a few years, radically affected religion, broken up the family, and revolutionised social custom. . . . It seems unlikely that the conditions of life can be transformed in this way without some injury to the standard of living (to wrest the phrase from the economist): improvisation can hardly replace the delicate traditional adjustments, the mature inherited codes of habit and valuation, without severe loss, and loss that may be more than temporary. It is a break in continuity that

threatens: what has been inadvertently dropped may be irrevocable or forgotten.[7]

What has been lost is the quality of life in English towns and villages, he believes, before the advent of machinery and the values imported with machinery: the "codes, developed in ages of continuous experience, of relations between man and man, and man and the environment in its seasonal rhythms":[8] the skills of the craftsmen and the manner in which these skills affected the craftsmen's relations with their products, as well as the folksongs and dances, the customs and traditional values that had humanised and created a community.

The methods of mass production and the consequent "standardisation" and "levelling down" have infected almost every facet of life in modern civilization (Leavis continues): the workplace where the division of labour in the factory has robbed labour of interest and made work merely a matter of earning money; the press where the main aim, as defined by newspaper proprietor Lord Northcliffe, is to "give the public what it wants," by appealing to the lowest common denominator; films—"They provide now the main form of recreation in the civilized world; and they involve surrender, under conditions of hypnotic receptivity, to the cheapest emotional appeals"; and radio broadcasting—"in practice mainly a means of passive diversion."[9] There is no point in claiming that modern technology has made it possible for the mass of the population to enjoy more leisure, for leisure itself has been corrupted by the modern technological malaise. The compensation offered for the degradation of work in modern industry is the fantasy world provided by film and radio; later Leavis adds addiction to television, bingo and one-armed bandits as well as the drug culture and the sexual promiscuity of the young to the list of symptoms revealing that the art of recreation, of genuine re-creative play, has been replaced by a "de-creation," a process every bit as deadly for our humanity as the processes of factory work. If alive today, Leavis would most likely add TV "soap operas," the celebrity culture and the volume of pornography available on the Internet, the press and much popular literature to the long list of features symptomatic of the degrading influence of modern culture; and what he would say about the sheer rapidity of technological change in modern life and the social and cultural impact of the digital revolution is anyone's guess—although he makes it clear in his late comments that he firmly believes that technology will continue to develop. Writing when he did, he is in no doubt that the modern cultivation of "optimism," "improvement" and "progress" is largely delusory; the main thrust of our civilization is downwards; civilization is in rapidly accelerating decline.

It is because English culture has reached such a low ebb that a "strong current of criticism is needed as never before," that the protection of standards is in the hands of a minority even more beleaguered than in the days of

Matthew Arnold,[10] and that it is incumbent upon "us to be as aware as possible of what is happening and, if we can, to keep open our communication with the future."[11]

Mass Civilization and Minority Culture and the two accompanying works I have mentioned constitute an early "manifesto" that underlies all of Leavis's subsequent writings and endeavours. It lies behind the decision to found *Scrutiny* and to keep it going, free of all advertising revenue despite the recurring threat of financial collapse, for twenty years, and his own individual and partisan approach to English literature. It also underpins his idea of a university and of the part to be played in the university by the English School or department. For while he acknowledges the inevitability of the ascendancy of "the machine," of technological advance, while he accepts that there is no going back to the conditions that obtained in a previous age, Leavis is not one to lie down and surrender without a struggle. And the force that should be brought to bear on modern technological advance and the human ills it has generated is the university. "The universities are recognised symbols of cultural tradition—of cultural tradition still conceived as a directing force, representing a wisdom older than modern civilization and having an authority that should check and control the blind drive onward of material and mechanical development, with its human consequences."[12] In *The Idea of a University* (1943) Leavis begins by insisting on the need to avoid the temptation to hammer out an agreed philosophy or *Summa* before starting to work. In particular, there is no "received doctrinal frame or conceptual apparatus which for Dante or Herbert was natural or inevitable"; and the notion of a religious revival, though it may be legitimate, is not the course Leavis is advocating. Rather he sees the values he is seeking as still enshrined within the notion of a liberal education traditionally provided by the "two older universities" in England. "Our age will, before it can stand in hope of its *Summa*, have been turned into something very different from what it is now. But education cannot wait upon the synthesis, and the enormous effort that makes the synthesis possible will not be merely philosophical; it will be the effort that creates the age, and the educational effort will be an essential part of it."[13] The aim is to produce "the educated man"—"the man of humane culture who is equipped to be intelligent and responsible about the problems of contemporary civilization." And for that there is needed a centre or focus within the university itself. Leavis proposes the English School or Department as such a centre or focus.

Leavis defends his proposal that the English School, of all the departments within the university, should be assigned such a privileged role or function by pointing to the non-specialist nature of English studies when compared with the kinds of specialisation going forward in other university departments. "'English,' because it is a humane school, and the non-specialist intelligence in which the various studies are to find that centre is the one that gets its own special training in literature. Its special—but not specialist—discipline is to be the literary-critical, a discipline of sensibility, judgment and thought which, of its essential nature, is concerned with training a non-specialist intelligence."[14] Rather than proposing a philosophical synthesis, which he considers an impossible ideal in contemporary England, Leavis suggests that we stick to the concrete as far as possible; and the concrete is the body of English literature, reaching back to Chaucer and beyond and coming down through Shakespeare and the seventeenth century to the present day. To study such a body of literature in its given historical periods is to move out beyond purely "literary" or "artistic" considerations and, drawing on relevant references in sociology, history, theology and any other disciplines, to perform discriminating judgments about "England as a civilization, a civilized community. . . . The student, it will be seen, would have to ponder his criteria, and that would mean a good deal of thinking and stock-taking of peculiarly valuable kinds. There would obviously be an implicit bearing on the present. . . . The aim is to produce a mind that will approach the problems of modern civilization with an understanding of their origins, a maturity of outlook, and, not a nostalgic addiction to the past, but a sense of human possibilities, difficult of achievement, that traditional cultures bear witness to and that it would be disastrous, in a breach of continuity, to lose sight of for good."[15]

I do not wish to enter here into the controversies that have surrounded Leavis's social analysis and his proposals concerning the function of the English School in the university nor to rebut the charge of "elitism" sometimes lodged against his preoccupation with the "two older universities." What I wish to do is to compare the general pattern of Leavis's thinking with Lonergan's. For it is in the elucidation of their pattern of thinking, and in the discriminating judgments that will have to be made as the similarities in this pattern begin to emerge, that the value of the comparison between Leavis and Lonergan, as I see it, essentially lie. In this chapter I shall trace briefly Leavis's proposal for the university's English School and Lonergan's treatment of what he terms "Cosmopolis" to Matthew Arnold's earlier proposal of an English Academy modelled on the role and function of the *Academie Francaise* in French literature and culture. I shall expand on this in a later chapter when I shall explore the Arnoldian influence on our two authors in greater detail.

We have seen how Leavis considers how the role of countering cultural decline might be performed by the English School in the university. I wish now to illustrate how Lonergan responded to the problems of cultural decline by adapting Arnold's proposal in his own unique fashion.

In chapter 7 of *Insight*, entitled "Common Sense as Object," Lonergan examines community, distinguishes three kinds of bias—individual bias, group bias and general bias—moves on to consider the nature of the longer cycle of decline and outlines his notion of "Cosmopolis." These topics illustrate the fact that Lonergan's chief preoccupation was to understand history; he is acutely aware that human existence is precarious, that human beings make themselves through their choices and decisions and that they are open to progress and its opposite, decline. Coming from Leavis, what strikes one most forcefully is the extreme generality of Lonergan's treatment of cultural decline and its reversal. Leavis considers the case of one country, England, he posits a particular cause of decline, the advent of mechanised civilisation, and illustrates its damaging ramifications by reference to particular instances. In proposing his "solution," which he admits can only be partial, he points to a concrete institution, namely the university, and to a particular kind of endeavour within that institution, namely a special kind of engagement with the literary products of that country. Lonergan does not restrict his treatment to any one country; he speaks of "man," "culture" and "decline" in a highly generalised fashion; he refrains from casting technology as the villain of the historical drama he depicts and he deliberately refuses to point to any one institution as providing the "solution," which at this stage in his book he admits can only be partial. The generality of his treatment, which is thrown into sharp relief following our examination of Leavis, at once highlights the difference in the styles of thinking of our two writers while also indicating their shared concern that cultural decline needs to be countered. The difference in thinking styles can be explained by the fact that in his book Lonergan is concerned with "insight," human understanding and intelligence, and he identifies progress with the accumulation and implementation over time of valid insights, and identifies decline with the flight from insight and understanding brought about by various kinds of bias. As I have said, Lonergan tends to work at the transcultural or transcendental level; or you might say that he deals in what is common to human nature everywhere—hence the generality of his treatment of decline, and its remedy.

In *Insight* Lonergan is not "doing" sociology or history but rather dealing in ideal types. He isolates the significant variables that make for particular kinds of change: he distinguishes three kinds of bias and posits two as the principles of decline. "There is the minor principle of group bias which tends to generate its own corrective. There is the major principle of general bias and, though it too generates its own corrective, it does so only by confronting human intelligence with the alternative of adopting a higher viewpoint or perishing."[16] Group bias depends on, and is supported by, the spontaneous intersubjectivity and the mutual self-interest of a given group within society which "is prone to have a blind spot for the insights that reveal its well-being to be excessive or its usefulness at an end." In time this leads to a distortion of the social reality so palpable as to be "exposed to the inspection of the multitude" and a reversal, that may be more or less peaceful, is eventually summoned.

General bias is the bias of common sense itself, which, though standing above the egoism of the individual and the bias of the dominant or depressed group that seeks only its own advantage, nevertheless lacks the theoretical framework to guide its choices or allow it to take a longer view; for common sense regards only the practical, and theory and higher viewpoints fall outside the sphere of the practical.[17] Consequently common sense on its own fails to appropriate the norms inherent in its own rationality which would permit it to be critical. Faced with the social surd, the social distortion generated by the systematic resistance to the cumulative emergence of new ideas, common sense conforms. The longer cycle of decline is kicked off by that major surrender on the speculative level, when the norms inherent in human intelligence are systematically ignored and there is a consequent "increasing demand for further contractions of the claims of intelligence, for further dropping of old principles and norms, for closer conformity to an ever growing man-made incoherence immanent in man-made facts." What emerges, in the limit, is the totalitarian regime which erects its own conscious myth to sustain the reality that has emerged, backed up by appropriate force. Amusingly (almost) common sense will in turn get out from under the totalitarian state and the ideological self-justification which common sense has helped to foster because it has no use for any theoretical apparatus. But on its own common sense is not equipped to reverse the process it has helped to initiate. (I cannot resist adding here, as a kind of aside, that the features of the "bias of common sense" Lonergan identifies and the rejection of "an alternative theoretical framework" have become all too visible and palpable in the politics of the United States since the election of 2016.)

The force that Lonergan would bring to bear on the decline brought about by group or general bias he terms "Cosmopolis." The function of Cosmopolis, which he refrains from identifying with any one institution, is to be a witness to the truth in adverse and unfavourable circumstances. "It is its business to satirize the catchwords and the claptrap . . .; it is its business to encourage and support those that would speak the simple truth though simple truth has gone out of fashion."[18] Cosmopolis "confronts the problems of which men are aware; it invites the vast potentialities and pent-up energies of our time to contribute to their solution by developing an art and a literature, a theatre and a broadcasting, a journalism and a history, *a school and a university*, a personal depth and a public opinion, that through appreciation and criticism, give men of common sense the opportunity and help they need and desire to correct the general bias of their common sense."[19] However, like Leavis, Lonergan is aware of the tremendous moral effort by a critical minority that is required to combat general bias. As he says, "It is by moving with that bias rather than against it, by differing with it slightly rather than opposing it thoroughly, that one has the best prospect of selling books and newspapers, entertainment and education."[20]

It would be wrong to say that Lonergan is not being empirical for he is being empirical while working at a more general level than either Leavis (or Arnold). The latter offer analyses of English society in given periods of its history; they quote contemporary authors and newspapers and cite specific instances. Now Lonergan clearly has recent modern history in mind as he writes about the longer cycle of decline: he speaks of Russia and Germany leaping to fairly thorough brands of totalitarianism. But his thinking is not grounded in this or that historical happening, and Cosmopolis is not directed to this or that historical situation. His analysis is grounded in human intelligence and its failures and, having indicated the biases that propel decline, he brings in Cosmopolis to show how decline can and ought to be countered. Whether or not western culture is involved in a longer cycle of decline Lonergan's analysis does not say. It does, however, help us to make up our minds and to understand the causes of decline with reference to human reason.

A little historical digging at this point may throw light on the concerns that Leavis and Lonergan hold in common and what it is that distinguishes them. Matthew Arnold was concerned with the "external" and "practical" character of Victorian English society, its cultivation of materialism, financial success and narrow utilitarian ideals. As one of Her Majesty's Inspectors of schools, he was dismayed by the threat to the educational ideal of character formation represented by the displacement of traditional liberal studies by science. He writes,

> To have the power of using, which is the thing wished, the data of science, a man must, in general, have first been in some sense "moralised"; and for moralising him it will be found not easy, I think, to dispense with those old agents, letters, poetry, religion. So let not our teachers be led to imagine, whatever they may hear and see of the call for natural science, that this literary cultivation is unimportant. The fruitful use of natural science itself depends, in a very great degree, on having effected in the whole man, by means of letters, a rise in what the political economists call the standards of life.[21]

In *Culture and Anarchy*, Arnold preaches the need for the pursuit of culture, which he in turn defines as "the study and pursuit of perfection," "an *inward* condition of the minds and spirit . . . at variance with the mechanical and material civilization in esteem with us"; which is like poetry in uniting "sweetness and light" and wishing to inform society with these characteristics. "Culture seeks to do away with classes; to make the best that has been thought and known in the world current everywhere; to make all men live in an atmosphere of sweetness and light, where they may use ideas, as it uses them itself, freely, nourished and not bound by them."[22] A practical man deeply concerned with the school curriculum, Arnold in his essay, *The Literary Influences of Academies*,[23] puts forward the notion of an English Academy on lines similar to the French Academy, founded by Richelieu in 1637 with the aim of purifying and embellishing the language (and thereby allowing French to replace Latin and Greek as the central force in French cultural life), and acting as a kind of "literary tribunal."

My reasons for embarking on this brief historical excursion are to show that Leavis and Lonergan have, in a sense, a common ancestry, in Arnold (and Coleridge), but each has adapted Arnold's proposals to his own purposes. Of the two Leavis probably owes more to Arnold; indeed he has frequently been compared to Arnold, and he deliberately places himself in the Arnoldian tradition. The opening words of *Mass Civilization and Minority Culture* are, "For Matthew Arnold it was in some ways less difficult," and his work is sprinkled with references to his great Victorian predecessor. Leavis is similar to Arnold in his preoccupation with the threat of "the machine" to English culture and his concentration on specifically literary values, the values inherent in the English literary tradition, as constituting a cleansing and redemptive force within the culture. Arnold's academy is transformed into the university English school or department, the notion of an "English Academy" clearly having been firmly scotched by Leavis's day, while the university department is now there—and in Leavis's thinking in need of a clearly defined role and purpose. By contrast, Lonergan takes what he has learned from Arnold and transposes it onto a transcultural plane, by grounding his analysis in what he terms "that inner core"—in this case humanity's natural propensity to accumulate, and its biased propensity to resist, valid insights. Lonergan translates Arnold's "English Academy" and Leavis's university English School into the transcultural entity he terms "Cosmopolis," which he refuses to identify with any one institution but which refers to a critical *moral function* that a wide range of social institutions are capable of performing.

It may be helpful here to indicate clearly what Leavis and Arnold are *not* saying. They are not saying or even suggesting that serious literature is the sole "moralising" influence in anyone's life, or even that it is the most important. Clearly there are many influences one could point to as having a serious influence on a person's moral development, such as parents, family, significant others and the problems and set-backs an individual might encounter and overcome, and so forth. But Leavis and Arnold were educationists who believed in the power of education to shape and influence those who might well be opinion-formers and authoritative figures in society—such as authors, journalists, broadcasters, politicians, teachers, lecturers, professors, theatrical producers etc. As a member of the Schools Inspectorship, and eventually Chief Inspector, Arnold was well placed to exercise a strong influence on educational thinking in his time; and Leavis was very conscious of Cambridge as a leading university with the potential to be a force for good in the cultural life of England and beyond. Arnold and Leavis were intent on influencing public opinion in England in their day by introducing the best that had been known and thought in the past, as they saw it, to students entering higher education. Their focus was the health and well-being of English culture and civilisation, the means they chose to use was the great literature of the past. Nor can the morally beneficial effects claimed for the study of literature be separated from the central norm or criterion—of right reason or self-transcendence—by means of which Arnold, Leavis and Lonergan measure the authenticity of a person and the moral health of a nation.

It is surely significant that Leavis, who had studied history at Cambridge for one year before going off to take part in the First World War, chose, on his return at the end of the war, to change subjects and devote his remaining two years to the study of English literature. The horrors he had witnessed in the war caused him to opt for a subject he believed to be capable of upholding and disseminating humane and civilising values, values he believed to be badly needed in a society traumatised, and possibly brutalised, by the experience of warfare.

PART TWO: CLASSICISM AND THE TURN TO THE SUBJECT

I wish shortly to indicate how Leavis's plans for an English School in the university accord in certain important respects with Lonergan's account of the functional specialities of theology, and have certain features or emphases that are not unlike those espoused by Lonergan. But first I must say something—to adapt phrases of Lonergan's—about Leavis's "turn to the subject" and his resistance to "the classical conception of culture." Once more, to grasp what Leavis is about it is best to start with a concrete instance. At one point Leavis satirizes Arnold Bennett's self-confessed "modesty about poetry."[24] Bennett had explained to an inquirer that he gave poetry "a miss" because he had "no technical knowledge of prosody . . . you cannot properly assess poetry without knowing a lot about prosody." Leavis finds Bennett's comments ridiculous and also rather dangerous since they hark back to the notion of prosody, the so-called "science of versification and metrical composition," which had dominated the thinking of the dilettante group of poetry critics before "Cambridge English" came into being. It is to I. A. Richards and the influence of his early book, *Principles of Literary Criticism*,[25] that Leavis attributes the honour of removing so much of the clutter associated with prosody. "The benefit it conferred was liberation. To be released from the thought-frustrating spell of 'Form,' 'pure sound value,' prosody and the time-honoured quasi-critical futilities had a positively vitalizing effect that can hardly be done justice today."[26] Richards's book helped rid the criticism of poetry of such notions as "pure Beauty" and "the specifically aesthetic emotion" deriving from Kantian metaphysics; in their place it offered an analysis of the psychological processes which the impact of a poem brings about. Its originality can be gleaned from this brief quotation: "Its (metre's) effect is not due to our perceiving a pattern in something outside us, but to our becoming patterned ourselves. With every beat of the metre a tide of anticipation in us turns and swings, setting up as it does so extraordinary extensive sympathetic reverberations."[27]

The importance of this "liberation from prosody" for Leavis can only be appreciated if it is seen as paving the way for the subject or reader to take responsibility for their response to a given poem. By getting rid of the pseudo-scientific terminology of prosody that came between the reader and the poem the way is cleared for the reading of poetry to become a truly personal response.

An analogous development can be seen in Lonergan's approach to metaphysics by way of cognitional theory. Traditional scholastic philosophy had begun with the concept of "Being," which was categorised under a number of objective headings: the one, the true, the good, the beautiful, substance and accident, nature, person, and so forth. Lonergan switches the starting point away from such objective categories to the inquiring subject. He turns scholastic philosophy around one hundred and eighty degrees. And so his epistemology is grounded in a cognitional theory and his metaphysics or ontology is grounded in his epistemology. The notion of "substance," for example, is "subjectified" by being recast, from the perspective of the inquiring subject, as a "unity-identity-whole"; and objectivity is seen to be the consequence of authentic subjectivity.

For neither Leavis nor Lonergan is this "turn to the subject" simply an incidental phenomenon. For both it is of tremendous significance, intrinsic to their whole approach to their respective disciplines, that on which their more fully developed positions hinge. It goes along with their respective rejections of the dominance of the classical notion of culture. For Leavis the threat of the "classicist mind" arose because English was a new subject when he studied it at Cambridge shortly after the First World War, and there was a danger (which Leavis fought against all his life) that it would not be thought a sufficiently rigorous discipline or, alternatively, that in the name of rigour it would be dominated by classically trained academics. This, Leavis believed, was the fate of Oxford English, which set fixed limits to the modernity of the books it considered fit to be studied—at one time the syllabus included no Victorian novels and certainly no works by twentieth century authors. On Oxford English and the classicist mind, Leavis says this:

> Everyone knows the reasons given, the classical reasons, for seeing the Greek and Latin classics as the supremely appropriate *literae humaniores* for humane education: "the literatures are complete"—that is, finished; "all the rules are known." The same habit betrays itself in the objection to recognising the

works of living writers . . . as fit subjects for academic study: in this modern field, we are told, too much depends on the vagaries and prejudices of personal taste and judgment. As if personal taste and real judgment—the hazards of self-commital—weren't entailed in a genuine approach to literature, and as if it were not of the utmost importance that the student's sense of this truth should never be blunted, but should inform his work everywhere![28]

If Leavis had to contend with the "classicist mind" if English were to be freed to be a living discipline and not a taxonomy of dead texts, Lonergan was faced with an even more daunting task. For in his youth Catholic scholastic philosophy and theology had been shackled for centuries with the classical view of culture, of science and of human nature. In the first page of the Introduction to *Method in Theology*, we read:

> The classicist notion of culture was normative: at least *de jure* there was but one culture that was both universal and permanent; to its norms and ideals might aspire the uncultured, whether they were the young or the people or the natives or the barbarians. Besides the classicist, there is also the empirical notion of culture. It is the set of meanings and values that inform a way of life . . .
>
> When the classicist notion of culture prevails, theology is conceived as a permanent achievement, and then one discourses on its nature. When culture is conceived empirically, theology is known to be an ongoing process, and then one writes on its method.[29]

But I cannot conclude this section without a comparison of how Lonergan and the Leavises see how one "gets on" in a classicist dominated world. First, Lonergan:

> On classicist assumptions there is just one culture. This one culture is not attained by the simple faithful. . . . None the less, career is always open to talent. One enters upon such a career by diligent study of the ancient Latin and Greek authors. One pursues such a career by learning scholastic philosophy and theology. One aims at high office by becoming proficient in canon law. One succeeds by winning the approbation and favour of the right personages. Within this set-up the unity of the faith is a matter of everyone subscribing to the correct formulae.[30]

The following is Queenie Leavis's account of the rise of George Gordon to the Chair of English Literature at Oxford:

> Gordon was the able Scots student who collects Firsts and prizes by cannily directed industry. Coming from Glasgow as already a brilliant Classic . . ., he saw possibilities, as others have done, in the more recent department of English and transferred his attention thither—English studies being, apart from the linguist's claim on them, notoriously the prerogative of your Classic. . . . So he attracted Raleigh's attention by editing a typically academic collection of es-

says, *English Literature and the Classics*, to which he himself contributed a piece on Theophrastus; this, he wrote, convinced Raleigh that he would do for the English School. . . . His chief productions are his two inaugural lectures. . . . The discipline of letters, he proclaims, is represented by the Oxford School of English. This is twofold. On the one hand, linguistic-philological studies as an end in themselves. On the other, scholarship—the ideal of perfect editing. . . . He followed this up by an attack on the Royal Commission's *Report on English*, apparently because that proposed that English should take the place traditionally occupied by Classics, and should, in short, be taken seriously as an educational and cultural study. To take literature seriously, he declared, is "an affront to life."[31]

PART THREE: METHODOLOGIES

F. R. Leavis was a critic of culture and an educational thinker, but his reputation rests primarily on the substantial body of his literary critical work, which is probably more penetrating in analysis and more far-reaching in its consequences as well as being more substantial in terms of sheer range and output than the work of any other critic of literature in the twentieth century. While many would question his judgments and his re-drawing of the map of English literature, with its implications for the reputations of particular authors, no one would question his influence, his range or the acuity of his analyses. I cannot here hope to reproduce the depth and range of Leavis's critical writing, but what I shall try to do is give the flavour of his work, to suggest the direction his analysis commonly takes, to examine his critical vocabulary so that the underlying critical method begins to emerge and an appropriate comparison can be made with Lonergan's "transcendental method."

Leavis often illustrates his critical method by comparing two poems. Take, for instance, his comparison of the two poems, *Heraclitus* and *Proud Maisie*, and how he arrives at the judgment that the latter, considered strictly as a piece of literary art, is superior to the former. Of *Heraclitus* he says that it offers us only emotion as such while "the alleged justifying situation, the subject of comment, (is) represented by loosely evocative generalities." In *Proud Maisie*, by contrast, the emotion generated in the reader is through the actual realization of the situation by the artist, "the emotion develops and defines itself as we grasp the dramatic elements the poem does offer—the data it presents (that is the effect) with emotional disinterestedness. For 'disinterestedness' we can substitute 'impersonality.'"[32] As we become familiar with Leavis's critical standards, it becomes clear that what he is against is the making of a "dead set" at a particular emotional effect, going straight for what he calls "an emotional debauch"; what he is for is accurate and concrete particularity in the realization of a scene or situation or predicament, with the result that the emotion is not "out there on the page," but is re-created in the reader through their engagement with the scene or situation realized. It is a contrast between the work of imagination that "does and gives," that "shows and realizes," on the one hand, and, on the other, that which simply tells or talks about or insists without core or substance.

Elsewhere Leavis defends the critical reading of a poem against the charge of "murdering to dissect":

> We can have the poem only by an inner kind of possession; it is "there" for analysis only in so far as we are responding appropriately to the words on the page. In pointing to them (and there is nothing else to point to) what we are doing is bring into sharper focus, in turn, this, that and the other detail, juncture or relation to our total response. . . . Analysis is not a dissection of something that is already and passively there. . . . It is a re-creation in which, by a considering attentiveness, we ensure a more than ordinary faithfulness and completeness.
>
> As addressed to other readers it is an appeal for corroboration. . . . In the work of an English School this aspect of mutual check—positively, of collaboration "in the common pursuit of true judgment"—would assert itself as a matter of course.[33]

In the next chapter I shall attempt to show how Leavis's account of art squares with the experiential basis of Lonergan's epistemology and how Leavis's account of his critical method accords in remarkable fashion with Lonergan's analysis of the process of coming to factual and evaluative judgments. Here let me point to just a few of the salient points of agreement between our two authors, points that all too easily elude us when we are dealing with the tricky realm of meaning. Leavis's saying of the poem, "it is 'there' for analysis only in so far as we are responding appropriately to the words on the page" has a strong resemblance to Lonergan's general position that reality is not already-out-there-now but consists of the raw data of experience ("marks on the page," "sounds in the air") being intelligently understood and reasonably affirmed in judgment by the knowing subject. While insisting on the poem being "there" only in the creative response of the reader, Leavis wishes to avoid any accusation of subjectivism by his insistence on pointing to the words on the page. Again the resemblance between this and Lonergan's use of data in his cognitional theory is striking. For without the intelligent inquiry of the subject, data for Lonergan are inert; at the same time the givenness of the data acts as a check on unbridled speculation since it is the data that have to be explained or interpreted. Finally, Leavis's appeal for collaboration "in the common pursuit of true judgment" echoes Lonergan's notion of "ongoing collaboration" and the need for "dialectics."

While acknowledging the need for mutual correction, both Lonergan and Leavis insist on the personal nature of judgment. As Leavis puts it, "an approach is personal or it is nothing; you cannot take over the appreciation of a poem, and, unappreciated, the poem isn't 'there.'" This accords with Lonergan's account of the nature of judgment: "A judgment is the responsibility of the one that judges. It is a personal commitment."[34] In both authors there is a repudiation of norms external to the subject by means of which valuations are achieved and validated; the norms are within the reader or the subject who makes the judgment. And this takes us to the central criterion by means of which Leavis judges any piece of literary art, what Lonergan terms the "eros for self-transcendence." Leavis has a highly developed sense of self-transcendence as the criterion of the true and the good, the real and the genuine. His critical vocabulary is alive with words—disinterestedness, impersonality, love, spontaneity, intelligence, creativity, life, self-knowledge, maturity, precision—all of which can be seen as contributing to an understanding of intellectual and moral self-transcendence, which produce in the reader or hearer the experience of emotional self-transcendence. Leavis deploys the notion of self-transcendence in the context of aesthetic judgments in ways which are highly instructive to those who, while accepting that self-transcendence is the touchstone of intellectual, moral and religious authenticity, are less well versed in art appreciation. Let his comments on dramatic tragedy make the point.

Why is it, Leavis asks, that while in dramatic tragedy we "have contemplated a painful action, involving death and destruction of the good, admirable and sympathetic, . . . yet instead of being depressed we enjoy a sense of enhanced vitality"? His answer points to levels of experience which "though they tend constantly to be ignored, are always, in respect of any concern for life and health, supremely relevant":

> The sense of heightened life that goes with tragic experience is conditioned by a transcending of the ego—an escape from all attitudes of self-assertion. "Escape," perhaps, is not altogether a good word, since it might suggest something negative and irresponsible. . . . Actually the experience is constructive and creative, and involves a recognising positive value as in some way defined and vindicated by death. It is as if we were challenged at the profoundest level with the question, "In what does the significance of life reside?," and found ourselves contemplating, for answer, a view of life, and of the things giving it value, that makes the valued appear unquestionably more important than the valuer, so that significance lies, clearly and inescapably, in the willing adhesion of the individual self to something other than itself.[35]

The aesthetic emotion, we can see from this quotation, is tied inextricably to moral judgment. It is not just that we recognise and admire self-transcendence in the work of art but that our own need for self-transcendence, which is spontaneous and basic to our humanity, results in the powerful emotions which its enactment evokes in us when we witness it.

Self-transcendence is at the heart of the criteria by which Leavis judges works of literature and, as I say, there is much that those familiar with Lonergan's use of this term can learn from Leavis when literature and art are in question. It is important to note that Leavis *argues for* his evaluative judgments. There is no pretention that we can simply claim that this is good, or this is better than that; the critic's function is not to pontificate or simply proffer inspired intuitions. Leavis is particularly hard on what he labels "Christian Discrimination," a kind of litmus paper test of what is good or significant which some Christians, he believes, practise in the name of criticism—though criticism, that is argument, is usually missing from their writing because they know in advance the views they consider important.[36]

In his practice of literary criticism, Leavis does not move immediately to claim that such and such a poem or novel has the vindicating attributes of self-transcendence. He begins with an examination of the data—the words and images, and their movement on the page—in considerable detail. As with Lonergan, the value of the data is their givenness but in literature the data operate in their own distinctive way. If such qualities as precision and concreteness of realization are prized, this is because they provide sure signs of "the elimination of ego-interested distortion and all impure motives." If a situation is artistically realized our emotional response is guided and directed by the situation; a situation that enacts itself is, we might say, honest. When, on the other hand, the situation is not artistically realized, when for example all the poem has to offer is an emotional drum-beat or a flurry of colours or an emotion-charged vocabulary—with words like "great," "fantastic," "wonderful"—then it is not the situation or human predicament that speaks to us, but the writer. We are, in fact, since it is the aim of art to evoke or structure a response in the subject, being manipulated. The writer is interposing her own egocentric response to the experience being described between the experience and the reader. As DH Lawrence says, "Never trust the teller, trust the tale." If, on the other hand, our emotions are being trained on a human situation barely presented in all its concrete and exact specificity, then our emotional response is defined by the object held before us for our contemplation. We have, we might say, been given the "evidence" on which to base our response; the reader's intelligence as well as emotions are engaged. It is the opposite with the reader or listener who is simply the victim of stimulus-response techniques, frequently found in pornographic writing, when biology takes over from thought and the emotions gallop, free of any intellectual control or accompaniment. If, in the context of coming to know, Lonergan can rightly say that objectivity is the consequence of authentic subjectivity, then, in the context of art, taking our cue from Leavis, we can rightly say that *artistically created objectivity fosters authentic subjectivity.* That rather philosophical way of expressing the point helps to explain, if ever so awkwardly, Leavis's passionate motivation for, and advocacy of, the teaching of English literature. The moment of emotional development and growth comes with the reader's response, when the reader, guided by the artist's objectivity, has the poem "by a kind of inner possession."

I have been attempting to show the value and relevance of Leavis's aesthetics to Lonergan's thought. But I also believe that Lonergan's epistemology and transcendental method have much to offer Leavis and his intellectual allies, by providing a needed philosophical basis for Leavis's critical method. I mentioned before that Leavis was wary of becoming entangled in philosophical disputes in his earlier writings and indeed tended to be somewhat hostile to philosophy. Given that the dominant philosophical movement in England at the time was Logical Positivism, Leavis's wariness can be appreciated. In one of his later works, *The Living Principle*, Leavis is inclined to be more sympathetic to the cross-fertilisation of philosophical and English studies. "The presence of philosophy in the university should be important for 'English'; the profit would accrue in the fields of both disciplines." He immediately adds that this is not to be understood as suggesting the subordination of English to philosophy. But it is an important concession and several reasons for Leavis having made it suggest themselves. First, he was increasingly aware that his own aesthetics and critical method were shot through with philosophical and epistemological assumptions. Second, he believed he had found in Marjorie Greene's *The Knower and the Known* and Michael Polanyi's *Personal Knowledge*[37] works that supported and explored the role of the subject in coming to know along with a rejection of Cartesian mind-body dualism.[38] Third, by this stage philosophical issues—sometimes referred to as "theory"—were beginning to invade traditional English studies at the university in the form of questions raised by critics of Marxist, structuralist, post-structuralist and deconstructionist persuasions. It was important for Leavis to nail his philosophical colours to the mast, to "come out" philosophically and to defend, for example, his view that behind the "meanings" in language there is an intending author: that "words 'mean' because individual human beings have meant the meaning."[39] Lonergan's epistemology provides Leavis with formidable support for such a statement. Moreover, I believe that Lonergan provides greater support for Leavis than either of the two other philosophers mentioned on account of the moral dimension—the role he attributes to self-transcendence and authentic subjectivity in his epistemology, while steering clear of subjectivism. It is not possible to talk about Leavis's critical method without taking account of this moral dimension and of the objectivity claimed for his critical judgments.

The insistence by Leavis on the importance of English as a discipline for the training of intelligence and sensibility together (he always insists on that "together"), his adducing the English School in the university as an instantiation of what Lonergan means by "Cosmopolis," a force with which to combat the dehumanising influences abroad in our culture—this insistence begins to make very clear sense once we have grasped the central role played in Leavisian criticism by self-transcendence. This point will be further emphasized if I turn now to show the relevance to the Leavisian approach to English Literature of the eight functional specialities that make up the work not only of theology but of any human discipline that seeks to bring the past into a significant relationship with the present and the future. Lonergan spells out the eight functional specialities in his book, *Method in Theology*. They are research, interpretation, history, dialectics, foundations, doctrines, systematics and communication. The first three of these—research, interpretation, history—look to the past. They need to be, in Lonergan's view, complemented by dialectics, foundations, doctrines and systematics, which look to the present and the future. It appears to me that Leavis can profitably be seen as being primarily engaged in the four functional specialities that look to the present and the future, within the context of literary studies. This need not surprise us. As Lonergan has said, the functional specialities "would be relevant to any human studies that investigated the past to guide its future."[40] And again in *Method*, "If one assimilates tradition, one learns that one should pass it on. If one encounters the past one also has to take one's stand toward the future."[41] Leavis's criticism, and the kind of English School he envisages within the university, are all about taking stands. And the over-riding criterion which determines what stand should be taken has to do, as we have seen, with self-transcendence.

There are, of course, eight functional specialities according to Lonergan, and each is necessary for English studies. In inveighing against the "classicist mind" and the attempt to establish philology and textual editing as the proper concern of English studies, Leavis does not wish to decry the need for research, for accurate and reliable texts, and so forth. What he is opposed to is any attempt to *reduce* English to these necessary and proper, but in his view, delimited functions. Underpinning all of his efforts is the perceived need to draw out the relevance of the past to the present and the future. That is what he is getting at when, describing his envisaged English School, he says, "The aim is to produce a mind that will approach the problems of modern civilization with an understanding of their origin . . . and . . . a sense of human possibilities . . . that traditional cultures bear witness to . . ."[42] Like all students of literature, he investigates the past, but he does so from a particular perspective. He is aware that every new and important author changes our view of the past, reshapes the tradition. And in a particularly pregnant formulation he says, "It is only from the present, out of the present, in the present, that you can approach the literature of the past. To put it another way, it is only in the present that the past lives."[43] The past that should live in the present is one that Leavis took great pains to define through the body of his critical work. He, in effect, redrew the map of English literature and in so doing profoundly influenced the selection of authors studied in British universities and schools.

He did so out of a central conviction, the need to inform the present with the best of the past, where that best has been judged by reference to the human norm of self-transcendence. At all times he tried to bring what he saw as salvific and sane in the tradition into a living relationship with the present. Hence the value of the study of literature as a discipline and its distinctiveness. The student of literature, as Leavis conceives it, is not dealing with a specimen out there that may be discussed, analysed and defined with little or no personal involvement. His insistence on the irreplaceable role of English, within English culture, in training not only intelligence but what he calls "sensibility" along with intelligence suggests the *change* in the student that a living engagement with literature might effect—a development and refinement of moral-aesthetic acuity and awareness. English is not a neutral discipline. It is not too much to say that Leavis sees the value of literary studies as residing in an openness to be formed and changed, and even transformed, for the better—that is what is living in the discipline, its existential dimension. Leavis is committed to the education of the students' feelings, the training of their sympathies, their emotional maturation. The preparatory "positive" work of researching, reporting, classifying the various meanings, tracing the sources, textual editing etc, is important and indispensable. But there is little doubt that for Leavis more important still is the task for which this positive work is preparing, the normative task in which he himself is supremely engaged, the task of responding, judging and placing. And, he believes, it is in the execution of this normative task that the main educational value of literary studies resides. Attempting to summarise, we might say that judgment for Leavis is a moral commitment, summoning forth the full authenticity of the one who judges in response to the authenticity grasped in the work of art, which is, in turn, inseparable from the authenticity of the author.

I hope I have said enough to show that the shape Leavis would give to English studies conforms in many important respects to the shape Lonergan would give to theological studies. Profit may be gained, however, from reflection on the functional speciality which Lonergan terms "Foundations" for the light that it throws on both Lonergan's and Leavis's approach. Foundational reality for Lonergan is conversion. In the context of theology it is a triple conversion: intellectual, moral and religious. He says, "It is a decision about whom and what you are for and, again, whom and what you are against. It is a fully conscious decision about one's horizon, one's outlook, one's world-view. It deliberately selects the framework, in which doctrines have their meaning, in which systematics reconcile, in which communications are effective."[44] F. R. Leavis can, in these terms, be seen to operate from a foundational reality of one who is intellectually and morally converted; of one who has been seized by the all-importance of self-transcendence if intellectual truth is to be grasped and if what is morally and aesthetically right, good and beautiful is to be properly appreciated. No one who understands his work can doubt that it is this overarching criterion that constitutes the framework of his thinking, informs the detailed and rigorous analyses and the literary judgments he makes, determines the "canon" of literature to which he gives approval, and determines further the "placement" of the many authors within that canon.

Lonergan also makes the penetrating point that conversion is operative in the "prior" phase of research, interpretation, history and dialectic. He comments, "However, in this earlier phase conversion is not a prerequisite; anyone can do research, interpret, write history, line up opposed positions. Again, when conversion is present and operative, its operation is implicit: it can have its occasion in interpretation, in doing history, in the confrontation of dialectic; but it does not constitute an explicit, established, universally recognized criterion of proper procedure in these specialities."[45] He goes on to add: "Neither the converted nor the unconverted are to be excluded from research, interpretation, history, or dialectic. Neither the converted nor the unconverted are to follow different methods in these functional specialities. But one's interpretation of others is affected by one's understanding of oneself, and the converted have a self to understand that is quite different from the self that the unconverted have to understand."[46] These comments, I believe, throw a sharp light on Leavis and the kind of impatience he shows towards "mere scholarship": "I do not like . . . the way in which scholarship is commonly set over against criticism, as a thing separate and distinct from this, its distinctive nature being to cultivate the virtue of accuracy. . . . Again, how does one acquire the necessary scholarly knowledge? Some of the most essential can be got only . . . in the interpretation and judgment . . . of poems (say) where it can be assumed that the text, duly pondered, will yield its meaning and value to an adequate intelligence and sensibility."[47] Though less tolerant than Lonergan of "unconverted" scholarship, Leavis is well aware of the foundational relevance of conversion—what he terms "earnestness of conviction"—and that it works, so to speak, "backwards" (to research, interpretation, history and dialectics) as well as "forward" (to doctrines, systematics and communications—though these are not, of course, Leavis's terms).

CONCLUDING REMARKS

F. R. Leavis, though he frequently speaks with great sympathy of religion, remained an agnostic till his death. Perhaps for that reason his witness to the foundational reality of what Lonergan terms "conversion" is all the more important. For he gives witness to the importance of this reality from a thoroughly independent standpoint, thereby showing a community of conviction and concern that it is most valuable for the theologian, and the methodologist of theology, to have. Theology is not on its own in these matters. Like Lonergan, Leavis sees the threats to our full humanity in the modern world. Like Lonergan, he sees the turn to the subject, accompanied by a rejection of the classicist mindset, as necessary prerequisites for the personal commitment that judgment is, and hence for "conversion"; they are not merely "emblems of modernity" but remove what can become powerful obstacles on the way to moral and religious earnestness of conviction. Like Lonergan, Leavis sees in "conversion"—earnest conviction—the only standpoint that is commensurate with the dangers that threaten. And he is at one with Lonergan in attesting that conversion is not another form of bias in its own right, a betrayal of scholarly and academic objectivity ("academic" becomes a pejorative term in Leavis's later writings), but rather, grounded in the human need for self-transcendence as it is, a realization of our authentic humanity. Conversion is the foundational reality of his own scholarly labours and the motivating force behind his plans for an English School. I have not found Lonergan's functional specialities to be a procrustean bed onto which Leavis has had to be forced; on the contrary, they have provided a most useful framework for a full and genuine understanding and sympathy for the kind of English School that Leavis sought to create; Lonergan's eightfold division of human studies has provided a most valuable instrument enabling me to explore and fathom the depth and reach of Leavis's recommendations. It has helped me to grasp the various aspects of his thought and to see how they relate to each other and, taken together, add up to a coherent viewpoint.

It is worth noting that there is a distinct shift within Leavis's mode of thinking when, following his analysis of the malaise affecting modern English society—which he attributes to the arrival of "the machine" and of "mechanised civilization"—he moves to his method of reading and appreciating a poem or work of literature. For the latter, his appreciation of literary art, is performed by means of a criterion that is truly transcultural, namely the criterion of self-transcendence, which is central to our humanity and hence independent of particular cultures, languages or nationalities; it is because of this, for example, that *Hamlet* or *King Lear*, to cite only two obvious examples, can be appreciated as great art in countries as disparate as Italy, Russia or Japan. The emotional response to self-transcendence is the same worldwide.

By adopting self-transcendence as the central criterion for the appreciation of literary art, Leavis joins Lonergan on the transcultural plane—and this, I would suggest, is greatly to his advantage when other approaches to literary criticism are put forward in opposition to his. In his Marxist book on literary theory, for example, Terry Eagleton throws out a strong challenge to the kind of approach advocated by Leavis, which he labels "the liberal humanist" approach. He says,

> The strength of the liberal humanist case . . . is that it is able to say why dealing with literature is worthwhile. Its answer . . . is roughly that it makes you a better person. There is also the weakness of the liberal humanist case . . . because it grossly underestimates (literature's) transformative power, considers it in isolation from any determining social context, and can formulate what it means by a 'better person' only in the most narrow and abstract of terms.[48]

While this might win the sympathy of students of literature with a minimal acquaintance with Leavis's writings, it is not difficult to show that it does less than justice to the kind of literary criticism Leavis sought to promote when he was alive and teaching at Cambridge. First, Leavis did not overlook the historical or social context in which a work of literature was produced but, rather than adopting a narrow "literary" or "artistic" approach to a poem or novel, urged that it be studied with reference to history, sociology, theology, or any other relevant discipline that might throw light on its meaning and import.[49] While he refused to adopt a Marxist approach to literature, this was not because he considered the social and material conditions in which works of literature were produced to be unimportant: as he says in *The Common Pursuit*, "If the Marxist approach to literature seems to me unprofitable, that is not because I think of literature as a matter of isolated works of art, belonging to a realm of pure literary values (whatever they may be)."[50] Second, I hope I have said enough to refute Eagleton's claim that the Leavisian approach "grossly underestimates literature's transformative power . . . and can formulate what it means by a 'better person' only in the most narrow and abstract terms." The central Leavisian—and Lonerganian—criterion of self-transcendence might sound abstract but its concrete realization is not hard to grasp since it meets a basic human need and is an essential requirement if truth and honesty are to flourish in our personal and social lives; since it requires us to set aside our biases and personal preferences in order to let the evidence speak for itself; and since, in considering any work of literary art, it enables our intellectual and emotional response to be determined and shaped by the human situation or predicament artistically realized in words. These are not "narrow" terms but refer rather to the cultivation of honesty, respect for evidence and the appreciation of artistic excellence; they clearly illustrate the value of studying literature as a humanising and civilising influence grounded in its fostering of authentic subjectivity.

As for the charge that the criterion of self-transcendence is, in some pejorative sense, "abstract," let it be answered by reference to a highly charged and all too palpable phenomenon at present taking place in our world—namely, the rise and influence in the Middle East of Isis, the Islamic terrorist organisation (it claims to be a state). In the British *Independent* newspaper for the 12 December 2015, the author and journalist, Howard Jacobson, who studied English Literature under Leavis at Cambridge, advocates novel-reading and a lively engagement with literature as an antidote to Islamic terrorism. He refers to a question asked by Paul Vallely: "What kind of person becomes a Jihadi terrorist? Specifically, what kind of educated person?" By way of an answer, Vallely says that "The overwhelming majority of graduates recruited into Islamic terrorism studied engineering, science and medicine. Almost none are social science or arts graduates." Jacobson advances his argument by quoting from a study issued by the British Council entitled *Immunising the Mind*, in which the author wonders if "embracing violence" might be "connected to education in certain subjects failing to encourage the questioning of received ideas or alternative arguments or viewpoints." The same author wonders if there might not be a particular "mindset which is attracted to the simple solutions and lack of ambiguity, nuance or debate sometimes seen in technical subjects—and that is vulnerable to radicalisation for similar reasons." He points out that the terrorist group known as Isis, which has displayed many acts of gross and barbaric brutality as part of its propaganda, has "eliminated law, fine arts, archaeology, philosophy and political science from curricula in areas it controls." As Jacobson asks, with a seriousness underneath the humour, "how come no one has ever been mugged by a person carrying a well-thumbed copy of *Middlemarch* in his back pocket?"

I might also add here that Isis is not the only political expression of the flight from reason in today's world; and that the stress placed in transcendental method on intelligence, rationality and responsibility is ever more urgently needed in a society or culture in which truth is considered an optional choice, something that, it is suggested, depends on the say-so of whoever wields political power; in which unpleasant truths can be ignored and sidelined because they interfere with a political leader's personal wishes and preferences; in which the central criterion of right and wrong is the ego of the leader.

As I have said, Leavis was concerned with the impact of education not only on the students' intelligence but also on their feelings. In *Method* Lonergan devotes a valuable section to feelings, which helps to bring out their importance in human life. He begins by distinguishing between non-intentional states and feelings, on the one hand, and feelings as intentional responses, on the other. The first are feelings or states such as fatigue, hunger or anxiety whereas the latter are responses to what is intended, apprehended or represented; among these are feelings that are intentional responses to values, "whether the ontic value of persons or the qualitative value of beauty, understanding, truth, virtuous acts, noble deeds."[51] He adds that "response to value both carries us towards self-transcendence and selects an object for the sake of whom or of which we transcend ourselves."[52] In this way feelings help to orientate us in the world since they invest an object or an action with value and importance and in so doing drive us on to do certain things and avoid others. Feelings are closely allied to decision and action, and feelings that have become habitual direct our behaviour over time. An absence of appropriate feelings in a situation can be ruinous. One of the problems besetting people suffering from autism is an inability to interpret and internalize the emotional life of others. Studies of autistic people watching films reveal that they often fail to understand what is going on because of their inability to grasp what is emotionally significant in the scenes they are watching: they simply do not know what to attend to, they are bewildered.[53] That is why so much importance is attached nowadays to the ability to understand and empathise with others. It is the development of empathy and fellow-feeling that enables us to prioritise certain objects or actions over others, to distinguish between what is truly important and what is less important or trivial. And while habitual self-transcendence is difficult to achieve, those who achieve it become "principles of benevolence and beneficence, capable of genuine collaboration and true love. . . . It is, finally, only by reaching the sustained self-transcendence of the virtuous man that one becomes a good judge, not on this or that human act, but on the whole range of human goodness."[54] These reflections on the role and value of feelings in human life surely vindicate Leavis's insistence on the literary-critical as a "discipline of sensibility, judgment and thought."[55]

One final word. Frederick Crowe has noted that "the university, as we know it today, will not be a wholly adequate institution for the kind of theology Lonergan envisages."[56] Towards the end of his long life Leavis wrote, "Let me say then that I know that it would be mere dream-indulgence to suppose that we might establish a university answering to the ideal implicit in my argument. I see little prospect of there being in any university an English School of which (say) half of the teaching staff were qualified to work in the spirit of my suggestion." However, he continues:"The massively ignored human need in such an age as ours achieves self-recognition and voices in the relatively few; but—as I have said before—the measure of importance in this realm is not quantitative; decisive changes of consciousness are initiated by tiny minorities; our civilization affords much excuse for dwelling on those truths."[57]

NOTES

1. For a clear, if sympathetic, account see William Walsh, *F. R. Leavis*, (London: Chatto and Windus, 1980).
2. See *Insight*, p. 666.
3. Apart from his extensive writings on philosophy and theology, Lonergan has written on subjects as various as the foundations of mathematics and macroeconomics. His *Collected*

Works, including English translations of his Latin works, amount to 25 volumes, published by the University of Toronto Press.

4. For a fuller comparison of Lonergan and Polanyi, see chapter 4 of my book, *Philosophical Encounters*, (Toronto: University of Toronto Press, 2005).

5. Bernard Lonergan, *Method in Theology*, (London: Darton, Longman and Todd, 1972), p. 265.

6. F. R. Leavis, first published as a pamphlet in 1930; reprinted in *Education and the University* (London: Chatto and Windus, 1943).

7. Leavis, *Education and the University*, p. 146.

8. F. R. Leavis, *A Selection from Scrutiny*, Vol 1, (Cambridge: Cambridge University Press, 1968), p. 169.

9. Leavis, *Education and the University*, p. 149–150.

10. Leavis, *Education and the University*, p. 156.

11. Leavis, *Education and the University*, p. 143.

12. Leavis, "The Idea of a University" in *Education and the University*, p. 2.

13. Leavis, "The Idea of a University," p. 26.

14. Leavis, "The Idea of a University," p. 43.

15. Leavis, "The Idea of a University," p. 56.

16. Lonergan, *Insight*, p. 235.

17. *Insight*, p. 225.

18. *Insight*, p. 240.

19. *Insight*, p. 241; my italics.

20. *Insight* , p. 241–2.

21. Matthew Arnold, "General Report for the Year 1876" in *Reports on Elementary Schools 1852–1882*, (London: HMSO, 1908), p. 178.

22. Matthew Arnold, *Culture and Anarchy*, 1869, (Cambridge: Cambridge University Press, 1950) p. 46–54.

23. Matthew Arnold, first published 1864, reprinted in *Essays Literary and Critical*, (London: Everyman, 1906), pp 27–28. The notion of an "Academy" or "Cosmopolis" has deeper historical roots in Coleridge's notion of the "Clerisy," whose business would be "general cultivation." See S. T. Coleridge, *Constitution of Church and State*, (London, 1839).

24. *Education and the University*, p. 156.

25. I. A. Richards, *Principles of Literary Criticism*, first published 1924 (reprinted by London: Routledge and Kegan Paul, 1963).

26. F. R. Leavis, *English Literature in Our Time and the University*, the Clark Lectures 1967, (Cambridge: Cambridge University Press, 1979), p. 17.

27. IA Richards, op. cit., pp. 139–40. This quotation points to a feature common to Leavis and Lonergan when exploring human experience; this is their preference for appeal to concrete experience, to what they are aware of occurring in their psyche, over against appeal to abstractions, the "futilities" Leavis associates with Kant.

28. *English Literature in Our Time and the University*, p. 68.

29. Lonergan,*Method in Theology*, p. xi.

30. Lonergan, *Method in Theology*, p 326–7.

31. *A Selection from Scrutiny*, Vol 1, p. 8–9.

32. F. R. Leavis, "Thought and Emotional Quality," 1945; reprinted in *The Living Principle*, (Chatto and Windus, 1975) p. 71–72.

33. *Scrutiny*, Vol 9, p. 309.

34. *Insight*, p. 272.

35. F. R. Leavis, *The Common Pursuit*, (London: Chatto and Windus, 1952), p. 131–2.

36. Leavis, *The Common Pursuit*, p. 248f.

37. Marjorie Greene, *The Knower and the Known*, first published by Basic Books, 1966; Michael Polanyi, *Personal Knowledge*, (London: Routledge and Kegan Paul, 1958).

38. Leavis, *The Living Principle*, p. 29f.

39. Leavis, *The Living Principle*, p. 58.

40. In "Bernard Lonergan Responds" in *Foundations of Theology*, ed. Philip McShane (Dublin: Gill and Macmillan, 1971), p. 233.

41. Lonergan, *Method in Theology*, p. 133.
42. *The Idea of a University*, p. 56.
43. *English Literature in Our Time and the University*, p. 68.
44. Lonergan, *Method in Theology*, p. 268.
45. Lonergan, *Method in Theology*, p. 268.
46. Lonergan, *Method in Theology*, p. 271.
47. F. R. Leavis "The Function of Criticism at any Time" in *A Selection from Scrutiny*, Vol 2, p. 281.
48. Quoted by Brian Wicker, "After the Deluge: criticism as reconstruction," *NewBlackfriars*, Vol 69, No 814, March 1988, p. 115.
49. *The Idea of a University*, p. 56.
50. F. R. Leavis, "Literature and Society," *The Common Pursuit*, p. 183. In this book Leavis writes about the relationship of literary criticism to philosophy and sociology and repudiates Romantic notions of how great literary works come to be written.
51. Lonergan, *Method in Theology*, p 31.
52. Lonergan, *Method in Theology*, p. 31.
53. This example is taken from Jason King, "Feelings and Decision Making," *New Blackfriars*, Vol 97, January 2016; the author makes extensive use of Lonergan's reflections on feelings as intentional responses to value, while locating his comments among more recent treatments of the subject.
54. Lonergan, *Method in Theology*, p. 35.
55. *The Idea of a University*, p. 43.
56. Frederick E Crowe, *The Lonergan Enterprise*, (Cowley, Cambridge, Massachusets, 1980), p. 94.
57. Preface to *The Living Principle*, p. 9.

Chapter Three

Poetry

Lonergan, Leavis and Langer

In this chapter I shall argue that Lonergan's basic cognitional theory, or transcendental method, can be shown capable of integration with the nature and function of literary language. It is surely a sound test of any account of how language functions that it can explain how and why poetry affects us as it does. This, so far as I know, has never been done in the case of Lonergan. In his brief comments on art and aesthetics in both *Insight* and *Method* there is no attempt by Lonergan to explain or analyse from the basic perspective of his cognitional theory the inner workings of poetry or literature or the structure of a reader's response to a poem or work of art.

PART ONE

I have no idea how a Wittgensteinian would even attempt to *justify* the poetic use of language. If, indeed, it is the task of the Wittgensteinian philosopher to sort out confusion caused by the "bewitchment" of language, to outlaw a-typical or deviant uses by bringing words back to how they are normally used,[1] poets would seem to be the principal enemy. For poets are continually using language in deviant and a-typical ways; they are forever making language afresh, forcing words into new and startling combinations that appear to defy all logic, forever deserting the well-worn paths of grammar and syntax most of us plod along in "ordinary discourse." They even declare it their object to "delight" and this is surely not far removed from bewitchment. The point is that Wittgenstein laid it down as a methodological principle that the central meanings of words should be grasped in what we might call their normal surroundings. But poets delight in wresting words from their normal surroundings and putting them to new uses in strange and unexpected places. It may well be that, after the manner of Plato, some Wittgensteinian philosopher-ruler would feel obliged to banish the poet from his Republic.

The empiricist philosopher-ruler might not be so drastic, but the poet could surely hope to occupy but a humble position in *his* Republic. For the empiricist is all for something called "literal meaning" and those metaphors not reducible to literal equivalents are necessarily regarded as nonsense. The reduction of poetry to its literal sense is all that A. J. Ayer can hold out as a means of crediting it with meaning in *Language Truth and Logic.* The compensation offered poetry not so reducible is rather meagre: "If the author writes nonsense, it is because he considers it most suitable for bringing about the effects for which his writing is designed."[2] These effects, it should be noted, could have no cognitive but only emotive value. In an intriguing article entitled *Professor Tillich's Confusions (Mind,* 1965), another empiricist philosopher, Paul Edwards, takes the famous theologian to task for his use of metaphor in his theological writings. Again, it is not metaphor as such that is condemned but only what Edwards terms "irreducible metaphor," that is metaphor for which no literal equivalent can be found. It is for his use of such irreducible metaphor that Tillich is censured, and the many poets who would surely deny that their metaphors and images are capable of restatement in some literal form of language must be equally condemned on empiricist grounds. It strikes me that in speaking of reducing metaphor to its literal equivalent both Ayer and Edwards are involved in a *petitio principii,* since such a reduction would seem to imply that the meaning of any metaphor be grasped before it could be rephrased in so-called literal language. In other words, the metaphor is an adequate vehicle of meaning *as it stands.* But it is easy to see that the empiricist's preference for literal language stems from his assumption that language gets its meaning from pointing to things "out there" in the world. The basic terms or propositions of our language, to which all other uses of language can be reduced, are those which point to facts in the world or can be translated into language about sense data. Such so-called literal language, the empiricist believes, is necessarily prior to metaphorical language which, when used validly, is only a more roundabout or "flowery" way of saying what can be expressed more simply in literal terms. The poet, therefore, who is notorious for dealing in metaphor and image, is, at best, an ornamenter merely; at worst, he writes nonsense.

For Lonergan, by contrast, the primary reference of language is not "out there" to "facts in the world" but rather inwards to acts of understanding, acts of judgment, and acts of valuing and choosing. Speaking and writing are instrumental acts of meaning; they express or mediate the primary acts of meaning which consist of understanding, judging and deciding, as well as wishing, longing, commanding, requesting, and so forth. And so there is continuity and discontinuity between understanding, for example, and language. There is continuity in so far as the language I speak expresses my understanding; there is discontinuity in so far as the hearer who understands my meaning can express it in the same or in quite different words.[3] The distinction between primary and instrumental acts of meaning allows for meaning to be expressed in non-linguistic modes, such as music, sculpture, painting, gesture, dance and mime. Therein lies a problem for those philosophies which would equate understanding with language or see language as the sole repository of meaning: the meaning of the non-linguistic arts may possibly be described in language but it can hardly without special pleading be regarded as purely linguistic in nature.

But our concern here is with literary art and clearly there are profound implications here for the metaphors, images and various mimetic devices employed by the literary artist to convey meaning. So long as they are grounded in acts of understanding, judging or valuing, then all of these, on Lonergan's terms, are valid carriers of meaning. There can be no question of an enforced reduction to so-called literal equivalents for cognitive meaning to be safeguarded. The poet is free to claim that he has at his disposal a range of means for the expression of certain meanings with a precision outside the scope of ordinary language. Indeed, Lonergan sides with those linguistic scholars who consider metaphor to be prior to literal language, poetry prior to prose. In *Method* he writes, "With GiambattistaVico, then, we hold for the priority of poetry. Literal meaning literally expressed is a later ideal and only with enormous effort and care can it be realised, as the tireless labours of linguistic analysts seem to show."[4] This is supported by Vygotsky who says of primitive language: "The primary word is not a straightforward symbol for a concept but rather an image, a picture, a mental sketch of a concept, a short tale about it—indeed, a small work of art."[5] It is only with the passage of time, Vygotsky notes, that "the image that gave birth to the name," and the feelings originally tied to it, lose out and conceptual meaning becomes uppermost. Susanne K. Langer is in agreement claiming, with some caustic force, that with time "speech becomes increasingly discursive, practical, prosaic, until human beings can actually believe it was invented as a utility, and was later embellished with metaphors for the sake of a cultural product called poetry."[6] Contrary to empiricist assumptions, then, metaphor appears to operate at the growing end of language so that a novel conception requires the employment of metaphor to pin it down and body forth the new meaning. Indeed, so pervasive is metaphor that philosophy—even empiricist philosophy—is full of the residue of past metaphor: just think for a moment of the source-meaning of such words as "matter," "form," "ostensive definition," "concept," "intention," "phenomenon" and so forth.

I have been at some pains to defend the cognitive value of metaphor against the strictures of empiricism, and to prevent possible distortion I should immediately add that the empiricist is right in recognising the emotive power of images and metaphors. After the manner of primitive words the images and metaphors of poetry release, discharge and distil in us feelings of all kinds—anger, sorrow, joy, fear, anxiety, nostalgia, absurdity and so forth. And the manner in which they do this is by the poet reversing, as it were, the process described by Vygotsky by which conceptual meaning becomes uppermost—by restoring the original *physical* properties of words. An image, after all, is directly related to our senses, whereas an idea or concept is directly related to our understanding and it is to our sensory imagination by means of images and the movement of words that the poet primarily appeals. Lonergan's distinction between experience and understanding begins to throw light on how poetry works and how it differs from more prosaic or practical language. But before developing that point it is necessary to say something about Lonergan's hierarchical ordering of consciousness.

As previously explained, coming to know for Lonergan is a structured activity consisting of experiencing, understanding that experience and judging the truth or falsity, probability or improbability of that understanding.[7] Experience and experiential are words I shall be using rather a lot and so a brief explanation of what Lonergan means by them in the context of his cognitional theory might prove useful. Experience has many meanings. It can mean "long and accustomed practice" as when we speak of "the man of experience," and I shall use the word in that sense later. But when Lonergan speaks of experience in relation to understanding and judgment he uses it in a more primitive sense, referring to the deliverances of sense and the deliverances of consciousness. Since my theme is art I shall concentrate on the deliverances of sense by which Lonergan means simply the contents of acts of seeing, hearing, smelling, touching, tasting. Lonergan's distinction between sense experience and understanding contradicts the notion entertained by Hume that there are atoms of meaning already constituted "out there" which the human mind receives passively through the senses. The data of sense for Lonergan are not-yet-meaningful. They give rise to inquiry—what is that? how does it work? how often does it happen? why does he do that? etc;—and inquiry, if successful, yields understanding and it is by the act of understanding that meaning—interpretation or explanation—is achieved. The data of sense are concrete and particular whereas the meanings that are found in them are general and universal: in saying that I am simply drawing attention to a basic feature distinguishing sensation from understanding. Experience, then, is what I interrogate in order to generate the hypothesis that will account for it, and it is to experience also that appeal is made at the third step in the triad of knowledge when I attempt to verify my hypothesis by testing how well it fits the data. What I wish to draw attention to here is that when I speak later of experience and the "experiential mode" in reference to how art works I am referring to a mode of operation that appeals primarily to our senses or sensory imagination.

Experience, understanding and judgment are the first three stages or levels of consciousness. But there is a further, fourth, stage of consciousness in which judgments of value and decisions to act are made. In the normative pattern of coming to know and coming to value each stage is passed through in sequence, though it is true to say that the later stages also hold sway over the former: thus, for example, principles of value frequently direct inquiry and suggest in advance what lines of investigation are to be followed up. Clearly Lonergan's hierarchical ordering of human consciousness—or the operations which this ordering objectifies—is more flexible and intricate than it is possible to indicate here, but certain features of it are central to my purposes in this chapter. At each stage there is a heightening of consciousness: at judgment, for instance, one is done with hesitation and takes a stand on what is so or is not so. With value judgments one not merely takes a stand but decides what one stands for. As the existentialists are aware, it is by our value judgments, choices, decisions and actions that we constitute our habitual responses, build our characters, make ourselves. That is why Lonergan speaks of the subject at the fourth stage moving from consciousness to self-consciousness or what we refer to as "conscience": it is not just some state of affairs that has to be affirmed or denied but the subject's very personality is at stake.

The transition from one stage of consciousness to another is brought about by the subject asking questions in a manner that most of us will recognize as spontaneous and irresistible. The *criterion* of what is true or good is self-transcendence: in other words, in acts of rational judgment I submit to the evidence irrespective of my own preferences, and in judgments of value I subordinate my own interests to pursue the value that promotes what is good or right in the particular situation. In both knowing and valuing, then, the meaning is independent of the subject but the criterion of what is known to be true or judged to be good is not some external norm but resides in the subject's personality, in the capacity for self-transcendence.

Feelings are related to both knowing and valuing in the sense that they accompany these activities, indeed constitute the driving force behind them. There are the feelings of pleasure and displeasure, of comfort and discomfort by which I respond to my experience; and there are all sorts of feelings associated with what I understand and judge. Feelings are also powerfully associated with values in the sense that the valuations we place on certain objects, actions, people arouse in us feelings of joy and sadness, pity, awe, fear and so forth. But not only do values arouse feelings in us but feelings, for their part, are often so immediate and deeply felt as to propel us spontaneously towards certain value judgments. In the normative pattern described by Lonergan judgments of value arise as a *fourth* stage after the process of coming to know is completed. But feelings can cause the normative pattern—as we all know—to be short-circuited: they possess us and catapult us into value-judgments, or they lean us so strongly in a particular direction that value judgments emerge without hesitation (sometimes rashly). But feelings can also be deep-seated and permanent, the fruit of long and patient cultivation, making me a moral agent in some permanent sense and not the plaything of every passing emotion. Of this kind are the feelings that incline me to the habitual self-transcendence of the virtuous man and it is in no small measure the task of education to cultivate such feelings.[8]

For in the last analysis it is the judgment of the man of cultivated feeling and long experience and not some putative external criterion that will decide what is right or wrong, good or bad in any field where value judgments are made.[9] The need for maturation not only holds true at the level of value judgments but also at the level of understanding and interpretation, as Lonergan's derogatory remarks on the "Principle of the Empty Head" make clear.[10] This is hardly surprising in view of the link that exists between the fourth level of consciousness and the previous three. Lonergan's transcendental method runs counter not only to empiricist assumptions of basic facts "out there" before which one should "sit like a little child" (the maxim of T. H. Huxley), but it also, as I hope the foregoing analysis makes clear, overcomes the empiricist is/ought poser, since there is no question of deriving a value judgment from an empirical proposition or of simply sticking on, in Humean fashion, approval or disapproval to what is otherwise a statement of fact. The fourth level of consciousness presupposes the first three but remains distinct from them as they remain distinct from each other: just as understanding presupposes experience but cannot be reduced to a construct out of sense data, so valuing and acting presuppose judgments of fact but are at the same time of a different, and in terms of personality, of a more interior order. That explains why the facts established at the third level (judgment) are also the *particular criteria* by which an evaluation is formed at the fourth: the shift from "facts" to "criteria" takes place because a different kind of question, namely a value question, is now being asked.[11] But let me turn back for the moment from the fourth level of consciousness to the first.

As I said previously, the fundamental experiential component of knowledge begins to throw light on how poetic language affects us and how it differs in this respect from more prosaic language. For it is largely through the sensuous features of language that poetry "works." When Seamus Heaney writes,

> The cold smell of potato mould, the squelch and slap
> Of soggy peat, the curt cuts of an edge

. . . we are not merely *informed of an activity*. as we would be in more prosaic language, but actually *participate* in it by imaginatively seeing, smelling and hearing it. A slightly more complex example is provided by Donne:

> On a huge hill,
> Cragged and steep, Truth stands, and he that will
> Reach her, about must, and about must go;
> And what the hills suddenness resists, win so,
> Yet strive so, that before age, deaths twilight,
> The soule rest, for none can work in that night.

Here the harshness and ruggedness of the verse, the brokenness of rhythm and syntactical complexity, impart the feeling of hard muscular effort that seems to enact the meaning. As Leavis observes, "poetry can communicate the actual quality of experience with a subtlety and precision unapproachable by any other means."[12] The stops/starts, fast/slow tempo, line stops and enjambments, rhymes, cadences and sound effects of poetry are the poet's devices for re-creating in the reader the actual *experience* being described. The mathematician, the scientist and the philosopher (normally) are not concerned that their readers re-enact an experience but only that they re-enact their understanding. The words they deliberately choose are those words whose sensuous root and associated feelings have long since withered and whose conceptual meaning is uppermost. The poet will give you meaning and sensuous stimulation at once; will give you the sensuous, experiential basis upon which the burden of meaning rests. It is this fusion of the sensuous and intellectual that is so distinctive of literary art, what Eliot commended in the Metaphysical Poets as "a direct sensuous apprehension of thought."[13] In the more comprehensive art-forms such as drama a huge number of devices are available to effect this: set, music, verse, movement, voice modulation, the juxtaposition of scenes etc. The principle is the same: it is first to our *sensory* imagination that the literary artist appeals. Lonergan's insistence on the experiential basis of knowledge integrates admirably with the way the artist works; we might say that the experiential basis is the artist's special domain, since it is the function of art to structure by means of artifice a response in readers by having them enact imaginatively an experience.

I am not saying that art is not concerned with the other levels of consciousness such as understanding, judging, valuing. Indeed, art would seem to be particularly concerned with values and with the feelings that are associated with values in the manner described above. But as Leavis says, "works of art *enact* their moral valuations,"[14] and this enactment, I would add, is highly concrete and particular, in a word "experiential." Lonergan's intimate linking of experience—understanding—judging—valuing helps us to understand, I am suggesting, how something that is primarily experiential and concrete can also be said to enact moral judgments and to be at once concrete and universal. Unlike other kinds of language, literary language is concrete and particular because the literary artist is concerned to communicate the raw material of experience and its attendant feelings from which insights, judgments and valuations will spring. It is, in fact, the mark of the inferior writer that he cannot deliver the experiential "goods," but simply *tells* us what his characters are like and how they relate to each other. It was this apparent failure in the novels of C. P. Snow that drew the famous condemnation from Leavis that he did not understand what a novel was.[15]

But we do not stick at the level of experience, at the concrete and particular. The Lonerganian distinction between experience and the other stages of consciousness helps to explain how the artist works by co-opting the creative powers of readers: the bare artistic presentment of scene or episode has the effect of forcing the reader to engage with the text and enter into the process of creation; the emotional engagement and the insights and judgments the bare artistic presentment evokes are the reader's; the reader has to work from the basic experiential data to realise its meaning, But it would be misleading to stress overmuch the distinction between experience and the other levels of consciousness as if they were not also intimately related. In art many things are happening at once and to insist overmuch that we simply move from one level of consciousness to another, after the manner of some neat pattern, would be to distort by oversimplifying. Where Lonergan's cognitional theory can help us is by suggesting how in art the later levels of consciousness are not simply *based on* experience (this is true of all first-hand knowledge), but seem to be *collapsed into* experience. Art presents its judgments and values in the experiential mode: in George Herbert's "Easter Wings," to take an obvious example, despair and faith, sin and resurrection are bodied forth in the form of the poem; in the novels of Graham Greene we can "smell" the spiritual condition of certain characters, and so forth.

Much of the thrill of any art form derives from this element of discipline: that within the limitations imposed by the medium so much feeling and meaning can be effectively communicated. At the same time, the experiential mode of art gives it its power to convince: the artist does not simply tell us that two people are in love, for example; he shows us. Defective art is frequently a failure to provide an adequate experiential basis for the quality and volume of the emotional reaction manifested by the author or sought from the reader. The actuality of experience acts as a check on exaggerated emotionalism or empty posturing. What I have called art's experiential mode helps explain that other feature of artistic appreciation, what Coleridge referred to as "that willing suspension of disbelief for the moment, which constitutes poetic faith." No doubt a certain suspension of disbelief is required in other disciplines, such as philosophy: we must understand before we can criticise. But because the literary artist is primarily concerned to organise (or re-organise) our experience and allows us to *realise* the meaning being conveyed, the suspension of disbelief in art is of a much more thorough-going character than the kind of engagement required in other disciplines.

PART TWO

So far I have attempted to explain from a Lonerganian perspective how literary art works and inevitably this has led to a consideration of how we, as readers, respond to literary art. To assess the capacity of Lonergan's transcendental method to illumine the nature of critical response we could do no better, I think, than compare the structure of that method with the recorded practice of F. R. Leavis, who has arguably contributed more than any other critic to our understanding of the nature of critical engagement with literature. Both Lonergan and Leavis emphasize the need to train and cultivate the feelings if moral maturity is to be achieved and, as a literary critic, Leavis is especially insistent on the ability of literature to effect this and, indeed, would largely justify the place of English in the university on these grounds.[16] But it is on Leavis's analysis of the structure of critical response to literature that I should like to focus.

It may seem paradoxical to compare Leavis to a philosopher since he was at some pains to decline the invitation of the philosopher Rene Wellek to state "more explicitly" and "more abstractly" the assumptions underlying his practice and was especially resistant to the philosophical notion of a *norm* by which poems and poets are measured. It has been suggested, however, that Leavis was less philosophically innocent than he protests to be and that it was the dominant logical-scientific paradigm of philosophy at that time (1937) to which he was so resistant. In any case, in his reply to Wellek and in several other places in *Scrutiny* he sets out the manner in which he comes to appreciate a poem and reach a critical evaluation. The importance of such recorded practice to Lonergan's method is that Lonergan claims to be thoroughly empirical in approach, that his mapping out of method is simply the objectification of the processes that occur spontaneously in actual practice.[17] In his reply to Wellek Leavis writes:

> By the critic of poetry I understand the complete reader: the ideal critic is the ideal reader. The reading demanded by poetry is of a different kind from that demanded by philosophy.... Philosophy, we say, is "abstract" ... and poetry "concrete." Words in poetry invite us, not to "think about" and "judge" but to "feel into" or "become"—to realize a complex experience that is given in the words. They demand, not merely a fuller-bodied response, but a completer responsiveness—a kind of responsiveness that is incompatible with the judicial, one-eye-on-the-standard approach suggested by Dr Wellek's phrase: "your 'norm' with which you measure every poet." The critic—the reader of poetry—is indeed concerned with evaluation, but to figure him as measuring with a norm which he brings up to the object and applies from the outside is to

misrepresent the process. The critic's aim is, first, to realize as sensitively and completely as possible this or that which claims his attention; and a certain valuing is implicit in the realizing. As he matures in experience of the new thing he asks, explicitly and implicitly: "Where does this come? How does it stand in relation to . . .? How relatively important does it seem?" And the organization into which it settles as a constituent in becoming "placed" is an organization of similarly "placed" things, things that have found their bearings with regard to one another, and not a theoretical system or a system determined by abstract considerations.[18]

I suggest that we can find here many points of significant agreement with Lonergan's analysis of how evaluation is achieved and validated. There is agreement on how feelings can lean us towards particular valuations, and on the need for a maturing process if feelings are to be cultivated and lead spontaneously and with a certain practised facility to weighing and placing a poem. There is the same repudiation of any empiricist notion of norms external to the subject by which poems and poets are measured: the emphasis throughout is on the man of experience acting as his own criterion. Implicit in this is a rejection of what Lonergan calls "the Principle of the Empty Head." Leavis's writings make it clear that a literary training is one in which the student moves gradually from relatively straightforward analysis and judgment to more complex areas calling for the refinement and subtlety of response that only the practised critic can provide.[19] And clearly there is no worry in Leavis's mind about deriving a value judgment from descriptive statements; at the same time the act of evaluation is taken to be cognitively serious: it is not a matter of adding approval to what is otherwise a purely empirical observation. Rather, "a certain valuing is implicit in the realizing." This, as we have seen, is on all fours (almost) with Lonergan's notion that in reaching value judgments we move from judgments of fact to judgments of value, from the third level of consciousness to the fourth. There is the slight query as to whether Leavis would recognize *any* difference between descriptive and evaluative utterances, though in view of the position he is reacting against his emphasis is understandable. Elsewhere (*Scrutiny,* Vol. 13, p. 60), he speaks of the critic (of Shelley's poetry) "passing *by inevitable transitions,* from describing characteristics to making adverse judgments about emotional quality; and from there to judgments that are pretty directly moral." If for the words in italics were substituted, "by the spontaneously generated questions effecting a transition from one level of consciousness to another," his position would be identical with Lonergan's. Lonergan, as we might expect in a philosopher, articulates his position with much greater elaboration than does Leavis, who is simply recording, in that wonderfully condensed and energetic manner of his, his own critical practice, and hence the vocabulary of the two writers is somewhat different; but the similarity is undoubtedly there.[20]

This similarity becomes more remarkable when we consider a later piece of writing by Leavis in which he reflects on what he means by analysis of a poem. Wellek, interestingly, had suggested that Leavis, on account of his insistence on the actual, was inclined more to realism than idealism, but what he has to say on poetic analysis suggests less a simple-minded realism (or idealism) and something remarkably like Lonergan's "critical realism." Leavis is defending the critical reading of a poem against the charge of "murdering to dissect" in a passage quoted at length in the previous chapter of this book which it is worth quoting again in the context of Wellek's questions to Leavis:

> We can have the poem only by an inner kind of possession; it is "there" for analysis only in so far as we are responding appropriately to the words on the page. In pointing to them (and there is nothing else to point to) what we are doing is to bring into sharp focus, in turn, this, that and the other detail, juncture or relation in our total response. . . . Analysis is not a dissection of something that is already and passively there. What we call analysis is, of course, a constructive or creative process. It is a more deliberate following-through of that process of creation in response to the poet's words which reading is. It is a re-creation in which, by a considering attentiveness, we ensure a more than ordinary faithfulness and completeness.
>
> As addressed to other readers it is an appeal for corroboration: "the poem builds up in this way, doesn't it? This bears such-and-such a relation to that, don't you agree?" In the work of an English School this aspect of mutual check—positively, of collaboration "in the common pursuit of true judgment"—would assert itself as a matter of course.[21]

Apart from being a trenchant affirmation that artistic appreciation is a re-creation, this quotation bears a close resemblance to certain central features of Lonergan's cognitional theory. Leavis's saying of the poem, "it is 'there' for analysis only is so far as we are responding appropriately to the words on the page" (on the previous page he had written, "an approach is personal or it is nothing: you cannot take over the appreciation of a poem, and unappreciated, the poem isn't 'there')"—this has an uncanny resemblance to Lonergan's general position that reality is not already-out-there now but consists of the raw data of experience ("marks on the page," "sounds in the air") intelligently understood and reasonably affirmed in judgment. And by referring to "having" the poem "only by an inner kind of possession" Leavis is, by implication, endorsing Lonergan's view of language as instrumental, as having meaning only in so far as it expresses the meaning proceeding from such interior acts as understanding and evaluation. While insisting on the poem being "there" only in the reader's creative response, Leavis clearly avoids the accusation of subjectivism or idealism by his insistence on pointing to the words on the page—"there is nothing else to point to." Again one cannot fail to be struck by the resemblance between this and Lonergan's use of data in his cognitional theory. For without the intelligent inquiry of the subject, data for Lonergan are simply inert and indeterminate; at the same time the givenness of the data acts as a check against unbridled speculation: explanations and interpretations must continually be confronted with the data, for it is the data that have to be explained and interpreted. Leavis's insistence that an appreciation is something personal that cannot be taken over from another corresponds to Lonergan's stated account of the nature of judgment ("A judgment is the responsibility of the one that judges. It is a personal commitment"),[22] while his reference to the inwardness of the movement towards possession suggests Lonergan's position that with each stage of consciousness the subject enters more deeply into herself till, with judgments of value, consciousness becomes self-conscious. Leavis's approach to the critical appreciation of a poem is open on traditional empiricist premises to the accusation of subjective interference with a meaning already "out there" on the page and yet Leavis affirms that by it "we ensure a more than ordinary faithfulness and completeness." There is implicit here a clear repudiation of the notion that subjectivity is the enemy of objectivity and again remarkable accord with Lonergan's statement that "objectivity is simply the consequence of authentic subjectivity."[23] Finally, the appeal in the second paragraph of the quotation for collaboration "in the common pursuit of true judgment" echoes Lonergan's finding that insights are cumulative and mutually corrective and that it is only by "ongoing collaboration" that true judgment in any field of inquiry, but more particularly in human studies,[24] can be ever more closely approached.

In his writings Leavis maintains that there can be no proof of a critical evaluation, certainly no laboratory demonstration of its correctness (as opposed, say, to the attempt at this made by I. A. Richards).[25] This is of a piece with his rejection of any external norm by which poets and poems can be measured. But he also maintains that certain features of a poem or novel can be pointed to in an invitation to evaluate or place the poem in a particular way, and he holds up the ideal of "the perfect reading" and speaks of "the one right total meaning that should commonly control his (the student's) analysis."[26]

This ideal would be warmly welcomed by Lonergan who speaks of the potential Universal Viewpoint grounded in the realisation that meaning is not "out there" but has its primary sources immanent in the interpreter.[27] It is by appealing to the self-correcting process of understanding (or understandings) that Lonergan would overcome the problem of relativism and Leavis's methodological formula, "This is so, isn't it?," inviting the reply, "Yes, but . . ." encompasses a similar understanding of understanding.

But the criterion of correctness for Lonergan is ultimately the subject's self-transcendence. Does Leavis have anything corresponding? I would suggest that the features Leavis picks out as leading to a positive evaluation and ultimate approval are on a par with what Lonergan describes by the term "self-transcendence." The set of terms Leavis uses to signify the positive qualities of a poem are actuality, intelligence, self-knowledge, life, maturity, reality—and these are set against another set of interrelated terms such as sentimentality, immaturity, day-dreaming, self-indulgence, failure of intelligence, lack of self-knowledge, and so forth. Leavis's critical vocabulary[28] comes close to a definition of what Lonergan means by self-transcendence, a notion which incorporates the actuality of experience, intelligent response and maturity of judgment and evaluation. If for Leavis "reality" and "sincerity," as Casey puts it, "come close to being equated,"[29] this is also true of Lonergan in the sense that sincerity ("authenticity" is Lonergan's term) is the ultimate criterion of what is real, true and good, and this resides in the subject. If Leavis maintains an indissoluble link between form and content then this is patently true of Lonergan whose ontology is isomorphic with the structure of cognitional process. The real is what is *intelligently* understood and *reasonably* affirmed (the true is the real): the *how* of the subject determines the *what* that is affirmed. For Leavis the *how* of the writer indicates his contact with reality and this in turn indicates his moral seriousness. When Leavis speaks of form he is not referring so much to a poet's technical skills as to the qualities of intellectual acumen and moral maturity that are manifested in a poem's concrete organization. As I said previously, what is distinctive about artistic form is that it is expressed in the experiential mode: valuation and meaning are encapsulated and enacted in the concrete. To illustrate the point further would require close examination of the detailed analyses of poetry and the comparative judgments that Leavis's work offers, but I think I have said enough for the point to be taken. One possible objection that should be anticipated is that for Leavis a poem's failure is *not necessarily* a reflection on the poet as a person, just as for Lonergan, although error *may be* due to culpable bias, this is by no means universally true as his references to historical, cultural, intellectual and physical limitations clearly suggest.

One other important point. Rene Wellek had thought Leavis's insistence on actuality inclined him towards a realist philosophy. But John Casey finds much of his critical writing to be couched in the language of romantic or expressionist, as opposed to mimetic, theory . His final judgment is that Leavis "produced a synthesis of mimeticism and expressionism" and he adds, "For a critic to have arrived at such a theoretical position is a very remarkable achievement."[30] Mimeticism and expressionism correspond roughly in philosophy to certain traits in empiricism and idealism respectively. If the degree of agreement between F. R. Leavis, the literary critic, and Bernard Lonergan, the philosopher-theologian, is as great as I have argued it is, this is not unconnected with the fact that Lonergan saw his philosophical enterprise as a correction of both empiricism and idealism and, as in the case of Leavis, that correction is not primarily opposed to the excesses of empiricism and idealism but to what each leaves out.[31] If Lonergan overcomes Cartesian dualism by a synthesis of the givenness of the data and the subject's cognitional processes, Leavis overcomes the aesthetic dualism of form and content by a synthesis consisting of the actuality of experience, artistically realized, and the poet's (and ultimately also the reader's) response to that actuality. Anyone looking for the epistemological basis of Leavis's aesthetic theory will find it, I believe, in Lonergan. And anyone seeking Lonergan's aesthetic theory as applied to literature will find it in Leavis. (I hope it is clear that I can say this without implying that Lonergan must agree with Leavis's every individual judgment). The agreement between the two men is, I believe, a remarkable tribute to both. It testifies to the courage of Leavis who in the face of a hostile philosophical tradition remained faithful to principles he found himself practising as a critic. For Lonergan Leavis's practice and his faithful recording of that practice are a wonderful vindication of his *transcendental method.*

PART THREE

In the light of the comparison I have made between Lonergan and Leavis, I am about to make a bold claim: Lonergan has got his theory of art wrong; and the reason it is wrong is because it is non-Lonerganian. It is not the aesthetic theory of a critical realist, but of an expressionist, S. K. Langer. In *Insight* Lonergan seeks to integrate mathematical and scientific knowledge with his cognitional theory and in doing so reveals a grasp of these subjects from the inside, but when in that work and in *Method* the subject of art makes a brief appearance he hands us over to Mrs Langer. "Here I borrow from Susanne K. Langer's *Feeling and Form,*" he tells us in *Method* (p. 61) and, as if to emphasize the derivativeness of what he has to say he adds in a footnote: "For an application of the above analysis to different art forms . . . the reader must go to S. K. Langer, *Feeling and Form* . . ." (p. 64).

Mrs Langer's theory of aesthetics is a particular kind of expressionism which is fundamentally Kantian, and for a philosopher like Lonergan who wrote *Insight* as a correction of Kant to take over without radical qualification a neo-Kantian theory of aesthetics is enough surely to put us on our guard. However, to say that Lonergan has got his theory of art wrong is, as I say, a bold claim requiring careful substantiation. Such substantiation will take the form of comparing Langer with Leavis and both with the structure of critical realism.

Feeling and Form is S. K. Langer's sequel to *Philosophy in a New Key*[32] where she worked out and presented her notion of symbol, distinguished it from sign, and applied it to the art form of music. *Feeling and Form* widens the application to include all art forms. Signs (or signals) merely indicate the existence of something, past, present, or future; a bell indicates that dinner is being served, for example. Symbols, however, are *"vehicles for the conception of objects."*[33] Black cloth is not simply the sign of mourning, but symbolises it, acts as a vehicle of our conception of mourning. With this understanding of symbol, Mrs Langer gives her definition of art: "Art is the creation of forms symbolic of human feeling." Music, to take Mrs Langer's primary example, is a tonal projection of the forms of feeling: crescendo, diminuendo, adagio, rallentando etc. It delineates the contours of human sentience, the pattern of life itself as it is felt and directly known.[34] Unlike discursive language, art is not denotive but gets its meaning or import from human feeling which it articulates in a manner beyond the powers of discursive language: art communicates the unspeakable. The feelings articulated by art are not just any of the feelings that beset the artist; rather, the work of art bespeaks the artist's understanding of the forms of feeling, what he knows about the "inner life"; the artist "objectifies 'our subjective being' the most intimate 'Reality' that we know."[35] Mimeticism or the representational function of art is dismissed as distracting from the true nature of art which is symbolic and expressive (pp. 52, 361). The artist's sole concern is with form whose content is the feeling of which the work of art is the form: form and content dissolve into one. When she comes to applying her general theory to literature once more it is the *emotional* value of each detail of a poem or play that is stressed.

No one can gainsay the brilliance and scope of Susanne Langer's philosophy of art. Her analysis of the techniques by means of which art articulates movement, growth, vitality and sentience are quite stunning. And unlike other aestheticians who hold form to be the essence of art (Clive Bell, for instance) she insists on the relationship of form to life—namely, as an expression of our emotional being. But is that one relationship enough? She cares not a jot for *what* literary artists have to say—"their alleged personal feelings and moral attitudes, their hopes and fears for the actual world, their criticisms of life."[36] All that matters is their creation of an experience, "wholly formed, wholly expressive. . . . All this concern with the philosophical and ethical significance of the hero's sufferings, however, leads away from the *artistic* significance of the play, to discursive ideas about life, character, and the world."[37] Art's reality is illusory (though not delusory), quite cut off from the practical problems that face us in everyday reality: likewise, poetry is treated as ahistorical, and moral evaluations (either of a character or of a poet) are resisted.[38] Lonergan is clearly taken with this notion of art as a couple of quotations should make clear: "Art, then, becomes symbolic, but what is symbolized is obscure. It is an expression of the human subject outside the limits of adequate intellectual formulation or appraisal"*(Insight,* p. 185); and "He (the subject contemplating a work of art) has ceased to be a responsible inquirer investigating some aspect of the universe or seeking a view of the whole. He has become just himself: emergent, ecstatic, originating freedom" (*Method* p. 63). All this is in violent contrast with Leavis's insistence that literature bears directly on life, that it can teach us, and that it is fraught with moral choices and decisions for both artist and reader. Leavis is insistent that a serious interest in literature cannot "confine itself to the kind of local analysis associated with 'practical criticism,' to the scrutiny of the words on the page in their minute relations . . .; a real literary interest is an interest in man, society, and civilisation, and its boundaries cannot be drawn."[39] And again: "I don't believe in any 'literary values,' and you won't find me talking about them; the judgements the literary critic is concerned with are judgments about life."[40] For this reason, it seems to me that Mrs Langer diverges from and Leavis converges with the normative pattern of Lonergan's transcendental method. It follows, naturally, that I believe Lonergan's espoused aesthetic theory to be inconsistent with the method he has elaborated and articulated with such rigour and applied fruitfully to fields as various as mathematics, science, history and theology.

John Casey pinpoints the most obvious objection to Mrs Langer's theory: "How do we *know* that works of art stand in a relation of logical analogy to forms of feeling? Have we any way of becoming acquainted with these 'forms' apart from their artistic . . . expression, so that we can compare them with the works in which they are said to be instantiated, and so decide whether they have been satisfactorily realized?"[41] The answer is that we cannot since the forms of feeling are essentially ineffable, comparable to Kant's *noumena,* things-in-themselves, unknowable except in so far as they are expressed in art.[42] Mrs Langer replies to the question, "How is the import of a work known?" by falling back—she has nowhere else to go—on "intuition."[43] One consequence of this is that her theory fails to be critical: we have no way of evaluating a work of art and placing it by comparison with other works. We know by intuition that art expresses feeling and is, therefore, good. The only criterion Mrs Langer appears to allow is art's powers of expression: when art fails to be expressive and lapses into the alien mode of discursive language then it has to that extent failed. Mrs Langer's theory—and this is obvious in her practice of poetic analysis—forces us to take poems and plays at their own valuation; and necessarily so, since she can offer us no vantage point from which the quality or adequacy of the emotion registered by the poet or playwright might be gauged and assessed.

This takes us to the heart of the matter. Mrs Langer's theory is monistic in the sense that art is simply the symbolic expression of the artist's subjective being. Critical realism is dualistic, though (I hasten to add) with a "small d," for its dualism is one that is overcome by means of synthesis. But there are two points in critical realism where idealism offers us only one—there is the subject's explanation and there are the data of experience; or, in poetry, there is the experience that is artistically realized and there is the poet's response to that experience. Immediately we have grounds for a critical judgment: does the explanation fit the data? Is the poet's emotional response adequate to the experience he is describing? Time and again this is the question Leavis asks: it is the touchstone of the poet's maturity, sincerity, intelligence etc. as manifested in the poem. For Lonergan, judgment is reached when the explanation of the data has been subjected to suitable tests. A poem is a self-subsistent artefact and the "test" of the poet's emotional response is for Leavis the poem's "concrete organization." Shelley is criticised for his deliberate striving after emotional effect as compared with "the Shakespearean mode, which is one of presenting something from which the emotional effect . . . derives."[44] The following remarks about George Eliot in *Middlemarch* make the point more fully.

> (At her "highest level" her) sensibility is directed outwards, and she responds from deep within. At this level "emotion" is a disinterested response defined by its object, and hardly distinguishable from the play of intelligence and self-knowledge that give it impersonality. But the emotional "fulness" represented by Dorothea depends for its exalted potency on an abeyance of intelligence and self-knowledge, and the situations offered by way of "objective correlative" have the day-dream relation to experience. . . . They don't, indeed, strike us as real in any sense; they have no objectivity, no vigour of illusion.[45]

It is such a standard of objectivity that Mrs Langer's theory of art so clearly lacks. In following her so unreservedly Lonergan has failed to integrate his theory of art with his own critical realism and married it instead to post-Kantian idealism. The result, unfortunately, is an impoverished theory of art, attenuating art's relevance to life and divorcing it from morality, and so making of the subject engaged in literary appreciation, to use Lonergan's phrase, a *truncated subject*, her mind uncoupled from the difficult business of critical thinking and evaluation. No doubt Mrs Langer's theory was extremely attractive to Lonergan, especially in view of the prevailing positivistic attempts to reduce art to mere ornamentation or empty babble. The irony is that even when he was writing *Insight* the foremost literary critic in England, F. R. Leavis, was practising criticism in accordance with the principles of Critical Realism and transcendental method.

The Leavis-Snow Controversy

It is difficult to speak of F. R. Leavis without commenting on his famous/infamous controversy with the scientist and writer, C. P. (Charles Percy) Snow. At this distance in time—well over fifty years—there is little new that can be said about this clash of ideas, but in the light of what has been said above about Leavis (and Arnold and Lonergan), it might be possible to explain the fury of Leavis's reaction to Snow's lecture and, in so doing, to draw attention to certain preoccupations of Leavis that, perhaps, have not so far been sufficiently emphasised. And without drawing Lonergan into the controversy—since he took no part in it—it might, nevertheless, be possible to lend some support to Leavis's side of the argument by noting some aspects of Lonergan's philosophy, including the understanding of culture that Lonergan and Leavis (and Arnold) share, which simply do not feature in Snow's presentation.

The basic historical fact is that in May 1959 C. P. Snow delivered the annual Rede lecture in the Senate House of Cambridge University.[46] By this time Snow was something of a public figure. Having obtained a Ph.D. in science at Cambridge at a time of great scientific activity and having undertaken scientific research for a few years, he was temporarily drafted into the British Civil Service in 1939 to recruit and deploy physical scientists in order to help the war effort. This did not involve working at the forefront of scientific research but was high level administrative work and gave Snow an insight into how people in positions of influence arrived at important decisions; the theme of how power is achieved and exercised was to be a major theme of his writing. Between 1940 and 1970 Snow produced a series of novels that established his reputation as an author; his novels were successful, sold well and were translated into several languages. So by 1959 Snow was well known and well connected, both at Cambridge and in literary circles in London. He titled his Rede lecture "The Two Cultures," by which he meant to refer to two groups of highly educated men (well, mainly men at that time), namely "scientists," on the one hand, and what he called "literary intellectuals," on the other.

These two groups, he asserted, were unable to communicate with each other on the plane of their major intellectual concerns and, indeed, he claimed that the literary intellectuals looked down on and were hostile to the members of the scientific community. Each group represented a "culture" and the two cultures were divided by mutual incomprehension. Snow deplored this division and wished to remedy it by suggesting changes to the English education system, including the education provided by a university such as Cambridge. He went on to claim that the shape and content of the English education system meant that literary intellectuals, who—he claimed—were the dominant opinion-formers of the day, did not appreciate the importance and impact of the industrial revolution or of the scientific revolution taking place at that time.[47] The industrial revolution had transformed the living standards of millions of people resulting in reduced infant mortality, longer life expectancy and sufficient food to eat. But this happy state obtained only in those countries that had industrialised. The world was now divided between the rich countries, which had industrialised, and the poor countries, which had not.[48] Snow proposed that scientists were the ones who could improve this situation—scientists and engineers, practical people who could help to transform the world by exporting science and technology to the developing world.[49] He warned that if the West did not take on this task of exporting science and technology, the Communists would[50] —it is worth recalling that in 1959 the cold war was at its height and fear of what the Communists might get up to was a strong motivating force. The conclusions to be drawn from Snow's argument were that, if poor countries were to achieve the high standards of living enjoyed in industrialised nations, they would have to industrialise; for this to happen, science and technology would be necessary and for this to happen, scientists would be needed; and for scientists and technologists to be provided in sufficient numbers, there would need to be a revision of the English education system and, above all, an expansion of the provision of science at the level of higher education.

Set out like that, Snow's argument looks pretty straightforward and uncontroversial. But it turned out to be highly controversial and the most vehement and violent reaction to Snow's observations came from F. R. Leavis. In many ways, I believe, it was the word "culture" in the title of Snow's lecture that did the damage. To avoid controversy, Snow would have been well advised to leave out this word and to have called his lecture, as he first intended, "The Rich and the Poor."[51] His comments on the theme of "rich and poor" came towards the end of his lecture and in his retrospective remarks, made four years after his Rede lecture, he said, "In my own mind the latter part of the lecture was always the more pressing."[52] But he began by talking about two distinct and opposing "cultures," and it was his observations about the views of the "literary intellectuals" that were found to be offensive. He said that intellectuals, and particularly literary intellectuals, were "natural Luddites"[53] and implied that they were the main reason why science and technology did not enjoy the same status in England as they did in the US and Russia. These literary intellectuals were fixated on the past and in this respect contrasted with the scientists, who were generally of a more optimistic disposition and who looked to the future. Snow's lecture was deliberately designed not only to raise the status of science and scientists in public opinion but he went on to suggest that the scientists were morally superior to the literary intellectuals of his day.[54]

It is not surprising that Leavis was deeply hostile to much of what Snow said in his lecture. He did not react quickly to Snow's comments, indeed refrained from reading the text of the lecture until he found that it had become a regular topic of conversation and that the subject of the "two cultures" was turning up in the essays submitted by sixth form students applying for admission to Cambridge. In 1962 as Leavis was about to retire from his duties at Cambridge, the students at Downing College, where Leavis was a Fellow, invited him to deliver the annual college Richmond lecture. Leavis chose to make the subject of his Richmond lecture a response to C. P.

Snow's Rede lecture of 1959; the title of his lecture was "The Two Cultures? The Significance of C. P. Snow." A feature of Snow's lecture that Leavis strongly opposed was the recommendation that there should be a major expansion of higher education with a particular focus on the expansion of the provision made for science. Leavis had developed a carefully worked out view of the role of the university, particularly where culture was concerned, and the proposed expansion of education, including the focus on science education, cut across this view and threatened its implementation. Leavis believed that science and technology would continue to advance; he was concerned about the human consequences of this advance and proposed the university as "representative of a wisdom older than modern civilization and having an authority that should check and control the blind drive onward of material and mechanical development, with its human consequences."[55] And, as we have seen, he saw the English School in the University as being committed to the cultivation in its students of the moral discrimination needed for the development of an authentically human society. The universities were to play a central role in the creation of a morally discriminating public. For Leavis, therefore, as for Matthew Arnold and Lonergan, culture is about the cultivation of the intelligence and sensibility, the education of the feelings and adherence to right reason. As Arnold put it, "To have the power of using, which is the thing wished, the data of science, a man must, in general, have first been in some sense 'moralised'; and for moralising him it will be found not easy, I think, to dispense with those old agents, letters, poetry, religion."[56] For Arnold, culture consisted of "the best that had been known and said in the world," and for him this meant to a large extent the study of poetry and classical literature.[57] Lonergan put it in his own way: Cosmopolis (his version of Arnold's Academy or intellectual metropolis) "invites the vast potentialities and pent-up energies of our time to contribute to their solution (the problems of society) . . . by developing *a personal depth and a public opinion*, that through appreciation and criticism, give men of common sense the opportunity and help they need and desire to correct the general bias of their common sense."[58] Like Leavis, Lonergan is aware that the creation of a morally discriminating public will require the tremendous effort of a critical minority, but, unlike Leavis, Lonergan does not identify that minority with a single institution, the university, but assigns the role of performing this important critical function to "an art and a literature, a theatre and a broadcasting, a journalism and a history, a school and a university."[59] He clearly believes that there are several institutions capable of shaping public opinion on the basis of right reason and traditional moral values. This sharing of the role of critic among these several institutions is typical of Lonergan, the philosopher, and his more generalised manner of thinking; Leavis, by contrast, was a literary critic and dwelt in the particular; hence it is not surprising that he saw the critical function as being performed by the institution with which he was most closely identified. However, I would suggest that Lonergan's proposal might have saved Leavis some of the anguish he felt when he saw his view of the university being threatened by the recommendations coming out of Snow's lecture.

When reading Leavis, Arnold and Lonergan, one is aware that each of these thinkers draws on a considerable intellectual, specifically philosophical, hinterland. There is no evidence of such a hinterland behind Snow's comments about culture. Where those three stressed the relationship between the creation of a culture and the education of the intelligence and moral sensibility, Snow makes no reference to inwardness of this kind. Compared with Leavis and the others, Snow's understanding of "culture" looks decidedly threadbare. He sees a culture not as an inheritance from the past, what Chesterton once referred to as "the thrift of our forefathers," but as an ability to communicate with others at an intellectual level and a holding in common of certain assumptions and behaviours that cut across such labels as religion, politics or class.[60] And far from looking to the past, scientists, he affirmed, looked to the future and, indeed, "naturally they had the future in their bones."[61]

As was quickly pointed out shortly after Snow's lecture, his attempted definition, or re-definition, of "culture" does not stand up to scrutiny. Snow's main reason for referring to "cultures" was to draw attention to the inability of scientists and literary intellectuals to communicate with each other. Yet, in the same lecture he says that "biologists more often than not will have a pretty hazy idea of contemporary physics"[62] and he later says that "pure scientists and engineers often totally misunderstand each other"[63] —yet, in his lecture he includes these other groups within the "scientific culture." In his retrospective comments he admits that he left out of consideration a whole group of scholars who study how human beings live or have lived, such as sociologists and social historians, economists, political scientists and psychologists.[64] The question was asked whether, in terms of Snow's definition, there were only two cultures or one hundred and two! [65] The question has become more acute since Snow's day as divisions and sub-divisions within the university curriculum have multiplied with increasing specialisation. A scientist working on space exploration, for example, might well be unable to communicate with one working on a cure for cancer, and so on. Snow attempts to deal with these questions in his retrospective comments but his answers are unsatisfactory and his use of the word "culture" is, I believe, mistaken and misleading.

The fragmentation of knowledge is a problem confronting all of us in the modern world and is more variegated and far-reaching than the reference to two cultures suggests. The best response to this problem I have come across has come from followers of Lonergan who have conceded that we have to abandon the idea of a modern Renaissance man capable of understanding the methods and findings of all of the intellectual disciplines; rather we should talk about "cognitive integration" on the basis of Lonergan's transcendental method. The one constant in scientific and scholarly investigation, they argue, is the method of gathering the data, forming hypotheses to explain the data, and testing the hypotheses to find which one is true or probable. And this method has to be performed responsibly. The beauty of transcendental method is that it is a meta-method that applies not only to the disciplines we classify as science but to all the intellectual disciplines in the university curriculum. All without exception have to comply with the four transcendental imperatives—Be attentive, Be intelligent, Be rational, and Be responsible—and their merits can be judged by being tried against these imperatives.

It is, I believe, Snow's impoverished notion of "culture" that justifies Leavis's judgement that "Snow is in fact portentously ignorant."[66] The word "portentously" is significant here since Leavis sees Snow as a portent of contemporary civilization. The fact that he can be taken seriously as a "sage" or "master-mind" on both sides of the Atlantic signals for Leavis a profound loss of critical acumen and moral discernment on the part of the educated public. He points out that the "literary intellectuals" that Snow is acquainted with belong to "the modish literary world; his 'intellectual' is the intellectual of the *New Statesman* circle and the reviewing in the Sunday papers. Snow accepts this 'culture' as the *haute culture* of our time; he accepts it as the age's finer consciousness so far as a culture ignorant of science can."[67] Leavis, in fact, has nothing but contempt for the metropolitan literary establishment, including the book reviewers in the Sunday papers, regarding them with some justice as compromised and corrupted by overriding commercial interests; they represent cronyism, forming a coterie bent on serving each others' interests; they lack the detached disinterestedness that alone guaranteed honest opinion and helpful criticism. (This is a sentiment Lonergan would have agreed with, suggesting at one point that *The New York Review of Books* might be more accurately called *The New York Review of Each Others' Books*.) Leavis concludes by describing Snow's "literary intellectual" as "the enemy of art and life."[68]

Leavis was also justified in his reaction to Snow's insulting reference to "literary intellectuals" being "natural Luddites" (in contrast with the scientists who "had the future in their bones"). The Luddites smashed machinery and tried to put a halt to technological progress; they were truly addicted to past ways of doing things. Leavis had no wish to halt or impede technological progress; indeed he considered it to be inevitable. In so far as he wished to explore the past, in the form of great works of literature, it was with a view to bringing the "best that had been known and said" in the past into a living and significant relationship with the present and the future. As he said, "it is only from the present, out of the present, in the present, that you can approach the literature of the past. To put it another way, it is only in the present that the past lives."[69] And he said of his envisaged English School, "The aim is to produce a mind that will approach the problems of modern civilization with an understanding of their origin . . . and . . . a sense of human possibilities . . . that traditional cultures bear witness to . . ."[70] Whatever might have been true of Snow's metropolitan literary associates, it was certainly the opposite of accurate to describe Leavis as a Luddite.

Leavis attacks Snow with the weapons of a literary critic, someone alive to the tone and texture of an author's language. He notes how from the outset Snow establishes himself as uniquely qualified to talk on the subject of the "two cultures" since he says of himself, "By training I was a scientist; by vocation I was a writer."[71] The frequency of occurrence of "I" and "my" in the opening section of Snow's lecture is revealing. He is establishing his credentials before offering his opinions and issuing his judgments. Leavis draws attention to the *tone* of Snow's comments, his self-assured and easy ability to pronounce with equal authority on science and literature. Leavis's opening comments must be ranked among the best put-downs in the whole of literature:

> If confidence in oneself as a master-mind, qualified by capacity, insight and knowledge to pronounce authoritatively on the frightening problems of our civilization, is genius, then there can be no doubt about Sir Charles Snow's. He has no hesitations. Of course, anyone who offers to speak with inwardness and authority on both science and literature will be conscious of more than ordinary powers, but one can imagine such consciousness going with a certain modesty—with a strong sense, indeed, of a limited range and a limited warrant. The peculiar quality of Snow's assurance expresses itself in a pervasive tone; a tone of which one can say that, while only genius could justify it, one cannot readily think of genius adopting it.[72]

In order to illustrate the tone of Snow's address, Leavis pounces on his pronouncement that Ibsen in old age was the only "world-class" author to understand the industrial revolution and his concluding comment that "there wasn't much that old man didn't understand."[73] This show of "knowledgeableness," Leavis points out, is characteristic of the tone of Snow's lecture. Snow makes many sweeping pronouncements on literature and science without feeling any need to support them with evidence or detailed references. We are expected to accept them as truths on the simple basis that Snow is uniquely qualified to pronounce on such matters; we are expected to accept them on the basis of Snow's own self-evaluation. As Stefan Collini observes in his excellent and not unsympathetic introduction to Snow's lecture, Snow "deploys the tropes of modesty to mask an assertion of authority."[74] Having pointed out that he is both a scientist and a writer, Snow comments with apparent modesty, "That was all. It was a piece of luck, if you like, that arose from coming from a poor home. But my personal history is not the point."[75] He then proceeds to tell us a good deal about his "personal history"—the first person singular, the word "I," is very prominent—and he burnishes his scientific credentials by describing how at Cambridge he had "a ringside view of one of the most wonderful creative periods in all physics." All of this on the very first page of the lecture—so much for Snow's comment about his "personal story" not being the point. The literary critic can see that these opening comments are precisely the point, that Snow is laying out the grounds which will justify his pronouncing on important matters based entirely on his say-so, without the need to support his claims with evidence.

Leavis was criticised for making his critique of Snow's lecture too personal, too *ad hominem*. The highly regarded American literary and cultural critic, Lionel Trilling, said of the tone of Leavis's lecture: "There can be no two opinions about the tone in which Dr Leavis deals with Sir Charles. It is a bad tone, an impermissible tone."[76] But in Leavis's defence it can be said that from the outset of his lecture Snow erected his comments on the grounds of his own authority. As Leavis said: "The general nature of his position and his claim to authority are well known: there are two uncommunicating and mutually indifferent cultures, there is the need to bring them together, and there is C. P. Snow, whose place in history is that he has them both, so that we have in him the paradigm of the desired and necessary union."[77]

It was the deeply personal nature of Snow's delivery that explained the personal nature of Leavis's attack and it is, I believe, a mistake to blame Leavis for this. Given the tone of Snow's delivery, we might say that Leavis had no option: it was not for nothing that he gave as the sub-tile of his Richmond lecture "The Significance of C. P. Snow." There is a good deal of artifice in the manner in which Snow shaped his lecture, especially the early sections where he seeks to establish his authority to speak as he does, and repeatedly draws attention to himself, if ever so modestly. He is adept at getting others to make his point for him, especially highly regarded scholars, such as the eminent mathematician, G. H. Hardy, on the literary establishment's annexation of the word "intellectual," or Rutherford, quoted by Snow in terms that suggest a kind of emotional kinship or camaraderie between him and the great scientist. Having quoted someone to voice opinions that are his, Snow concludes by saying, "he was absolutely right."[78] This is a tactic that enables him to assert his opinion without fear of challenge while appearing to be self-effacing.

In fact, taken as a whole, Snow's argument is that of an administrator or bureaucrat, albeit one used to working at a fairly high level. He has little to say about the excitement of scientific research, of the joy of discovery and intellectual breakthrough; indeed by 1959 he had not been involved in research for over twenty years. By this stage in his life he is an administrator who is out to change the shape and content of English education by advocating the case for increased investment in the teaching of science and technology. His argument won a great deal of support and it is not surprising that Snow was invited into Harold Wilson's governing Labour party in 1964 to act as second-in-command of the newly founded Ministry of Technology, was awarded a Life Peerage and became the government's spokesman on Technology in the House of Lords. In 1963 the Robbins Report recommended a major expansion of higher education and Snow endorsed its findings and principles. He also welcomed the foundation of new universities in the 1960s. The outcome of these changes is that today the uptake in higher education of science and technology courses, including those relating to information technology, dwarfs the uptake of courses in the arts and humanities. To that extent, Snow has emerged victorious from the controversy surrounding his Rede lecture of 1959, and Leavis as the loser. Leavis deplored and condemned the Robbins Report, claiming that it would lead to a decline in standards and that "more means worse." It is not clear if he truly believed it to be inevitable that standards would decline or that he wished to deprive more students of the opportunity to study at the level of higher education. After all, when he quit Cambridge he went to work as a Visiting Professor at the recently founded University of York. What is more likely is that he saw his plans for the University as a centre of national consciousness, and in particular his hopes for the English School within the University, becoming less likely to be realised as a result of the expansion. He might also have felt that expansion would result in a loss of influence in British intellectual life of the two "older" universities of Oxford and Cambridge. At one point in his lecture he refers to "Snow's designs on the university."[79]

To that extent, as I have said, Leavis was the loser. However, Leavis inflicted considerable harm on Snow's literary reputation. It is when he turns to Snow's assumption that he is "beyond question a novelist of a high order" that Leavis unleashes his most deadly and devastating criticism of "the significance of C. P. Snow." He says that as a novelist Snow "doesn't exist; doesn't begin to exist. He can't be said to know what a novel is."[80] In support of these judgments, Leavis points to the fact that in his novels Snow tells but does not show; his characters lack life; the dialogue in his novels is "inept; to imagine it spoken is impossible. And Snow is helpless to suggest character in speech."[81]

One of the ways in which Leavis invites the reader to assess the merits of Snow as a novelist is by comparing him with two English novelists Leavis considers to be truly great: George Eliot and D. H. Lawrence. The very mention of their names is sufficient to dwarf Snow's stature as a novelist. Leavis goes on to describe Lawrence as "the greatest English writer of our century" and uses a passage from *Women in Love* to mock what he considers to be Snow's inadequate "sense of human nature and human need."[82] Lawrence, of course, is one of Leavis's heroes, and Leavis rightly took pride in the fact that he had helped to establish Lawrence's reputation and standing (as well as that of T. S. Eliot). Leavis says that if Snow's lecture has any value for use in schools or universities "it is as a document for the study of cliché."[83] As examples of cliché, he cites Snow's saying that "history is merciless to failure" and that scientists "had the future in their bones." As an observation on Snow's style in his lecture, this reference to Snow's use of cliché is, I believe, the most acute part of Leavis's analysis. Reading Snow's lecture for the first time, I noted that its tone was a strange combination, being at once "chummy" and "authoritarian." I did not find myself referring to cliché exactly but noted Snow's fondness for what I termed "homely phrases," phrases such as "a formal touch of the cap"[84], "a ringside view," "a kind of frozen smile across the gulf," "screams of horror," "jam tomorrow."[85] Snow is a phrase-maker, the author of the phrase "the corridors of power" which has become part of everyday speech, as indeed has the phrase "jam tomorrow." Whether these are termed cliché or "homely phrases," Leavis is right to point out that they are not sufficient to qualify a writer as a "novelist of a high order."

But what Leavis, in my opinion, overlooks is that phrases of this kind work very well in a public lecture by adding an immediacy to what is being said. The audience—and when lecturing the audience's reaction is paramount—quickly gets the point. Leavis, of course, grasps this himself, remarking of this characteristic of Snow's delivery, "He clearly feels that it has an idiosyncratic speech-raciness that gives his wisdom a genial authority."[86] Leavis says this as a criticism but it might well have been said as a compliment, especially the reference to "raciness," the ability to get a point over quickly and with a small dash of humour. Audiences appreciate that and if Snow's lecture did become a subject of intense discussion not only in England but in other European countries and in the US, it was due in no small measure to Snow's ability to communicate with a mass audience. By contrast, the syntactic complexity of Leavis's sentences combined with the subtlety of his analysis probably worked against him, especially in the context of a lecture. (One of the more amusing criticisms of Leavis provoked by the language of his attack on Snow was that he was "a bad writer.")

Politicians are very fond of clichés since the point of a cliché is that it does not have to be explained; as a phrase that is well worn, its meaning is already "out there" and immediately obvious. For that reason, it is not surprising that Snow's lecture gained the attention of politicians and that he himself was invited into the world of politics as a government spokesman shortly after his lecture. As I have said, Snow's argument is the argument of a bureaucrat or administrator. In many ways it is quite simplistic, advocating science and technology as the means for achieving a higher standard of living, for bringing about an improvement in the material conditions of people's lives. Even at the scientific level it was simplistic, since Snow completely fails to advert to the scientific consequences of the mass industrialisation he advocates: consequences such as global warming and climate change, not to mention the degradation of the environment, massive problems we are acutely aware of today. He also fails to refer to the political infrastructure required for mass industrialisation to occur in the countries he considers to be poor. At a more philosophical or ethical level, Leavis is right to draw attention to Ruskin's distinction between wealth and well-being. Most people appreciate the improvements in the material conditions of life today which have been brought about by technology and the application of science, but Leavis points to the fact that the human need ranges far beyond what politicians and economists mean by "living standards." As Jesus observed, "Not by bread alone does man live": love, romance, friendship, family, human relationships, compassion, empathy, intellectual satisfaction, moral discernment, the excitement of discovery, fidelity, fortitude, endurance, forgiveness, reverence—human emotions of all kinds and the human situations and events that evoke them—all of these and more transcend the material conditions of life, but are the stuff of literature and poetry. This dimension of human life is totally missing from Snow's lecture which, surprisingly in a novelist, focuses exclusively on the material side of things. Leavis has an exalted view of the novel,[87] which he saw as, at its best as in Tolstoy's *Anna Karenina*,[88] the expression "of general truths about life." "Life" is probably the central criterion in Leavis's critical method: novels and stories that fail to do justice to the mature experience of human life, that fail to be life-enhancing and life-promoting, are the object of his negative judgments. Leavis wishes to draw attention to the deeper dimensions of human life. Despite the fact that he would appear to have lost the political argument, no one could deny the immense importance of what he wishes us to grasp and hold onto, as summarised in this quotation from his response to Snow:

In coming to terms with great literature we discover what at bottom we really believe. What for—what ultimately for? What do men live by?—the questions work and tell at what I can only call a religious depth of thought and feeling. Perhaps, with my eye on the adjective, I may recall for you Tom Brangwen, in *The Rainbow*, watching by the fold in lambing-time under the night-sky: "He knew he did not belong to himself."[89]

It is worth pausing at this point to ask what Leavis is doing here, by citing this comment on one of Lawrence's characters in his controversy with the novelist C. P. Snow. Leavis never lost his capacity to shock, to jolt the reader, and I think that is one reason why he refers here to questions of ultimate concern and Tom Brangwen's experience that "He knew he did not belong to himself." I believe he did so because he knew that the sentiment entertained in the novel by Tom Brangwen was well outside Snow's range, of a depth (which he terms "religious") that Snow's novels never penetrate or even approach. The sentence illustrates the distance separating Snow from a novelist of the stature of Lawrence. But what light does the reference throw on Leavis himself? I believe that Leavis's reference to this instance of Lawrence's insight into human experience (which he clearly endorses) is quite continuous with Leavis's central criterion of self-transcendence. We have seen this criterion in operation in Leavis's account of how dramatic tragedy affects us:

> The sense of heightened life that goes with tragic experience is conditioned by a transcending of the ego . . . it is as if we were challenged at the profoundest level with the question, "In what does the significance of life reside?," and found ourselves contemplating, for answer, a view of life, and of the things giving it value, that makes the valued appear unquestionably more important than the valuer, so that significance lies, clearly and inescapably, in the willing adhesion of the self to something other than itself.[90]

What Tom Brangwen experiences in Lawrence's novel we might call "real self-transcendence," the actual experience of leaving his ego behind, being taken out of himself, and, I believe, this is also for Leavis the aesthetic-moral experience of the reader when responding to great literature. To subscribe to self-transcendence as the criterion of the true and the right is to subscribe to the notion that the truth and the right are human imperatives: they make imperious demands on us human beings, demands that at times require us to overcome our spontaneous wishes and needs and, in a word, that we transcend ourselves. These are not demands we have chosen freely, but ones that lie beyond any voluntary choice—or perhaps "behind" might be the better word, since they are simply "there," exercising their authority and influence on our quest for what is true and what is right. It is when he broaches questions of ultimate concern or speaks of "the adhesion of the self to something other than itself" that Leavis manifests what can only be described as a religious sensibility—and, significantly, he uses the adjective "religious" in his comments on Tom Brangwen. Leavis, of course, was an agnostic in matters of religion (he described himself as "a Puritan without religion"), but I see no contradiction in claiming that someone who was a professed agnostic had a religious sensibility. Indeed, Muriel Bradbrook says of him, "his temperament was religious, but his upbringing cut him off,"[91] and John Harvey comments that in Leavis's "best writing" there "is the presence of a religious impulse which in another age might have been directed to God, but is here directed to civilisation."[92] The comment that comes nearest to what Leavis is referring to in these two citations, the one regarding Tom Brangwen in *The Rainbow* and the other explaining the impact of dramatic tragedy, is this from a Cistercian monk when speaking of his religious awakening: "I knew I carried something within me that reached beyond the limits of me."[93]

The novels of C. P. Snow are rarely referred to or borrowed from libraries today. It would appear that Leavis's criticism of the novels has hit home. Leavis's reputation also dipped for a time in the years following his death but a revival of interest in his critical method, his influence and his emphasis on inwardness has taken place in recent decades and looks set to continue well into the future. While the size and influence of science and technology departments in our universities might point to the triumph of C. P. Snow in this notorious controversy, who would deny that, given the problems of our civilization today, the areas of human living highlighted by Leavis—I am thinking primarily of the education of the feelings, and the cultivation of moral discernment and intellectual acumen—are of paramount importance? For it is by assisting the process of moral and intellectual maturation and growth that education will assist also the creation of an authentic public opinion. It would appear to me that today's world has more need of the wisdom of F. R. Leavis than of that of C. P. Snow, and that for this reason Leavis's is the more enduring legacy.

NOTES

1. 'What *we* do is to bring words back from their metaphysical to their everyday use.' Wittgenstein, *Philosophical Investigations*, 1, p. 116.
2. A. J. Ayer, *Language, Truth & Logic*, first published 1936; (London: Victor Gollancz, 1967) p. 44–45.
3. For an extremely useful commentary on Lonergan's view of language, see Joseph Flanagan's contribution to *Language, Truth and Meaning*, (London: Gill and Macmillan Ltd, 1972), edited by Philip McShane.
4. *Method*, p. 75.
5. L. S. Vygotsky, *Thought and Language*, (Massachusetts: Massachusetts Institute of Technology Press, 1962) p. 75.
6. S. K. Langer, *Philosophy in a New Key*, (Harvard: Harvard University Press, 1942), p. 126.
7. I hope this makes it sufficiently clear that I am in no way suggesting in what follows that "aesthetic knowledge" or whatever can be assigned to any *one* level of Lonergan's hierarchy of human consciousness. Knowledge of any kind for Lonergan consists of the three stages mentioned.
8. *Method*, p. 32.
9. *Method*, p. 40–41.
10. *Method*, pp. 157 and 159. Lonergan is contesting the view that we can only interpret honestly when we simply look at what is already "out there"; against this he argues that interpretation is best carried out by someone with proven experience and expertise in a particular area of inquiry.
11. On this, see my book, *Philosophical Encounters: Lonergan and the Analytical Tradition* (Toronto: University of Toronto Press, 2005), p 181–182.
12. *New Bearings in English Poetry* (Chatto and Windus, 1932), p. 17.
13. T. S. Eliot, *Selected Essays* (London: Faber and Faber Ltd, 1952), p. 286.
14. F. R. Leavis, *The Common Pursuit*, p. 110.
15. F. R. Leavis, *The Two Cultures? The Significance of C. P. Snow*, Leavis's response to Snow's 1959 lecture on 'Two Cultures.' See the next section.
16. In "Education and the University," *Scrutiny*, Vol. 9.
17. *Method in Theology*, p. 4.

18. *Scrutiny*, Vol. 6, p. 60–61.
19. "Education and the University," *Scrutiny*, Vol. 9.
20. The literary journal, *Scrutiny*, was first issued quarterly in 1932 and ran till 1953, with Leavis as editor. It has been re-issued as volumes, with this first volume representing the years 1932–33 and subsequent volumes corresponding to the years following that.
21. "Education and the University," *Scrutiny*, Vol 9, p. 309.
22. *Insight*, p. 272.
23. *Method*, p. 265.
24. See, for example, Lonergan's comparison and contrast of historical with scientific knowledge in *Method*, p. 219.
25. See *Scrutiny*, Vol. 9, p. 310.
26. See *Scrutiny*, Vol. 9, p. 310.
27. *Insight*, chapter 17.
28. See John Casey's excellent chapter on Leavis in his book, *The Language of Criticism* (London: Methuen & Co Ltd, 1966) for a careful guide here. John Harvey links Leavis's critical comments on the perils of egotism with his own energetic "introspective moral vigilance" in *The Leavises*, op. cit., p. 179.
29. *The Leavises*, op. cit., p. 186.
30. *The Leavises*, op. cit., p. 177.
31. *Insight*, p. xxviii. I understand this as referring to the fact that empiricism leaves out understanding and idealism leaves out judgment, the process by means of which understanding is verified. Lonergan repudiates the notion that his critical realism is a halfway house between empiricism and idealism but rather considers idealism to be the halfway house between empiricism and critical realism.
32. S. K. Langer, *Philosophy in a New Key* (Harvard, 1942) and *Feeling and Form* (New York, 1953).
33. *Philosophy in a New Key*, p. 61.
34. Langer, *Feeling and Form*, p. 40.
35. Langer, *Feeling and Form*, p. 366.
36. Langer, *Feeling and Form*, p. 288.
37. Langer, *Feeling and Form*, p. 358.
38. Langer, *Feeling and Form*, p. 218, 361.
39. "Sociology and Literature" in *The Common Pursuit*, p. 200.
40. Leavis, *Nor Shall My Sword*, p. 97.
41. John Casey, op. cit., p. 67.
42. John Casey, op. cit., p. 67.
43. *Feeling and Form*, p. 375.
44. *The Common Pursuit*, p. 111.
45. F. R. Leavis, *The Great Tradition* (London: Chatto and Windus, 1948; Peregrine Books edition, 1966), p. 93.
46. In this section I shall be referring both to Snow's Rede lecture, entitled *The Two Cultures*, and to Leavis's response to Snow, entitled *The Two Cultures? The Significance of C. P. Snow*. Each has been published in book form with an Introduction and Notes by Stefan Collini, the former by Cambridge University Press in 1998, the latter by Cambridge University Press in 2013. To simplify, I shall refer to Snow's text as CPS and to Leavis's as FRL, adding the relevant page reference.
47. CPS, p. 22 ff.
48. CPS, p. 41 ff.
49. CPS. p. 47 f.
50. CPS, p. 50.
51. CPS, p. 79.
52. CPS, p. 53.
53. CPS, p. 22.
54. CPS, p. 47–8.
55. FRL, 'The Idea of a University' in *Education and the University*, p. 2.
56. Matthew Arnold, 'General Report for the Year 1876.' p. 178.

57. Matthew Arnold, *Culture and Anarchy*, p. 46–54.
58. Lonergan, *Insight*, p. 241.
59. Lonergan, *Insight*, p. 241.
60. CPS, p. 9–10.
61. CPS, p. 10.
62. CPS, p. 9.
63. CPS, p. 31.
64. CPS, p. 70.
65. CPS, p. 66.
66. FRL, p. 53.
67. FRL, p. 60.
68. FRL, p. 61.
69. F. R, Leavis, "English Literature in Our Time and the University," p. 68.
70. F. R, Leavis, "The Idea of a University," p. 56.
71. CPS, p. 1.
72. FRL, p. 53.
73. CPS, p. 25.
74. CPS, p. xxix.
75. CPS, p. 1.
76. Quoted by Stefan Collini in CPS, p. xxxviii.
77. FRL, p. 56–7.
78. CPS, said first of Rutherford on p. 5, and then of Cockroft on p. 45.
79. FRL, p. 74.
80. FRL, p. 57.
81. FRL, p. 58.
82. FRL, p. 67.
83. FRL, p. 62.
84. CPS, twice on p. 12.
85. CPS, p. 1, p. 17, p. 25 and p. 44 respectively.
86. FRL, p. 63.
87. In *Anna Karenina and Other Essays* (London: Chatto and Windus, 1973), p. 11, he quotes with approval D. H. Lawrence's judgment that 'The novel is a great discovery: far greater than Galileo's telescope or somebody else's wireless. The novel is the highest form of human expression so far attained.'
88. F. R. Leavis, *Anna Karenina and Other Essays*, p. 13.
89. FRL, p. 69.
90. F. R. Leavis, *The Common Pursuit*, p. 131–32.
91. *The Leavises*, op. cit., p. 35.
92. *The Leavises*, op. cit., p. 35.
93. Erik Varden, *The Shattering of Loneliness: On Christian Remembrance* (London: Bloomsbury), p. 6.

Chapter Four

The Arnoldian Influence

PART ONE: ARNOLD AS A SOCIAL COMMENTATOR

In this chapter I shall argue that much of what Lonergan says about ideas, progress, decline and "cosmopolis" in chapter 7 of *Insight* has its source in writings of Matthew Arnold. I hope to furnish internal evidence that Lonergan was influenced by Arnold's *Culture and Anarchy*[1] and by his essay "On the Literary Influences of Academies."[2] But there is much to be gained from setting these works in the unfolding evolution of Arnold's social philosophy so that the reader can grasp clearly the recurrent themes and concerns of Arnold, the basic pattern of his ideas. This should help the reader to place *Culture and Anarchy* and the "Academies" essay in their historical and social context and thereby distinguish Arnold's purposes from those of Lonergan. It should also help to explain the many references to Arnold in Leavis's writings on society and literature and why Leavis was keen to place himself in the Arnoldian tradition when commenting on the quality of England's cultural life.[3] Leavis commented that in his early years as a literary critic it was Arnold and Satayana "who really counted."[4] Like Arnold, Leavis combined literary criticism with reflections on the quality of English civilization, seeing the former as having an important bearing on the latter. In the second part of the chapter I shall focus on Arnold's long neglected writings on religion and argue that Arnold's influence extends to Lonergan's *Method in Theology*.

Of England's great nineteenth century men of letters and cultural prophets, Matthew Arnold was possibly the most rounded (a quality he personally admired): poet, literary critic, classicist, Oxford Professor of Poetry, political and social commentator, innovative religious writer, he earned his living for more than thirty years as a member of the Inspectorship of Schools. In many respects Arnold's views on culture and society were learned and tested "on the hoof"—through his meetings with people in England from all walks of life in his work as a school inspector, as well as by his travels abroad to study the educational systems of other European nations. His father, Dr. Thomas Arnold, the famous educationist and headmaster of Rugby School, was a vigorous clergyman of the Church of England zealous to promote the educational, social and religious changes he considered necessary while preserving those parts of church and state he most loved; he said that if he had had two necks he would have been hanged twice![5] Matthew was in many ways the son of his father; but as a school inspector he was freed from any specialist role, such as the one that constrained his father, and was able to play the role of the generalist man of letters, a role that appears to have suited his temperament and his purposes.

He had broad sympathies with each of the three classes—aristocracy, middle class and working class—which, on his diagnosis, constituted English society in his time (a three-part classification that remains the matrix of any analysis of British society to this day). From 1847 to 1851, before becoming a school inspector, he worked as private secretary to the Liberal peer, the Marquis of Lansdowne, a post which left him free to pursue his own interests while bringing him into contact with the aristocratic Whig ruling clique which could form and change governments without allowing any major office to get outside a few select families.[6] Although not himself an aristocrat, Arnold nevertheless retained courteous contacts with aristocratic friends and acquaintances all through his life. By birth Arnold belonged to the middle class, albeit on his father's side we have to go back to his great grandfather to find anyone who actually engaged in trade and on his mother's side his immediate ancestors and relatives were almost exclusively Anglican clergymen.[7] Through his membership of the professional class and his family's connections with the ruling Establishment, and also through his own quality of inwardness, Matthew Arnold had a profound sense of being outside or beyond ordinary class distinctions.[8] With regard to the working class, Arnold in some respects saw further than most of his contemporaries: in a letter to his wife as early as 1851 he wrote that "the lower classes . . . will have most of the political power of the country in their hands. . . ."

As Arnold's political and social thought develops and matures during the 1850s and 1860s his writing reflects a central preoccupation: that he is living in a time of change when power will be transferred from the aristocracy to the emerging middle classes before being transferred finally to the lower working classes. He seems to sense an inevitability in this gradual transfer of political power; the wheel of history is ineluctably turning in one direction and while change can be delayed it cannot be prevented. But if change is inevitable, Arnold is deeply conscious that there is no inevitability that change will be for the better. In many ways his life's work can be summed up as an effort to ensure that when change does occur it will be for the better; or at least that what is best in English and European culture will not be destroyed in the process. He does not see the working class coming into its inheritance of power in his own time. Therefore he concentrates mainly on the improvement through culture and civilizing forces of the middle classes.

The middle classes were, by and large, the mercantile and capitalist classes. They were the merchants, tradesmen, factory owners, financiers and entrepreneurs whose wealth derived from the industrial revolution. In religion many were dissenters wedded to the Protestant ideal of individualism as well as to the utilitarian values of Bentham and Mill. They had struggled to overcome their religious and political disabilities and were deeply distrustful of the Established Church and of State interference; they had a passionate belief in personal and economic freedom. Matthew Arnold encountered them frequently in his educational travels and was dismayed by their narrowness and provincialism, their cultivation of materialism and financial success, and by their estimation of worth by the utilitarian criterion of practicality and value for money. The vehicle for promoting the needed improvement of the middle classes, he believed, was education which, as a school inspector, he was in a strong position to advocate. In one of his earlier, non-polemical essays, which formed the introduction to his report on "Popular Education in France," first published in 1861 (and reprinted separately in 1879 with the title "Democracy"), Arnold sets out to win the middle classes to his conception of education. But Arnold's conception of education is one which he believes only the modern state can deliver and his intended audience was committed to the notion of voluntarism and free enterprise in education as in other matters and was notoriously resistant to any suggestion of state interference. He sets about his task, accordingly, by attempting to allay his audience's suspicions of state interference.

> I propose to submit to those who have been accustomed to regard all State action with jealousy, some reasons for thinking that the circumstances which once made that jealousy prudent and natural have undergone an essential change. The dissolution of the old political parties which have governed this country since the Revolution of 1688 has long been remarked. . . . These parties, differing in so much else, were yet alike in this, that they were both, in a certain broad sense, aristocratical parties.[9]

But despite its many virtues, Arnold goes on to say, "The time has arrived when it is becoming impossible for the aristocracy of England to conduct and wield the English nation any longer"[10] The reason is that democracy is making inroads on aristocratic rule.

> It is because aristocracies almost inevitably fail to appreciate justly, or even to take into their mind, the instinct pushing the masses towards expansion and

> fuller life, that they lose their hold over them. It is the old story of the incapacity of aristocracies for ideas, the secret of their want of success in modern epochs. The people treats them with flagrant injustice, when it denies all obligation to them. They can, and often do, impart a high spirit, a fine ideal of grandeur, to the people; thus they lay the foundations of a great nation. But they leave the people still the multitude, the crowd; they have small belief in the power of the ideas which are its life. Themselves a power reposing on all which is most solid, material and visible, they are slow to attach any great importance to influences impalpable, spiritual, and viewless. And it must in fairness be added, that as in one most important part of human culture, openness to ideas and ardour for them, aristocracy is less advanced than democracy, to replace or keep the latter under tutelage to the former would in some respects be actually unfavourable to the progress of the world.[11]

Democracy's day has dawned, Arnold contends, but "The difficulty for democracy is, how to find and keep high ideals."[12] For Arnold America is a warning to England and the rest of Europe, for America is the exemplar of "the dangers which come from the multitude being in power, with no adequate ideal to elevate or guide the multitude."[13]

Arnold has no wish to abolish the great public schools, like Eton or Harrow, which serve the aristocracy so well, but he does wish to replace the private schools of the middle classes, which he clearly considers to be shrines of mediocrity indifferent to high cultural values, with state schools like the French Lyceums. This would bring the instruction in the schools to the middle classes "under a criticism which the stock of knowledge and judgment in our middle classes is not in itself able to supply . . . it can confer on them a greatness and a noble spirit, which the tone of these classes is not of itself at present able to impart."[14] The reason for the present deficiency of the middle class is that while aristocracy has "culture and dignity" and "democracy has readiness for new ideas and ardour for what ideas it possesses," the middle class has only "ardour for the ideas it already possesses."[15] Arnold goes on to pay tribute to the role of Protestant Dissent, "that genuine product of the English middle class," for the "negative achievement" of liberty of conscience and freedom of opinion. But liberty and industry will not ensure "a high reason and a fine culture," the only guarantors of a "great nation," as opposed to a merely wealthy or energetic nation. He concludes his persuasive essay by suggesting that what will preserve England's greatness and allow her to prosper as a people, like the ancient Athenians, responsive to art and beauty, are "Openness and flexibility of mind. . . . Perfection will never be reached; but to recognize a period of transformation when it comes, and to adapt themselves honestly and rationally to its laws, is perhaps the nearest approach to perfection of which men and nations are capable."[16]

Remaining within the context of education, Arnold virtually repeats this argument in his essay of 1864, "A French Eton," subtitled "Middle Class

Education and the State." As in "Democracy" Arnold is looking beyond the day when power will reside in the middle class to the day when "this obscure embryo, travailing in labour and darkness"—the working class—will hold office. It is a prospect that fills him with not a little dread unless there is an "adequate ideal, a cultured, liberalised, ennobled, transformed middle class" to act as "a point towards which it (the lower class) may hopefully work, a goal towards which it may with joy direct its aspirations."[17] In advocating the transformation of the middle class Arnold has an ulterior motive—the transformation of the middle class is a necessary precondition for the transformation of the lower class. The alternative is graphically indicated in "Democracy": "But the calamity appears far more serious still when we consider that the middle classes, remaining as they are now, with their narrow, harsh, unintelligent, and unattractive spirit and culture, will almost certainly fail to mould or assimilate the masses below them, whose sympathies are at the present moment wilder and more liberal than theirs."[18]

The pattern of Arnold's argument is now quite clear. The aristocracy is about to be supplanted by the middle class; notwithstanding the high tone and ideals bestowed by aristocratic rule, particularly in England, its demise seems inevitable and, at least in part, is due to aristocracy's incapacity for new ideas. The middle class, however, is itself somewhat obtuse in the realm of ideas; it lacks culture, refinement and the capacity to respond to things of the spirit. The fact that it is successful in business, Arnold is saying, does not make it fit to govern, at least not a country that aspires to greatness. Finally, if the middle class cannot be reformed, shedding its limitations and its narrow "Millite" values, what hope is there for the transformation of the working class? In another document dealing with education, Arnold spells out more fully the means by which he thinks the transformation of the middle class might be effected, in a passage that would certainly have won the approval of Leavis and in many ways expressed the reasoning that drove the Leavisian project. As one of Her Majesty's Inspectors of schools, Arnold—like Leavis—was conscious of the threat to the educational ideal of character formation represented by the replacement of traditional liberal education by science. He writes,

> To have the power of using, which is the thing wished, the data of science, a man must, in general, have first been in some sense "moralised"; and for moralising him it will be found not easy, I think, to dispense with those old agents, letters, poetry, religion. So let not our teachers be led to imagine, whatever they may hear and see of the call for natural science, that this literary cultivation is unimportant. The fruitful use of natural science itself depends, in a very great degree, on having effected in the whole man, by means of letters, a rise in what the political economists call the standards of life.[19]

In "Democracy" and "A French Eton" Arnold's argument is offered as supporting the introduction of a state system of education along the lines of the great French state schools. In his essay on "The Literary Influences of Academies," published in 1864, Arnold deploys similar reflections on the condition of England to support the desirability of an English counterpart to another French institution, the French Academy. The French Academy was founded by Richelieu in 1637 with the aim of protecting and upholding the French language, and of being "a literary tribunal" or a "high court of letters." Quoting Renan, Arnold sees the academy as "a recognised master in matters of tone and taste . . . creating a form of intellectual culture which shall impose itself on all around."[20] The notion of an authority in matters of intellect and taste Arnold finds attractive but is aware that it is contrary to the English character and habits of mind. It has, however, served the French well, fostering that "openness of mind and flexibility of intelligence" the French have in common with the Athenians. The qualities of England are, by contrast, "energy and honesty." Energy, Arnold continues, is the characteristic of genius and England has produced Shakespeare in the realm of poetry and Newton in the realm of science. But this same energy makes England impatient with the idea of an authority in intellectual matters, with anything that would curb its freedom. Arnold's point at this juncture in the argument is that in terms of human advancement occasional bursts of genius are not adequate compensation for the absence of the generally high level of intelligence such as the French Academy helps to generate and sustain. The continuity between the thinking of Matthew Arnold on this issue and that of F. R. Leavis is revealed in Leavis's comments in the preface to *Education and the University*: "Such prepotency as this country may hope for in the English-speaking world of the future must lie in the cultural realm." He goes on to say that the university has the opportunity to become "if not the Athens of the English-speaking world, the unmistakeable main focus of the Athenian function it had done so much to confirm to this country."[21]

Expanding on his theme, Arnold observes that "the *journeyman-work* of literature, as I may call it (is) so much worse here than it is in France." Comparing the work of English scholars with their French counterparts he detects in the former curious and regrettable lapses in judgment and tone, and a distinctly provincial note; this he attributes to the absence of any institution similar in function to the French Academy. "I say that in the bulk of the intellectual work of a nation which has no centre, no *intellectual metropolis* like an academy, . . . like M. Renan's 'recognised authority in matters of tone and taste'—there is observable *a note of provinciality*."[22] The lapses and provinciality, the eccentricities of opinion and stylistic solecisms Arnold discerns even in reputable English authors are put down "to the critic's isolated position in this country, to his feeling himself too much left to take his own way, too much without any central authority representing high culture and sound judgment, by which he may be, on the one hand, confirmed against the ignorant, on the other, held in respect when he himself is inclined to take liberties."[23]

In the "Academies" essay Arnold is not discussing the class divisions in England or the characteristics of any one class. He simply argues, with a wealth of examples, the advantages to a society of a "sovereign organ of opinion," a central institution which by setting and maintaining standards helps to raise the general level of performance of its scholarly and literary output. Arnold's advocacy of two public bodies—a state system of education and an academy—should not be misunderstood; he is not advocating socialist ideas. Rather his support for institutions of this kind stems from his belief as a classicist in the power of right reason, *ratio recta*. This is the central tenet of Arnold's philosophy. It underlies just about everything he says on just about any subject. Another of his names for right reason is "disinterestedness." It is "the free play" of the mind, the freedom of the intellect to range over, to consider, to ponder without fear or favour; it is all that Arnold means by "light." Arnold sees the state as the instrument of right reason in matters of education because the state stands above classes and sectarian divisions and allegiances. As such it has the power to smash the narrow outlook that would perpetuate the mediocrity of middle class education. In the same way an English version of the French Academy is another means of enlarging the scope of right reason in public events.[24] In *Friendship's Garland* Arnold has Arminius say, "The victory of 'Geist' over 'Ungeist' we think the great matter in the world. The same idea is at the bottom of democracy; the victory of reason and intelligence over blind custom and prejudice."[25] And the advice of Arminius, who represents continental rationality and openness to ideas, to England and the English is: "*Get Geist.*"[26]

Friendship's Garland was written in the form of twelve letters between July 1866 and November 1870, and published in book form in 1871. Although it reworks many of Arnold's familiar themes it broadens the scope of their application and marks a change in his style. Its tone is satirical, mockingly ironic, as Arnold pretends to defend the good sense and probity of England and her customs against the penetrating criticism of an intelligent, rational, if somewhat choleric, continental upstart from Prussia. The format allows Arnold to be much freer in the targets he selects for mockery; the amused, satirical tone differs greatly from the tone of judicious reasonableness of his previous writings. It is as if, having tried judicious reasonableness without much success, Arnold has decided to assault his countrymen's minds and emotions by means of satire. The success of *Friendship's Garland* must have encouraged Arnold to continue in the same satirical vein in his next series of articles, which came to be published in book form under the title *Culture and Anarchy* (first published in 1869; in revised form in 1875). *Culture and Anarchy* was to prove to be Arnold's most popular and enduring work, a book whose phrases worked their way into the language, a set text in almost every English liberal arts course of higher education. Although there is evidence to believe that Lonergan had read widely in Matthew Arnold, it is *Culture and Anarchy* which appears to have been most obviously at the forefront of his mind when he wrote of bias and cosmopolis in chapter seven of *Insight*. It was Arnold's constant aim, as he said it was of Sophocles, to "see life steady and to see it whole." The success of *Culture and Anarchy* must owe something to its being Arnold's most complete attempt to diagnose the ills besetting England as he understood them and, as a corollary of this, his most sustained prognosis of the principles and approaches that could reverse England's decline.

The argument of *Culture and Anarchy* is set within the framework of the threefold division of English society—the aristocracy, the middle classes and the lower classes, now amusingly and famously entitled respectively the Barbarians, the Philistines and the Populace. The strengths and faults of each class are indicated. The Barbarians have a belief in personal liberty and a love of sport and physical accomplishment. But with them culture tends to be an exterior matter of "looks, manners, accomplishments, prowess." They are not resistant to ideas so much as unaware of them. To the Philistines, Arnold concedes, England owes most of her wealth and her standing in the world as a prosperous nation of free individuals.[27] But the Philistines are resistant to ideas; seduced by coal and property, free trade and money-making, they worship "machinery" and regard culture as frivolous and insignificant, adopting in this a thoroughly "realist" approach. Finally, the Populace deserves our admiration on account of the toil and grinding labour it is subject to, but it is absorbed in its own struggle to achieve power, and hence it thinks only of promoting its own class.[28] Indeed class promotion is common to all three groups as is the dogma that freedom is doing as one likes. Culture, by contrast, aims at "a *general* expansion of the human family," at "a *harmonious* expansion of human nature" and so is at variance with "our strong individualism, our hatred of all limits to the unrestricted swing of the individual's personality . . . with our inaptitude for seeing more than one side of a thing. . . ."[29] Arnold wishes to see the love of culture supplant the mere promotion of class interest. He perceives a tension between our "ordinary self" and "our best self"—the former is a prisoner of the class to which it belongs; the latter is free of class bias, recognizing "the paramount authority of . . . right reason."[30] He notes that "in each class there are born a certain number of natures with a curiosity about their best self, with a bent for seeing things as they are, for disentangling themselves from machinery, for simply concerning themselves with reason and the will of God, and doing their best to make these prevail;—for the pursuit, in a word, of perfection."[31] Since this bent always tends to take such people out of their class, Arnold calls them "aliens."

The remnant of "aliens" is yet another instance, along with the state and the notion of an academy, of a body or agency that stands beyond class divisions and can bring the force of right reason to bear on national affairs. But this particular expression of the idea is new. So also are the categories of Hebraism and Hellenism by which he strives to analyse the English character. The Hebraic tradition derives from England's Jewish inheritance and stands for energy, practicality, duty and self-control. At present, Arnold argues, it has ascendancy over Hellenism, the Greek tradition of intelligence, light, flexibility and openness of mind. This has lost out to the hebraising tendency in recent centuries, particularly under the influence of Puritanism.[32] Arnold makes no secret of his dislike of Puritanism and what he sees to be the negative side of Protestantism. He believes it has checked and frustrated the wonderful effect of the Renaissance in unleashing ideas, and has distracted England from the main current of modern thought. "For more than two hundred years the main stream of man's advance has moved towards knowing himself, the world, seeing things as they are, spontaneity of consciousness; the main impulse of a great part, and that the strongest part, of our nation has been towards strictness of conscience."[33] What is needed at present is "the development of our Hellenising instincts, seeking ardently the intelligible law of things, and making a stream of fresh thought play freely about our stock notions and habits."[34] Hellenism can break down the fanaticism and narrowness of Hebraism; it was because St. Paul adapted his Hebraism by Hellenism that he was able to destroy the mechanical worship of a fixed rule.[35] We (Arnold continues) need to go further than Paul, who persisted in perceiving man's moral nature to be his all, and apply fresh ideas in all our activities. Hebraism and Hellenism are at one in the final aim, the aim of perfection; and Hebraism, like Hellenism, is opposed to "the conception of free-trade, on which our Liberal friends vaunt themselves, and in which they think they have found the secret of national prosperity," but which, Arnold believes, "threatens to create for us, if it has not created already, those vast, miserable, unmanageable masses of sunken people"—paupers.[36] But by itself Hebraism cannot devise a system that would rectify the situation; for that the Hellenistic spirit—understanding and not just moral exhortation—is needed. It is the Hellenistic spirit that is needed if the mechanical worship of the fetish of free trade is to be destroyed.

Arnold concludes his argument by proposing to give "the heritage neither to the Barbarians nor to the Philistines, nor yet to the Populace; but we are for the transformation of each and all of these according to the law of perfection. Through the length and breadth of our nation a sense,—vague and obscure as yet,—of weariness with the old organisations, of desire for transformation, works and grows."[37] And he rounds off by calling the members of this invisible army of "best selfers," those capable of realizing the Socrates in themselves, "docile echoes of the eternal voice, pliant organs of the infinite will. . . ."[38]

That Arnold is a central source of Lonergan's commentary on ideas in chapter seven of *Insight* is a point that can be quickly established beyond reasonable controversy. The message Lonergan like Arnold wishes to drive home is that if you want to make progress and reverse decline, "Get Geist." Both authors share the same fundamental belief that right reason, Lonergan's "free, unrestricted desire to know the truth," is the motor of progress and its opposite—bias, distortion, Arnold's "Ungeist"—is the motor of decline. Lonergan's account contains the familiar Arnoldian vocabulary: "the multitude," "sweetness and light," "academy," "court," "claptrap," "culture," "class." More significant is the strong community of feeling and the shared concern that culture should retain its function of being critical of the operations of common sense and practical men of affairs. Should culture lose this function, either by being trivialized or restricted to an ivory tower or by being reduced to a mere prop or function of common sense practicality, then not only is its essential function gone but by that same token practicality is itself condemned to ruin. Culture is needed in order to save practicality from itself. And what is Lonergan's "cosmopolis" but a universalisation of Arnold's notion of an academy, "an intellectual metropolis," a supreme arbiter in matters of taste and judgment, because itself nothing more than the representative of right reason? Lonergan's plea that cosmopolis stands above all the claims of class or state because founded on "the native detachment and disinterestedness of every intelligence"[39] is in its way a mirror reflection of Arnold's urging that the remedy for England's ills rests in a remnant of "aliens" or "best-selfers," capable of rising above mere class interest because their first allegiance is to the paramount authority of right reason. But it is not only Lonergan's idea of "cosmopolis" that stems from Arnold. It is surely patently clear that the critical function Leavis assigns to the university, and the English School within the university, accords with Arnold's comments on the role of right reason—whatever institutional form it might take—in English society. As might be expected, Leavis's diagnosis of the ills besetting English culture comes closer to Arnold's than Lonergan's more generalised, and theoretical, comments in *Insight*. For Leavis is deeply worried by what he perceives to be the dehumanising effects of mechanised industrial practices on society at large. And as in the case of Lonergan, several of Arnold's terms and phrases can be found in Leavis's writings, such as the notion of "distinterestedness," which Leavis sought to convey by a variety of terms—such as "impersonality," "spontaneity," "intelligence," "creativity"[40] —while Arnold's "free play of the mind" and his references to "Athens" and the "Athenians" can also be found in Leavis's writings on culture and literary criticism.

Lonergan's analysis of the principles of progress and decline and his notion of cosmopolis are more than a simple repetition in the twentieth century of what Matthew Arnold said in the nineteenth. Leavis makes the valuable point that authors who stand later in a tradition serve to illuminate and give meaning to the tradition by drawing out where the tradition was heading for.[41] Lonergan takes up the themes of Matthew Arnold and by reworking them, systematizing them and placing them in a more contemporary and, it must be said, a transcultural context, he gives fresh meaning to the position Arnold stood for. Lonergan places Arnold's notions of class allegiance and resistance to ideas within the framework of a threefold bias to which human beings are prone. The treatment of the biases follows his outline of the development of community and his diagnosis of the tension within community. This tension is generated by the differing tendencies of intelligently devised social order, on the one hand, and the spontaneous drives and fears of individuals and groups, on the other. It is in the context of this tension in community that Lonergan carries out his analyses of the biases he identifies in human society and which he adds to a further bias—of egotism—stemming from the depths of the individual psyche, which he analysed in a previous chapter. The three biases are individual bias, group bias, and general bias. On individual bias, the bias of the self-seeking egoist, Arnold is, to the best of my knowledge, silent and so Lonergan's fascinating treatment of this topic will not be summarised here. Group bias corresponds to the class interest Arnold perceives to be at work respectively among the Barbarians, the Philistines and the Populace. Lonergan radicalises this idea by broadening the scope of its application beyond that of a social class. Groups are found in society, to be sure, but different functions within a technology, an economy or a political system are also performed by groups and Lonergan includes all of these within his designation of group bias.

> Were all the responses (to new ideas) made by pure intelligences, continuous progress might be inevitable. In fact, the responses are made by intelligences that are coupled with the ethos and the interests of the groups and, while intelligence heads for change, group spontaneity does not regard all changes in the same cold light of the general good of society. Just as the individual egoist puts further questions up to a point, but desists before reaching conclusions incompatible with his egoism, so also the group is prone to have a blind spot for the insights that reveal its well-being to be excessive or its usefulness at an end.[42]

Group bias, Lonergan continues, leads to its own reversal. For it is prone to generate a distortion of the social reality so palpable as to be "exposed to the inspection of the multitude" and a reversal, that may be more or less peaceful, is eventually summoned.[43] This is of a piece with Arnold's reflections on the inevitability of the transfer of political power from the aristocracy to the middle classes in his day. But Lonergan's treatment is more universally applicable than that of Arnold who restricts his analysis to a single society and who habitually argues by citing individual instances, events or personalities. Lonergan moves beyond the individual instance and the affairs of an individual nation to state a rule or generalization: group bias brings about its own reversal. And the reason is that beyond the group there is the much vaster multitude, whose interests are increasingly ill-served by one or several groups whose contribution to the general good has diminished or vanished but which, notwithstanding, is intent on promoting its own survival or even advancement. Lonergan's analysis can be vindicated by reference to historical events, such as the French Revolution, as well as events we witness in modern politics or commerce. In the end the shorter cycle of decline is brought to an end by force of the numerical superiority of those whose interests are poorly served.

General bias is the bias of common sense itself, a bias to which all men are prone. Common sense regards the practical, the here and now, getting on with the world's business, achieving short-term objectives. The higher viewpoint that would consider the general good of society, that would insist on due weight being given to the long-term results of any enterprise, falls outside the sphere of the practical here and now, and so is dismissed by common sense. Where group bias generates the shorter cycle of decline, common sense colludes with group bias in producing the longer cycle of decline. For common sense lacks the theoretical framework that would guide its choices and allow it to take the longer view. Faced with the distortion of the reality generated by the systematic resistance to the cumulative emergence of new ideas, common sense is powerless to propose an antidote that could be effective. Such an antidote would require the emergence of a human science or depth of analysis for which common sense has no regard. In the midst of the social anomalies that proliferate under the impact of the biases of dominant groups, culture retreats into irrelevance, the proposals of the detached and disinterested intelligence are scorned as impractical idealism and common sense conforms. Facts are facts. The longer cycle of decline is initiated by this surrender on the intellectual level, when the norms inherent in human intelligence are systematically ignored and there is a consequent "increasing demand for further contractions of the claims of intelligence, for further dropping of old principles and norms, for closer conformity to an ever growing man-made incoherence immanent in man-made facts."[44] But common sense is powerless by itself to reverse the process it has allowed to develop.

This rather crude summary of Lonergan's long and nuanced analysis of general bias should suffice to reveal at once how his notion is rooted in aspects of Arnold's thinking and yet takes us far beyond Arnold and the Victorian world he inhabits. Arnold's notion of Hebraism, the besetting fault of all classes of English society in his day, is akin to Lonergan's notion of general bias. Hebraism is concerned with doing, with energy, with practicality. It is contemptuous of thinking, of understanding, of seeing how things truly are. Against the habits of Hebraism Arnold enlists Hellenism, declaring that it is not the case, despite "what the majority of people tell us, . . . that things are for the most part to be settled first and understood afterwards."[45] But Lonergan's treatment is at once more radical and more contemporary. And more radical because more contemporary, since the neglect of the norms of rationality have by his day led to decline on a scale Arnold could not possibly have envisaged. As Leavis says in the opening words of *Mass Civilization and Minority Culture,* "For Matthew Arnold it was in some ways less difficult." Lonergan's account refers to the availability today of a terrifying range of means for the suppression of that liberty which is the principle of progress. "Its means include not merely every technique of indoctrination and propaganda, every tactic of economic and diplomatic pressure, every device for breaking down the moral conscience and exploiting the secret affects of civilised man, but also the terrorism of a political police, of prisons and torture, of concentration camps, of transported and extirpated minorities, and of total war."[46]

And if Lonergan joins Arnold in impugning the "old liberal views of automatic progress," he is also critical of Marxist dialectics which he considers to be founded on the grave error of erecting an instance of the corrective process of the shorter cycle of decline—class warfare—into the main principle of all progress. That is to confuse progress with decline.[47] And I suspect it was similar reasoning that kept Leavis from sympathising with Marxist attempts to define the role and method of literary criticism, which were powerful in academic circles in his time. For anyone, such as Arnold, Lonergan or Leavis, who esteems "right reason" or "disinterestedness" or "self-transcendence," as the motor of progress, the promotion of class warfare is not the answer to society's problems.

Matthew Arnold is less concerned with the transfer of power from one class to another, which he believes will be inevitable (as Lonergan observes, "the dialectic sooner or later upsets the short-sighted calculations of dominant groups"), than with releasing new and fresh ideas, with ousting us from the "comfortable straw of our old habits." But Lonergan, in the light of his analysis of the longer cycle of decline, confers on cosmopolis a more precisely defined role than any conceived by Arnold in his rather loose evocation of "Hellenism." The business of cosmopolis is "to prevent dominant groups from deluding mankind by the rationalisation of their sins; if the sins of dominant groups are bad enough, still the erection of their sinning into universal principles is indefinitely worse; it is the universalisation of the sin by rationalisation that contributes to the longer cycle of decline; it is the rationalisation that cosmopolis has to ridicule, explode, destroy."[48] Lonergan's cosmopolis is conceived as commensurate with the depth and breadth of the evil he has analysed. Cosmopolis, as Lonergan conceives it, is not identifiable with the state, an academy or any institution. As the evil it addresses is pervasive so cosmopolis itself has to be pervasive. Matthew Arnold calls for the release of fresh ideas to disturb our stock notions and habits. Lonergan acts in the spirit of his source material by taking up Arnold's suggestions and offering a programme that is more fully elaborated than Arnold's and is designed to meet the different order of magnitude of the problems encountered by people in this later day.

If we look closely at Lonergan's treatment of Matthew Arnold we can see that he is effecting a shift from scholarly common sense to theory. Lonergan's analysis places two sets of people in two different kinds of relationship with each other; depending on the interaction of the multitude with the self-promoting group(s) there results either the shorter or the longer cycle of decline (or both—the relationships are not mutually exclusive). The result is quite strictly a function of the relationship, and the relationship between the two sets of people can be in the field of commerce, economics, politics or whatever. Cosmopolis, in turn, is compatible with any body or institution that performs the designated critical function relative to general bias. Lonergan extracts the basic pattern of Arnold's ideas from their context in Arnold's writings; his analysis is detached from the arguments Arnold pursues, and there is no implication that Lonergan agrees or disagrees with Arnold's reflections on England in the 1860s and 1870s. He works out the implications of some of the relationships Arnold speaks about so that they come to form a model of human behaviour, a model free of any particular cultural context. He then applies the model in order to understand and interpret modern history. Matthew Arnold is not trying to establish general laws or principles of human behaviour, but rather to understand the words and actions of men in his own country at a particular time. He speaks from his experience and from his stock of inherited wisdom; he does not share the general bias of common sense but his understanding is, nevertheless, a type of developed common sense in that, as in Leavis, the focus is on a particular country and on particular events and occurrences in that country. Lonergan's use of Arnold brings about a transition from the scholarly differentiation of consciousness to the theoretical differentiation of consciousness.[49] Scholarly reflection has been transposed into theory, a conceptual structure of virtually unlimited application. The local colour and the topical references to be found in Arnold (and Leavis) are gone; but there is an immense, if unglamorous, gain in precision, system and range of application.

A point that perhaps needs to be stressed is that Arnold locates the solution to the problems he diagnoses in contemporary society *within human beings*—his particular focus is, as he puts it, on "moralising young men" (men being presumed to be the agents of the changes and developments expected to take place in England at that time.) And the main means for bringing about such moralising are, as he says, poetry, letters and religion. Leavis and Lonergan follow Arnold in pointing to what lies within human beings as the most radical solution to society's problems and discords. For Leavis, the principal means for "moralising" students was to be literature as it was taught and studied in the English School of the university. In Lonergan the principal means was to be found in the study of philosophy, at least of a philosophy that recognised self-transcendence or the "detached, disinterested desire to know the truth" as the central criterion of objectivity and authenticity. And, as I shall attempt to explain in the second part of this chapter, unlike Leavis but like Arnold, Lonergan also proposed religion—or at least a religion centred on conformity with right reason—as providing a powerful force for good in contemporary society. Lonergan's stated position is that "the intellectual, the moral and the religious are three phases in the single thrust to self-transcendence."[50] In their allegiance to right reason and self-transcendence both Leavis and Lonergan qualify to be counted as members of Arnold's "best-selfers" or "aliens"—the minority or remnant that Arnold identified as capable of rising above both self- and class-interest and, in so doing, as helping to bring about a culture that cleansed and purified society and kept it free from violence and internal division. It is all too easy to scoff at such idealism but without it society will continue to be troubled and disaffected. As we look around our world today we find that it is marked by ethnic, religious and cultural tensions and divisions, divisions that certain power groups and influential individuals are happy to exacerbate and exploit with violent and disastrous results on a scale that Matthew Arnold could probably never have envisaged; but the right reason, the *ratio recta*, that Arnold championed and praised, is, in the final analysis, the only way forward if humanity is to enjoy the sustained peaceful and harmonious coexistence that Arnold sought to bring forward in the England of his day.

The task I have been engaged with in this chapter clearly falls within the first of the eight functional specialties which Lonergan considers to be common to the practice of theology and of human studies: the specialty of research. Essentially I have been tracing the source of the ideas Lonergan expounds in a relatively small section of his vast work, *Insight*. Matthew Arnold can be regarded as one of a series of authors and thinkers who provided the questions, the agenda and some of the raw materials for Lonergan's own thinking and writing. Arnold is not a technical thinker and he is distrustful of systems and system-makers. Lonergan is a technical and systematic thinker. In particular there is Arnold's most profound belief—it is fundamental to all his thinking—that the solution to the problems he diagnoses is to be found in a renewed programme of inwardness; that an understanding of what is within human beings is fundamental to an understanding of what lies without, of the external, man-made world; and that this turn to the subject is the mark of modernity.[51] Both Leavis and Lonergan believed in inwardness, in bringing about beneficial inner change, intellectual and moral, in those who heeded what they had to say. Both Leavis and Lonergan also sought to improve the quality of cultural life by targeting our intelligence and sensibility—by means of what Lonergan termed "intellectual and psychic conversion." Arnold fears the uncommitted intellect. He believes in enlightened commitment, and asserts that personal and social transformation is the key to personal and social growth towards perfection.[52] We have here, in a general way, much of what Lonergan stands for. And we have here much of what Leavis stands for. "Ratio recta" is the root that Arnold, Lonergan and Leavis hold in common; it is from that common root that there grew their proposed solutions to the cultural challenges they encountered and diagnosed in their own distinctive and individual ways. The desire to educate people of common sense by awakening and refining their moral sensibility and authenticity is one that was shared by Matthew Arnold, Bernard Lonergan and F. R. Leavis. It was a goal that each of the three held dear and to which they devoted a great deal of their scholarly efforts.

PART TWO: ARNOLD ON RELIGION

Matthew Arnold had a profound concern for religion. He said that had he been born in a previous generation he would most likely have been an Anglican clergyman, like his father and many of his forebears. But Arnold belonged to a generation of English men and women whose religious faith had been assaulted by developments in science and in scholarship: the Darwinian theory of evolution in his native England and the historical criticism of the bible emanating at that time mainly from Germany. Arnold witnessed the painful loss of faith of his close friend and fellow poet, Arthur Hugh Clough, and the memory of Clough's experience remained with him in the years following his friend's premature death at the age of 43 in 1861. His feelings about the public change in attitudes towards traditional Christian religion are movingly expressed in one of his most quoted poems, "Dover Beach":

> The Sea of Faith/Was once, too, at the full, and round earth's shore/Lay like the folds of a bright girdle furled./But now I only hear/Its melancholy, long, withdrawing roar,/Retreating, to the breath/Of the night-wind, down the vast edges drear/And naked shingles of the world.[53]

When at the end of the 1860s Arnold elected to address the religious issue it was with the intention of effecting a reconciliation between traditional faith and the modern mind shaped by the new criticism and the new scientific outlook. Arnold was anxious to preserve what he considered to be most palpable and solid in the Christian tradition in order to preserve its beneficial effects on culture and society. What was not verifiable or truly "scientific" he was quite prepared to disown or discard or assign to the realm of "poetry." Arnold set out his new interpretation of Christian belief in four books, all published within the space of a decade. "The thing," he wrote, "is to recast religion."[54]

I shall argue that some of Lonergan's key theological notions, notions that were to help determine the basic orientation of his reflections on theological method, have their source in his engagement with Arnold's religious writings. I put it this way to deflect any suggestion that Lonergan simply repeats Arnold on religion, that he merely "takes over" Arnold. Far from it. As one might expect, a considerable intellectual distance separates the twentieth century Roman Catholic theologian of professed conservative views and the nineteenth century literary critic who has with justice been called "the founder of English modernism";[55] the systematic and technical thinker from the man of letters who championed "flexible common sense." When comparing Lonergan and Arnold the differences are as instructive as the similarities.

This section, then, has two objectives. The first is to argue, on the basis of a range of distinctive ideas held in common, that Matthew Arnold's religious writings positively influenced Lonergan's development of a method for theology. This objective will serve as a principle of selection in the first part of the article where I offer a summary of Arnold's religious thought. But while this part will be selective Arnold's central position will, I trust, emerge without distortion. The second objective will be to suggest further how the intellectual disagreement between Arnold and Lonergan influenced Lonergan to write *Method in Theology* as he did.

Arnold's Religious Thought

It is fairly safe to say that Arnold's religious writings are today the least read of all his work.[56] P. J. Keating expresses a widely shared view when explaining the exclusion of any of Arnold's religious writings from *Arnold's Selected Prose*, which he edited: "The writings on religion, to which Arnold gave pride of place when he anthologized himself in 1880, I have omitted completely, because, of all Arnold's work, these seem to me to carry least well to the modern reader."[57] F. R. Leavis makes a similar point when considering Arnold's essay on "The Study of Poetry": "The element that 'dates' in the worst sense is that represented by the famous opening in which Arnold suggests that religion is going to be replaced by poetry. Few now would care to endorse the unqualified intention of that passage, and Arnold as a theological or philosophical thinker had better be abandoned explicitly at once."[58] But in his day Arnold's religious books were, if anything, more widely read and discussed and the cause of greater controversy than his literary criticism or even his polemical essays on society and culture, which have stood up well to the passage of time. His religious thought is outlined in

St. Paul and Protestantism, published in 1870; *Literature and Dogma*, published in 1873; *God and the Bible*, published in 1875; and *Last Essays on Church and Religion*, published in 1877. A shorter, popular edition of *Literature and Dogma* was published in 1883.

In the opening paragraph of *St. Paul and Protestantism* Arnold challenges Renan's claim that Paul, who is identified with Protestantism, is coming to the end of his reign. Paul is not coming to the end of his reign, Arnold contends; indeed his reign is just beginning. What is coming to an end is Protestantism: "The Protestantism which has so used and abused St. Paul is coming to an end; its organizations, strong and active as they look, are touched with the finger of death."(pp. 1–2). Arnold sets about rehabilitating Paul and to achieve this he lays down a key methodological principle. What is important in a religious teacher, he says, and "gives him his permanent worth and vitality" is "the scientific value of his teaching," the "facts which can be verified" (p. 5). He continues, "The license of affirmation about God and his proceedings . . . is more and more met by the demand for verification" (p. 5). Terms like "science," "the scientific sense," "verification," "facts" abound in the early pages of the essay and recur in the books that follow. Arnold is propounding a critical instrument he hopes will be effective in religious discourse and put a stop to the theologians' habit of "proving anything about anything." In all of his religious writings Arnold suggests the need for Christian theology to look again at its foundations because science and critical scholarship have called in question much that was once taken for granted or considered susceptible of proof.

St. Paul and Protestantism is a sustained attack on the Calvinistic theological scheme or system, characterized by "original sin, free election, effectual calling, (and) justification through imputed righteousness" (p. 10). As Calvinism has developed, its doctrines have become harsher and more rigid: "and to complete the whole, a machinery of covenants, conditions, bargains and parties contractors, such as could have proceeded from no one but the Anglo-Saxon man of business, British or American" (p. 12). The basic mistake of the Puritan approach to Paul, according to Arnold, is to treat poetry as if it were a scientific treatise. Paul is a Hebrew, he "orientalises"—i.e., he speaks figuratively, metaphorically, symbolically. It is the methodology of Puritanism that is at fault. To read the bible correctly it is necessary to have an understanding of the human mind and its history, and acquaintance with many great writers (p. 19); "no man . . . who knows nothing else, knows even his Bible" (p. 31).

Focussing in particular on *The Epistle to the Romans*, Paul's "mature and greatest work," Arnold picks out what was for Paul the guiding thread in all he did and wrote. This was Paul's *"desire for righteousness,"* his master impulse, "the governing word of St. Paul's entire mind and life" (p. 34). Although Paul was not a scientific writer, he seized hold of a scientific fact:

that all men have a natural desire for righteousness, for right conduct. This is "the law as reason and conscience, God as moral law" (p. 31). The rule of reason and conscience is "an aim to which science does homage as a satisfying rational conception" (p. 31). To serve God is "to follow that central clue in our moral being which unites us to the universal order" (p. 32). Sin and righteousness can prove themselves scientifically, because they are based on human experience, on human self-knowledge. It is this basis in experience that establishes the desire for righteousness as scientific: "the moral law in human nature, however this law may have originated, is in our actual experience among the greatest of facts" (p. 30). Arnold's argument in the first chapter of *St. Paul and Protestantism* is curious but perfectly logical. On the one hand, Paul must not be mistaken for a scientific writer, the author of a scientific treatise; he is oriental, figurative, poetical. On the other hand, Paul's writing is not purely imaginative or fictional; because it is based on one crucial, scientific fact, the fact that men seek righteousness.

In the previous section of this chapter we saw how compliance with "right reason" stood at the centre of Arnold's advocacy of an English institution similar in function to the *Academie Francaise* as well of state education—these recommendations were based on Arnold's strong desire to help groups take the wider view of pursuing the common good, the good of all, and, in doing so, to move beyond the pursuit of class-interest. Arnold claimed that the pursuit of righteousness was a palpable fact, something that belonged to the very humanity of human beings; what emerges in his religious writings is that he sees this pursuit as uniting humans to "the universal order," to "God as moral law." In other words, right conduct is compliance with the divine will, something that unites us to God because right conduct is continuous with the very being or nature of God. So when in *Culture and Anarchy*, Arnold refers to the "best-selfers" as "docile echoes of the eternal voice, pliant organs of the infinite will" he is doing something more than employing fanciful metaphorical phrases to underline his point of view, but speaking what he considers to be the literal truth—"ratio recta" or conscience is that in human nature that is continuous with the divine nature itself. It is this philosophical-theological belief that explains Arnold's repudiation of the notion, gaining in popularity in his age, that human beings are nothing more than the products of Nature. His views are expressed powerfully in his poem *"To a Preacher"*:

"In harmony with Nature?" Restless fool,/. . . . Know, man hath all which Nature hath, but more,/And in that more lie all his hopes of good./ . . . Man must begin, know this, where Nature ends;/Nature and man can never be fast friends./Fool, if thou canst not pass her, rest her slave!

For Arnold "right reason" as the motor of progress and the opponent of decline has behind it the divine sanction; to be converted to the paramountcy of the search for righteousness is to be converted to God. And although

Leavis, as we have seen, sets great store by the criterion of "right reason," he would not appear to share Arnold's belief that this criterion unites us to the divine will—although he does appear to propose that compliance with right reason is or at least leads to something close to human fulfilment. Lonergan's references to "right reason"—what he terms "the detached, disinterested desire to know the truth and to do the right"—do appear to be closer to Arnold's position in that he claims that this desire can be verified by appeal to our experience as intellectual and moral beings but he also goes further than this and argues that the transcendental imperatives of "Be intelligent," "Be rational" and "Be responsible"—imperatives which mark us out as human—require the existence of a source that lies beyond human nature. However, as I shall argue, Lonergan's appeal to right reason—or religious conversion—as the foundation of the normative phase of theological method is more subtly nuanced than Arnold's promotion of "right reason" and "conduct" at the expense of the traditional doctrines of Christianity.

Arnold cites many texts from the psalms, the gospels and Paul's epistles to support his contention that the desire for righteousness was a central preoccupation of the Old Testament Jews and that Paul continued in the same vein. He refers to Paul's lists of moral habits to be pursued or avoided. The "superstructure" of Paul's theology, he says, was built on "the solid ground of his hearty desire for righteousness" (pp. 24–5). Arnold proposes that there are two sides to Paul's thinking. There is "The voluntary, rational and human world of righteousness, moral choice, effort, (which) filled the first place in his spirit." But he also regarded God as "the power by which we have been 'upholden ever since we were born.' . . . By this element we are receptive and influenced, not originative and influencing; now, we all receive far more than we originate" (pp. 39–40). Where the Puritan stresses man's passivity before God, concentrating exclusively on God's activity, Paul combines the influence of God's power in us, "that produces results transcending all our expectations," with our own agencies of reason and conscience (p. 40). It is a two-way process of acting and being acted upon. Arnold offers an analogy from human experience.

> Of such a mysterious power and its operation some clear notion may be got by anybody who has ever had any overpowering attachment. Everyone knows how being in love changes for the time a man's spiritual atmosphere and makes animation and buoyancy where before there was flatness and dullness. . . . And not only does it change the atmosphere of our spirits . . . but it also sensibly and powerfully increases our faculties of action. . . . An indolent man . . . will show energy quite easily from being in love. This, I say, we learn from the analogy of the most everyday experience. (pp. 40–41).

It is on the basis of such an analogy that Arnold explains Paul's conversion to Christ. It was for the sake of righteousness that Paul "felt himself *apprehended*, to use his own expression, by Christ" (p. 41). "For us, who approach Christianity through a scholastic theology, it is Christ's divinity which establishes his being without sin. For Paul, who approached Christianity through his personal experience, it was Jesus Christ's being without sin which establishes his divinity" (pp. 42–3). Arnold is here attacking the Puritan notion of conversion as instantaneous and "mechanical," a "miraculous" process in which the human being takes no active part but is simply the passive recipient of imputed righteousness. This is nonsense (Arnold argues) and lies at the heart of the Puritan misunderstanding of Paul. Rather, Paul felt that by perfectly identifying himself with Jesus, "by appropriating Jesus and in no other way," he could "get the confidence and the force to do as Jesus did" (p. 47). This was "*faith*." More fully he (Paul) calls it: "Faith that worketh *through love*." (p. 47) Paul combined "the world of reason and morals and the world of sympathy and emotion. The world of reason and duty has an excellent clue to action, but wants motive power; the world of sympathy and influence has an irresistible force of motive-power, but wants a clue for directing its action" (p. 51).

By dying with Christ, Arnold continues, "you become transformed by the renewing of your mind and rise with him. . . . You rise with him to that harmonious conformity with the real and eternal order" (p. 52). This is how faith, working through love, helped Paul. And because Jesus identified himself with our neighbours the process is completed by our attachment to all men (p. 54). "The three essential terms of Pauline theology are not, therefore, as popular theology makes them: *calling, justification, sanctification*. They are rather these: *dying with Christ, resurrection from the dead, growing into Christ*" (p. 55).

Arnold goes on to dispute belief in a physical resurrection, claiming that in Paul's mature writing it was the *spiritual significance* of resurrection that predominated—it is "a resurrection *now*, and a resurrection to righteousness." He accepts, however, that Paul believed in a physical resurrection and in life after death. There are other aspects of Pauline belief that Arnold finds uncongenial and these he tends to attribute to Paul's habit of "judaizing," his importation into his theology of the tenets and methods of Judaic scholasticism. Such habits were natural in someone with Paul's training and background, but they were secondary. Arnold's way with those aspects of Pauline belief that clash with his own interpretation is rather glib and sweeping. In a manner that is to become more pronounced in *Literature and Dogma*, he appears to fabricate a critical notion—in this case Paul's regrettable habit of "judaizing"—which is invaluable in excising from the "central" Pauline theology whatever Arnold considers to be a disposable accretion. Not unnaturally, Arnold's way with difficulties gave rise to the many objecting voices that were raised against him. Unfortunately, for many this meant that Matthew Arnold was cast as the author who called in question traditional Christian beliefs and the positive case he puts forward was overlooked.

In the final section of *St. Paul and Protestantism* Arnold reflects on a theme that he develops more fully in *Literature and Dogma*: namely, the mischief done to theology by the introduction of metaphysics and "the habits of the Greek and Roman schools." This is a process in which St. Augustine, albeit a great religious genius, was instrumental. Then came the "Protestant Phillistine": "Sincere, gross of perception, prosaic," he translated "Paul's mystical idea" into "a legal transaction, and reserved all his imagination for Hell and the New Jerusalem" (p. 79). Arnold concludes by re-emphasizing the need to adopt a scientific approach to theology (p. 80). Clearly, by appealing to righteousness, a notion he feels can be vouched for on grounds of experience, Arnold believes he has found the key to what such an approach would be.

In *Literature and Dogma* Arnold makes a bold and forthright statement of his position with all the power of rhetoric he can command. In the Preface he indicates that his object "is to reassure those who feel attachment to Christianity, to the Bible, but who recognize the growing discredit befalling miracles and the supernatural" (p. vii of the popular edition). Henceforth Christianity must be vindicated, not by miracles, but by "its natural truth." This truth is encapsulated in the Old Testament as "Salvation by righteousness" and in the New Testament as "Righteousness by Jesus Christ" (p. x).

Arnold develops the distinction made in his earlier essay between science and literature, and asserts that the bible should be read as literature. Metaphysics should have nothing to do with religion, which is not about ideas but about conduct, and as such is easy to understand, albeit difficult in performance. "Conduct is three fourths of human life," Arnold tells us again and again. "Religion is . . . ethics heightened, enkindled, lit up by feeling . . ., *morality touched by emotion*" (pp. 15–16). The Jews of the Old Testament saw God as a moral power and not as a First Cause whose existence is deduced by abstract reasoning. They had an experimental awareness of God because they perceived that there is so much in morality that is "not ourselves—its source lies elsewhere." The moral differentiation of consciousness (to employ Lonergan's term) arose when men looked to their permanent and not just their transitory happiness; the religious when they were thrilled at doing this (p. 37). The antithesis frequently posited between natural and revealed religion is false. "For that in us which is really natural is, in truth, *revealed*. We awake to the consciousness of it, we are aware of it coming forth in our mind; but we feel that we did not make it, that it discovered us, that it is what it is whether we will or no" (p. 37). The major perception of the ancient Jews was that "righteousness tendeth to life." Similarly God for them was no abstract idea but the "Eternal" or "the enduring power, not ourselves, which makes for righteousness" (p. 46). We should revert to the Jewish perception, place religion once more on a solid experimental basis, and be done with the metaphysics and dogma that are the source of disputes and disagreements (p. 44).

Arnold gives a number of naturalistic explanations of how, even among the Old Testament Jews, certain doctrines and beliefs came about. The experience of exile, for example, gave birth to the notion of the Messiah (p. 56). Such a belief shores up the will to live by righteousness, it lends support to the basic tenet that "righteousness tendeth to life." But unlike the basic tenet such a doctrine does not have a "firm experimental ground," is not verifiable. "It is exactly what is expressed by the German word, 'Aberglaube,' *extra-belief*, belief beyond what is certain and verifiable" (p. 58). As far as miracles are concerned, Arnold does not attempt to prove that they are impossible—in *God and the Bible* he accepts that there is no valid inductive proof of the impossibility of miracles; he simply *asserts* that they are impossible. The reason is that we know whence stories of miracles come: "the Time-Spirit is sapping the proof from miracles—it is the 'Zeit-Geist' itself" (p. 96). The eschatology attributed to Jesus is said to have been imported by the reporters who frequently failed to understand the words of Jesus they reported. Jesus transcended his time and his disciples, "and yet, . . . planting his profound views of thought in their memory along with their own notions and prepossessions, to come out all mixed up together, but still distinguishable one day and separable; and leaving his word thus to bear fruit for the future" (p. 120).

Jesus's contribution to the basic and verifiable Jewish belief in righteousness was to shift the focus from conduct to "*the feelings and dispositions whence conduct proceeds*" (pp. 67–68). Jesus refined the idea of righteousness by means of his method and his secret. His method is revealed in his emphasis on conscience, on man's heart and thoughts as the source of his actions; his secret is the law of the cross, the way of self-renunciation (pp. 126–28). Catholicism lays hold of Jesus' secret and therein lies its greatness; Protestantism lays hold of Jesus' method, stressing individual conscience and conversion, and therein lies its greatness. What is required is a balance of the two. Jesus' truth is grasped by living it; it is a practical rule. Arnold vehemently distances Jesus from philosophers and all metaphysics. It is true that Jesus applied certain traditional titles to himself but Arnold attempts to show that he used these terms in a spiritual sense only. Indeed Jesus seems to have foreseen how his words would be misinterpreted by his disciples, by Paul and Peter, by the author of the Fourth gospel. He "foresaw the growth of creeds, the growth of dogma, and so through all the confusion worse confounded of councils, schoolmen, and confessions of faith . . ." (p. 149). One cannot help wondering why if Jesus foresaw these dangers he did not take better care to ensure that they did not come about, but at this stage in his exposition Arnold is not disposed to pause and consider such objections.

Arnold's attitude to doctrines is ambiguous. He appears to consider it fairly inevitable that doctrines should have arisen and speaks of them in affectionate tones as "fairy tales," "extra-beliefs." At other times "aberglaube" becomes a term of abuse. The reason is that he wishes to deal gently with "popular religion" but harshly with "the pseudo-science of dogmatic theology" (pp. 198–99). His attacks on councils, schoolmen and creeds are sharp and sarcastic—the Athanasian creed is described as "learned science with a strong dash of violent and vindictive temper" (p. 152); again, "the age which developed dogma had neither the resources nor the faculty for such a criticism" (p. 155). This harshness derives from a belief that there has been a tragic reversal in the Christian order of things. From being "extra-beliefs" doctrines have developed to become the very point of Christianity, obscuring its true nature, causing dissension and bringing Christianity into intellectual disrepute by making its validity reliant on miracles and the fulfilment of prophecies. The true theological doctors are not Augustine, Luther, Bossuet or Butler but men such as the author of *The Imitation of Christ* (a book Arnold loved), St. Francis de Sales and the Anglican Bishop Wilson. Where the former mistakenly attempted to explain religious beliefs with the aid of concepts borrowed from philosophy, the latter correctly placed the emphasis on conduct and the cultivation of virtue. "Religion has been made to stand on its apex instead of on its base. Righteousness is supported by ecclesiastical dogma, instead of ecclesiastical dogma being supported on righteousness" (p. 161). He clearly hopes that his own efforts to rid Christianity of the clutter of dogma will clear the way for "the better time which will arrive" (p. 202). It was Arnold's hope that as time went on and legend and miracle ceased to be regarded as facts, the Christian legends would still be loved "as poetry."

God and the Bible is Arnold's response to the many criticisms provoked by *Literature and Dogma*. For the most part he is content to rehearse the arguments put forward in the earlier book, adding some new instances and illustrations. One remark may, however, be thought relevant to the present inquiry. Arnold accepts as true the observation of a "judicious Catholic" that the Protestant nations have greater freedom, order and stability than the Catholic nations; this he attributes not to the Protestant theology of the sixteenth century, but to the Protestant "return to the individual conscience—to the method of Jesus." If Protestantism could restore to Catholicism the method of Jesus, "it will have given to the Catholic nations what enables them to do the rest for themselves" (p. xix). This agrees with Arnold's general position on the future of Christianity and is reinforced when at the end of *Last Essays on Church and Religion* he says, "A Catholic Church transformed is, I believe, the Church of the future" (p. 227). This sentiment or statement of his outlook is representative of Arnold's independence of mind; for at the time it was uttered England was still a highly Protestant nation, and for a public intellectual to refer to Catholicism in such a respectful manner was most unusual.

In the second chapter of *Last Essays*, entitled "Bishop Butler and the Zeit-Geist," Arnold attacks what he perceives to be the attempt of the great English eighteenth century divine to ground Christian belief on rational argument. Whatever the merits of Arnold's observations in respect of Bishop Butler, they do reveal his strong opposition to any attempt to argue opponents into intellectual submission. The "ground belief" of Christianity is not demonstration based on miracles and metaphysics. But to believe that righteousness *is* salvation and that this is found in Jesus, this is "the ground-belief of all Christians . . . (and) is in itself an indestructible basis of fellowship" (pp. 58–60). What might be termed the "apologetics" approach to Christian belief is, in Arnold's reckoning, doomed to failure. The way of Jesus was not to argue but to reveal to men what they are; it is this which transforms them and makes them want to change their behaviour. Arnold continues, "the object of religion is conversion, and to change people's behaviour" (p. 92). Butler, he says, was on surer ground when he referred men "to a law of nature or virtue, written on their hearts. Butler did believe in the certainty of this law. It was the real foundation of things for him" (p. 143).

One of the most innovative and surprising features of Lonergan's proposed method for theology is his displacement of what is termed "fundamental theology." Traditionally, a student embarking on a Roman Catholic theological course began by studying fundamental theology under a series of headings: Inspiration, Revelation, The Church etc. The doctrines selected were considered fundamental because they acted as a foundation for the theological courses to be followed over succeeding years. Once it was shown that scripture was the inspired word of God, or that Jesus claimed to be God and "proved" it by performing miracles and fulfilling prophecies, or that the Church was founded with the authority to teach all nations, the way was open for a deductivist method of establishing theological conclusions. This approach to theology was not unlike the approach Arnold saw and criticised in Bishop Butler. It purported to place theology on a basis of rational argument. Now Lonergan would agree with Arnold's strictures on Butler: you cannot argue people into faith. "The apologist's task," Lonergan writes, "is neither to produce in others nor to justify for them God's gift of his love. Only God can give that gift and the gift itself is self-justifying. People in love have not reasoned themselves into being in love."[59] Instead of resting one set of doctrines on another set of doctrines supposed to have some logical priority, Lonergan displaces fundamental theology and proposes a new basis for theology's normative, mediating phase. This new basis is conversion.

At this point some clarification is required in order to distinguish clearly between what Lonergan strived to achieve and the religious claims made by Arnold. Anyone encountering Arnold's comments on religion in *St Paul and*

Protestantism and his other works could be forgiven for thinking that Arnold is addressing theologians and advising them on how to make their discipline of theology more rigorous, more "scientific." "The license of affirmation about God and his proceedings . . .," he says, "is more and more met by the demand for verification." He appears to be advocating a critical instrument that will put an end to theologians' habit of "proving anything about anything." In chapter two of *Last Essays on Church and Religion* he advises theologians that the methods used by Bishop Butler are obsolete; that they should abandon attempts at "proving" the Christian religion by demonstration on the basis of miracles and metaphysics. In *Literature and Dogma* he speaks of "the growing discredit befalling miracles and the supernatural" and urges that religion should have nothing to do with metaphysics since it is not about ideas but about conduct. All of this sounds as if Arnold is addressing the issue of method or methodology—the pitfalls to be avoided and the right approach to be taken.

But when we actually encounter the solid and verifiable fact that Arnold is proposing, we find that he is talking, not about method, but about content. He is referring to what he terms "the natural truth" of Christianity, which is "salvation by righteousness" and "righteousness by Jesus Christ." His comments turn out to be not about method, after all, but about the content of the Christian faith. Or it might be more accurate to say that Arnold slips from talking about method to talking about content and appears not to notice what he has done; his failure to distinguish clearly between method and content can be confusing for the reader. For Arnold religious conversion is adherence, joyful adherence, to righteousness. It turns out that the criterion of authentic conversion is to be judged by the same criterion—the criterion of "right reason"—that Arnold urges upon his readers in *Culture and Anarchy*. One cannot help feeling that religion for Arnold is but a prop for good citizenship. Religion is to be saved for the future because it supports the civic virtues based on right reason. Arnold's motivation was probably to "moralise" the young men who, he fully expected, would most influence culture and society in the years to come; his religious writings are, in truth, an adjunct to his commentaries on society and culture although he makes no effort to make this point explicit. But, in his favour, it has to be said that Arnold is fully aware of the close alliance between "moralising" and the cultivation of the feelings. T. S. Eliot spells out Arnold's position on Christianity with brutal clarity: he says of Arnold's religious writings that they are "negative in a peculiar fashion: their aim is to affirm that the emotions of Christianity can and must be preserved without the belief."[60] The reader can begin to see the truth in the criticism of Arnold as a philosophical or religious thinker made by Eliot, who said that "Arnold has little gift for consistency or for definition. Nor had he the power of connected reasoning at any length: his flights are either short flights or circular flights."[61]

Now Lonergan takes up Arnold's wish for theology to become a more rigorous and scientific discipline but he is careful to apply these terms strictly to theological method, a topic he had in mind from early on in his academic career. Lonergan's focus in *Method in Theology* is exclusively on method and he is at pains to separate method from the content of dogmas or doctrines. It is in the context of discussing the method that should guide theological inquiry that Lonergan appears to pick up Arnold's appeal to "right reason." As we have seen in previous chapters, Lonergan esteems the notion of self-transcendence, which he sees to lie at the heart of right reason, and he considers self-transcendence to be required at the intellectual, moral and religious levels of consciousness. He says that "the intellectual, the moral and the religious are three phases in the single thrust to self-transcendence."[62] It is in this context that Lonergan works out what he calls "transcendental method" and we have seen in a previous chapter how he applies this method in the form of the eight functional specialities that constitute the work of theology in both its positive and its normative phases. Crowe tells us that "the young Lonergan is already in search of 'a matrix or system of thought' that would stand outside of, and be a guide for, actual theology."[63] Lonergan saw such a matrix as parallel to the service rendered to science by mathematics: "The quantitative sciences are objective simply because they are given by mathematics an *a priori* scheme of such generality that there can be no tendency to do violence to the data for the sake of maintaining the scheme."[64] These two quotations should help underline the difference between Arnold's achievement in his religious writings and Lonergan's achievement in working out a method for theology. Lonergan's *a priori* matrix—that is, transcendental method—at once stands outside theology—has nothing to do with the contents of theological inquiry—but at the same time it acts as a guide to theological inquiry, conferring on it the rigour that goes with the thrust for self-transcendence. What I wish to draw attention to here is the possibility that the germ of the idea of applying a verifiable set of facts to theological method might have first occurred to Lonergan when he engaged with Arnold's religious writings and witnessed Arnold's desire to salvage what he could from the Christian message by being able to claim something solid and verifiable to be found in that message. He certainly appears to have had some sympathy for Arnold's critical comments on Butler. But what Arnold claimed to be the central truth—indeed the only truth—contained in the teaching of Jesus, Lonergan used as the basic idea behind the method he devised for theology. For what is transcendental method but an unravelling of *ratio recta* as it operates at the intellectual, moral and religious levels of consciousness? As I have said, Lonergan's use of a verifiable "matrix" is a good deal more nuanced than Arnold's reduction of Christianity to conduct.

Matthew Arnold lamented the fact that doctrines had taken priority over faith and conversion in the course of Christian history. Religion had been made to stand upon its "apex" instead of on its true base. Lonergan is in agreement for reasons I have explained and his conception of conversion has many similarities to Arnold's. Like Arnold, he repudiates the notion of conversion as a passive, mechanistic process.[65] Rather, conversion is a falling in love with God, an act of self-transcendence that grounds all self-transcendence. Faith, in turn, is the knowledge born of religious love.[66] A similar connection between faith and love in the context of conversion is made by Arnold. For both men conversion is not usually an instantaneous affair but rather something that takes time and effort.[67] For both, conversion yields "that harvest of the Spirit that is love, joy, peace, kindness, goodness, fidelity, gentleness, and self-control."[68] There is, then, a sympathy of understanding between Arnold and Lonergan on the nature of conversion and its place in Christian belief. This sympathy is reinforced by the analogy between being converted and falling in love. We have heard Arnold on this "analogy of the most everyday experience." In *Method in Theology* Lonergan quotes the old Latin tag, "Nihil amatum nisi praecognitum, Knowledge precedes love," and instances two exceptions to this rule.

> There is the minor exception . . . inasmuch as people do fall in love, and that falling in love is something disproportionate to its causes, conditions, occasions, antecedents. For falling in love is a new beginning, an exercise in vertical liberty in which one's world undergoes a new organization. But the major exception to the Latin tag is God's gift of his love flooding our hearts. Then we are in the dynamic state of being in love . . .[69]

Lonergan makes use of the analogy of a man and woman in love, as Arnold does, in order to illustrate how God's gift of his love works in human beings. For both authors religious conversion makes righteousness joyful. As Lonergan puts it, a person who has undergone conversion acts "with the easy freedom of those who do all good because they are in love."[70] And finally, Arnold claims that in Paul's thinking human beings are depicted not only as acting and striving through reason and conscience, but as "being receptive and influenced." Paul, he says, could "pass naturally" between the two worlds, the one voluntary, rational, morally striving, the other the "divine world of influence, sympathy, emotion."[71] As Lonergan's thinking progressed he appeared to achieve an enlarged appreciation of the significance of human and divine love. This is expressed by his comments on the "two vectors" he mentions in one of his later essays, the one from below upwards and the other from above downwards.

> For human development is of two quite different kinds. There is the development from below upwards, from experience to growing understanding, from

growing understanding to balanced judgment, from balanced judgment to fruitful courses of action. . . .

But there also is development from above downwards. There is the transformation of falling in love. . . . Where hatred only sees evil, love reveals values. At once it commands commitment and joyfully carries it out, no matter what the sacrifice involved. Where hatred reinforces bias, love dissolves it. . . . Where hatred plods around in ever narrower vicious circles, love breaks the bonds of psychological and social determinisms with the conviction of faith and the power of hope.[72]

Areas of Agreement

Let me close this section by summarising the features of Arnold's position which appear to have influenced Lonergan's thinking on theological method in a positive way.

- In a critical and scientific age, religion needs to be recast. Theology needs to find new foundations
- What is needed is an empirical theology, one that yields verifiable knowledge and, in that sense, is truly scientific
- Theological beliefs can no longer rest on so-called rational arguments such as "proofs" from miracles or appeals to inspired authority
- They should rest on the "natural truth" of Christianity, on what it makes of human beings as they are
- Human beings have a natural desire to know the truth and to do the good; this "quest for righteousness" is a fact that is manifested in every question we ask; it is a palpable fact, though not one verified by sensory data; it is not chosen by us but is what defines us as human
- The human quest for righteousness, our intellectual and moral nature, is the point of contact with God
- Human beings are intellectually and morally striving but also receptive of God's influence
- The object of religion is conversion, a falling in love with God, God's gift of his love
- Conversion is the true "ground-belief" of Christian theology in its normative phase. Doctrines should be founded on conversion, on righteousness, rather than righteousness on doctrines. Religion in the recent past has been made to stand on its apex instead of on its true base.
- The main hope for Christianity is a reformed Roman Catholic Church, one in which the importance of conversion, of conscience and self-transformation, has been rediscovered.

Now if I am right in claiming that these ideas are to be found in Arnold and that they are also key conceptions in understanding the method Lonergan proposes to guide the work of theology, then I conclude that Matthew Arnold's religious writings influenced Lonergan in a profound and positive way. Arnold's major agreement with Lonergan lies in the central role he ascribes to conversion and his linking of conversion to the quest for righteousness. His major disagreement is that for him conversion is a substitute for doctrines whereas for Lonergan conversion is a precondition for doctrines. In a way that is typical of Lonergan, he has salvaged what he finds informative and helpful in Arnold and put it to new use in his own developed thinking. Where others were content to reject or abandon Arnold's religious writings outright, Lonergan, having made some important distinctions, allowed his mind to be engaged and stirred and in this way he found aspects of Arnold's thought that enabled him to develop his own more nuanced position.

Criticism of Arnold

It is not very difficult to find fault with the cogency of many of Arnold's arguments or to indicate the weaknesses in his position. The most trenchant criticism of Arnold on religion came from F. H. Bradley who as a metaphysical thinker of some standing appears to have lost patience with Arnold's attacks on metaphysics and his habit of disarming criticism by protesting his "inaptitude" for "abstruse reasoning." My concern in this section is not to conduct a wholesale critique of Arnold but to present his position as source material for Lonergan's reflections on theological method. A critique of Arnold should emerge in the process of relating Arnold's thinking to Lonergan's. Nevertheless, Bradley's attack in his *Ethical Studies* should provide vivid illustration, should any be required, of the hazardous task facing anyone daring enough to "take over" Arnold. Bradley's attack can conveniently be offered here as representative of the questions anyone defending Arnold would have to answer.

> Nor does it help us to say (Bradley writes) that religion is "morality touched with emotion." . . . All morality is, in one sense or another, "touched by emotion." Most emotions, high or low, can go with and "touch" morality; and the moment we leave our phrase-making and begin to reflect, we see that all that is meant is that morality "touched" by religious emotion is religious. . . . Religion is more than morality. In the religious consciousness we find the belief, however vague and indistinct, in an object, a not-myself; an object, further, which is real. An ideal which is not real, which is only in our heads, cannot be the object of religion. . . . But when "culture" went on to tell us what God is for science, we heard words we did not understand about "stream" , and "tendencies" and "the Eternal"; and had it been anyone else we were reading, we should have said that, in some literary excursion, they had picked up a metaphysical theory, now out of date, and putting it in phrases, the meaning of which they had never asked themselves, had then served it up . . . as the last

result of speculation, or of that "flexible common sense" which is so much better. When the literary varnish is removed is there anything more? (Bradley adds in a footnote:) We hear the word "verifiable" from Mr. Arnold pretty often. What is to verify? Has Mr. Arnold put "such a tyro's question" to himself? If to verify means to find in outward experience, then the object of true religion can not be found as this or that outward thing or quality, and so can not be verified. It is of its essence that in this sense it should be unverifiable.[73]

In a gentler vein, G. K. Chesterton, an admirer of Arnold, makes the following remarks in the first chapter of his book on St Francis of Assisi:

> Since I have mentioned Matthew Arnold and Renan and the rationalistic admirers of St Francis, I will here give the hint of what it seems to me most advisable for such readers to keep in mind. These distinguished writers found such things as the stigmata a stumbling-block because to them a religion was a philosophy. It was an impersonal thing; and it is only the most personal passion that provides here an approximate earthly parallel. A man will not roll in the snow for a stream of tendency by which all things fulfil the law of their being. He will not go without food in the name of something, not ourselves, that makes for righteousness. He will do things like this, or pretty nearly like this, under quite a different impulse. He will do these things when he is in love . . . (St Francis) was a Lover. He was a lover of God and he was really and truly a lover of men; possibly a much rarer mystical vocation.[74]

Taking the longer, historical view of religious thinking, Arnold might be seen as belonging to that group of post-Enlightenment thinkers who have sought to save what they could rationally subscribe to in traditional Christian theological beliefs and then proposed that most of the rest could be discarded or, at best, treated simply as disposable props supporting the beliefs they consider acceptable. A. N. Wilson suggests that the person who started the trend of putting Jesus forward as a great moral teacher and exemplar, while cutting out any references to him as divine or as a worker of miracles, was Thomas Jefferson in his book, *The Philosophy of Jesus*.[75] But as later writers noted, Jefferson's Jesus bears a strong resemblance to Thomas Jefferson! The same might be said about Matthew Arnold's Jesus, who has been cut down to size by being made to conform to Arnold's hopes for society and culture and the central role to be played by "right reason" in maintaining peace and harmony at a time of precarious social change—in other words, Arnold's Jesus has been cast in the image of Arnold's general intellectual horizon, with all its limitations; he has been made to fit in with Arnold's concerns for society.

The one decisive feature of Arnold's thought that sets it apart from Lonergan's is Arnold's belief in the omnicompetence of common sense, something alluded to by Bradley. If Lonergan is correct in stating that "theological development is fundamentally a long delayed response to the development of modern science, modern scholarship, modern philosophy,"[76] then Arnold was not well equipped to recast religion. He knew little science and was wary of, if not hostile to, philosophy. He viewed theory and system with suspicion and, although he read the works of some philosophers,[77] he tended to place reliance on the common sense of the man of letters that he was. But Arnold's philosophical innocence leaves his statement of his position very vulnerable. To begin with, while purporting to exclude all metaphysics from Christian theology, he makes the criterion of experiential verification the test of the validity of Christian teaching. This is suspiciously like metaphysics and, as Bradley notes, so also are his definition of God and his statement that "righteousness tendeth to life." Furthermore, Arnold's suggestion that human beings' natural desire for righteousness is experiential and thereby satisfying to science is problematic: the experiential verification the natural sciences require involves the use of the senses and, as Bradley also notes, Arnold's notion of verification appears not to rely on the senses. To justify his appeal to verification, Arnold would need to appeal to the distinction Lonergan makes between the data of sense and the data of consciousness, for we can verify the human desire for righteousness by appealing not to the data of sense but only to the data of consciousness—we are conscious of such a desire and can verify it by reference to human behaviour based on this conscious desire.

Arnold's epistemological innocence also leads him to adopt a thoroughly ahistorical approach to Christian tradition. Arnold the man of letters blithely discards all the developments that have taken place over time in the Christian formulation of doctrines, claiming that they result from the blunder of treating poetry as if it were science. He is unaware that in the course of history there are ongoing differentiations of consciousness and that "with every differentiation of consciousness the same object becomes apprehended in a different and more adequate fashion."[78] Arnold has no conception of what common sense knowledge is, of what theoretical knowledge is, and of how the two relate. He cannot, therefore, see how the common sense and the systematic modes of thinking can be two different ways of apprehending the same reality. He is unable to see, for example, how the early Christian thinkers borrowed terms and concepts from Greek philosophy, such as "substance," "nature" and "person," words not found in the gospels or the Jewish tradition, in order to achieve a clear and precise understanding of many of the statements and claims to be found in the gospels. And so he is driven to the conclusion that the systematic development of theology is nothing less than a gross distortion of the original message.

There is a somewhat bland absence in Arnold of any awareness that his own intellectual horizon determines what he finds intelligible and unintelligible, acceptable and unacceptable, in the Christian tradition, determines his own selective approach to the interpretation of the bible and his understanding of history. Arnold's approach to miracles is in some ways surprising in view of his highly developed literary and religious sensibility. His horizon makes him reject miracles on the bare grounds that they are "incompatible" with the modern mind. He sees them rather crudely, like Hume, as nothing more than freakish occurrences, violations of the established laws of nature, and fails to grasp their significance as enacted parables. The miracles reported in the four gospels are not just presented as wonders—indeed Jesus is reported as refusing to perform miracles in order to impress the crowd. Rather the miracles he performs are carriers of meaning, they make sense within the totality of Jesus's ministry of mercy and compassion, of love of God and love of neighbour. His miracles of healing project his mission of restoring people to wholeness and health, of repairing human brokenness; his miracles of nature, such as his walking on water or stilling the storm, graphically convey the nature and power of faith. Given Arnold's sensibility, this is surely a prime example of the self-deluding short-sightedness of common sense practicality, which he had, ironically, argued it is the task of culture to overcome.

Also curious, in view of his previous writings, is Arnold's reduction of religion to conduct. In *Culture and Anarchy* he considers Hellenism, representative of reason, understanding and "light," and Hebraism, which refers to right conduct, duty and conscience, and comes to the conclusion that England has too much of the latter and not enough of the former. Right reason and those who, like the Athenians of old, follow its dictates are the heroes of *Culture and Anarchy*, though Arnold does insist that Hellenism and Hebraism have the same goal, the goal of perfection. But in his strictly religious writings Arnold is thoroughly Hebraic; he limits religion to conduct and sets up a barrier between doing and thinking. His reason seems to be the wish to demolish the dogmas of Christianity which he considers to be cloaking "the one thing necessary"—self-transformation, conversion. But this amounts to the supremacy of practicality over thought in a way he condemns in *Culture and Anarchy*. For similar reasons Arnold speaks of God only as a moral force and not as an intelligent being. Lonergan's transcendental method is not restricted to the moral imperative "Be responsible" but embraces also the intellectual and rational imperatives "Be intelligent" and "Be rational." Hence it is quite appropriate in Lonergan's scheme for faith to seek understanding: God is not only a moral force but the source of the universe's intelligibility and rationality. Arnold's reduction of religion to conduct overlooks the human need for intellectual satisfaction and hence also for emotional and aesthetic satisfaction. It is doubtful if his austere religion of duty and self-control could inspire people to build cathedrals, write poetry, compose sublime music or produce great art, as traditional Christianity has done.[79] It is ironic and rather tragic that Matthew Arnold, the poet and lover of literature and liturgy, the author of *Culture and Anarchy*, should find himself in this position. But it is also cheering that his labours over his religious writings have not been entirely in vain and that a theologian as significant as Bernard Lonergan would appear to have gained a great deal from his engagement with them. It may well be that the young Lonergan was inspired by Arnold's focus on inwardness to embark on his own life-long exploration of human intentional consciousness, which stands as one of the most important intellectual achievements of the twentieth century.

One final word. The name of Matthew Arnold occurs nowhere in the various indexes of the twenty-five volumes that make up Lonergan's Collected Works. That might appear to disprove my claim that, as a matter of fact, Lonergan's ideas, both in *Insight* and in *Method in Theology*, his two most important works, were influenced by the writings of Matthew Arnold. Had there been only one bond of similarity between Lonergan and Arnold my claim could rightly be ignored. However, there is not just one bond but, as I have sought to demonstrate, a multiplicity of bonds and, taken together, these would seem to indicate that the claim I have made needs to be taken seriously. As to the absence of Arnold from the indexes of Lonergan's books, there is really a very simple explanation or reason for this being so. For in his books Lonergan makes abundant references to the ideas and systems of thought of philosophers as varied as Aristotle, Aquinas, Hume, Kant, Heidegger, Husserl and Gadamer, and their names duly appear in the index. Lonergan does so because he is presenting their ideas as they expressed them, attempting to convey their intended meaning. In the case of Matthew Arnold, Lonergan is not presenting Arnold's ideas as Arnold intended them to be understood, rather he is expressing his adaptation of Arnold's ideas; he is expressing his own ideas. It would have been extremely tedious and, indeed, distracting, if he had broken off what he wanted to say and explained, first, what Arnold actually said and then, second, how he had changed and adapted Arnold, in order to make Arnold's thinking more systematic and coherent. He had to get on with the task of saying what he had to say.

Lonergan took what he found interesting in Arnold, adapted it and built it into his own systematic treatment of progress and decline in *Insight* and of theological method in *Method*. And what would Arnold, that notorious enemy of system, have made of this transformation of his position? Given the verdict of history on his position, especially his religious position, Matthew Arnold could, I feel, be nothing less than flattered.

NOTES

1. Matthew Arnold, *Culture and Anarchy* (First published 1869; Cambridge: Cambridge University Press. 1950,) edited by J. Dover Wilson.

2. Matthew Arnold, "The Literary Influence of Academies" in *Essays Literary and Philosophical*, ed. G. K. Chesterton (London, 1907).
3. See *Anna Karenina and Other Essays*, (London: Chatto and Windus, 1973), p. 177.
4. *Anna Karenina*, p. 177.
5. Patrick J. McCarthy, *Matthew Arnold and the Three Classes* (New York, London, 1964), p. 2.
6. McCarthy, *Arnold and the Three Classes*, p. 54.
7. McCarthy, *Arnold and the Three Classes*, p. 107.
8. McCarthy, *Arnold and the Three Classes*, p. 107.
9. *The Complete Prose works of Matthew Arnold 11: Democratic Education*, ed. R. H. Super (Ann Arbor, 1962), p. 4.
10. *Democratic Education*, p. 6.
11. *Democratic Education*, p. 11–12.
12. *Democratic Education*, p. 17.
13. *Democratic Education*, p. 18.
14. *Democratic Education*, p. 22.
15. *Democratic Education*, p. 23.
16. *Democratic Education*, p. 29.
17. *Democratic Education*, p. 324.
18. *Democratic Education*, p. 26.
19. Matthew Arnold, "General Report For the Year 1876" in *Reports on Elementary Schools 1852–1882* (London, HMSO, 1908), p. 178.
20. Matthew Arnold, "The Literary Influence of Academies," in *Essays Literary and Philosophical*, ed. G. K. Chesterton (London, 1907), pp. 27–29.
21. Op. cit., p. 11.
22. Op. cit., p. 38. First italics mine.
23. Op. cit., p. 45.
24. Arnold does not make his proposals for state controlled education and for an academy with equal force. In the case of the former he is in deadly earnest; he was able to exert crucial influence on his brother-in-law, the government minister William Forster, author of the English Education Act of 1870. With regard to the academy, Arnold concludes his essay by suggesting that he hardly expects such an institution to emerge in the form he describes and urges, in turn, that writers enforce their own self-discipline. The germ of Arnold's proposal for an academy was earlier contained in the original version of his survey of "Popular Education in France," where the institution held up for English emulation is the French Institute (see Super, op. cit., pp. 156ff). This supports the view that Arnold was less concerned with the practical aspects of his proposal and more with the general philosophical point that right reason should be brought to bear on national affairs.
25. Matthew Arnold, "Friendship's Garland," in *Matthew Arnold: Selected Prose*, ed. P. J. Keating [London, 1970), p. 304. This is the most accessible and inexpensive selection of Arnold's prose writings.
26. Arnold, *Selected Prose*, p. 306.
27. Arnold,*Culture and Anarchy*, p. 64.
28. Arnold, *Culture and Anarchy*, p. 105.
29. Arnold, *Culture and Anarchy*, p. 49.
30. Arnold, *Culture and Anarchy*, p. 110.
31. Arnold, *Culture and Anarchy*, p. 108.
32. Arnold, *Culture and Anarchy*, p. 142.
33. Arnold, *Culture and Anarchy*, p. 143.
34. Arnold, *Culture and Anarchy*, p. 162.
35. Arnold, *Culture and Anarchy*, p. 159–60.
36. Arnold, *Culture and Anarchy*, p. 193.
37. Arnold, *Culture and Anarchy*, p. 210.
38. Arnold, *Culture and Anarchy*, p. 210.
39. B. Lonergan, *Insight: A Study of Human Understanding* (London, 1958), p. 238.

40. F. R. Leavis, *The Great Tradition*, p. 13. Leavis is speaking of Jane Austen's relation to the tradition of the English novel: "If the influences bearing on her hadn't comprised something fairly to be called tradition she couldn't have found herself and her true direction; but her relation to tradition is a creative one. She not only makes tradition for those coming after, but her achievement has for us a retroactive effect: as we look back beyond her we see in what goes before, and see because of her, potentialities and significances brought out in such a way that, for us, she creates the tradition we see leading down to her. Her work, like the work of all great creative writers, gives a meaning to the past."

41. F. R. Leavis, *The Great Tradition*, p. 13. Leavis is speaking of Jane Austen's relation to the tradition of the English novel: "If the influences bearing on her hadn't comprised something fairly to be called tradition she couldn't have found herself and her true direction; but her relation to tradition is a creative one. She not only makes tradition for those coming after, but her achievement has for us a retroactive effect: as we look back beyond her we see in what goes before, and see because of her, potentialities and significances brought out in such a way that, for us, she creates the tradition we see leading down to her. Her work, like the work of all great creative writers, gives a meaning to the past."

42. Lonergan, *Insight*, p. 223.
43. Lonergan, *Insight*, p. 225.
44. Lonergan, *Insight*, p. 225.
45. Arnold, *Culture and Anarchy*, p. 205.
46. Lonergan, *Insight*, p. 232.
47. Lonergan, *Insight*, p. 235.
48. Lonergan, *Insight*, p. 239.
49. Lonergan, *Insight*, p. 239.
50. Lonergan, *A Second Collection* (London: Darton, Longman and Todd, 1974), p. 133; see also p. 127.
51. See Arnold's essay on Heinrich Heine in *Essays Literary and Critical*, p. 105, where he says of Goethe, "he puts the standard, once for all, inside every man instead of outside him" etc; also *Culture and Anarchy*, pp. 6–7.
52. See Arnold's comments on Wilhelm von Humbolt in Super, op. cit., pp. 312–313; also the Conclusion of *Culture and Anarchy*.
53. First published 1867, but reckoned to have been written in 1851.
54. Matthew Arnold, *Literature and Dogma*, (London: 1873), p. xviii. In the rest of this article, when reference is made to *Literature and Dogma*, it is to the shorter, popular edition of 1883.
55. B. Willey, *Nineteenth Century Studies: Coleridge to Matthew Arnold*, (London, Chatto and Windus, 1949); Penguin Ed., 1973, p. 276.
56. Arnold's religious works were out of print for decades; they are by now included in the *Complete Prose Works of Matthew Arnold*, edited by R. H. Super. Just about the only "modern" academic to place himself in the line of Arnold is R. B. Braithwaite who argued in a famous essay that religious language is ethically but not factually significant, in the course of which he said, "But the patron saint whom I claim for my way of thinking is that great but neglected Christian thinker Matthew Arnold . . . " See "An Empiricist's View of the Nature of Religious Belief," [1953] in *The Existence of God*, edited by John Hick (London: 1964), p. 247.
57. P. J. Keating, *Arnold's Selected Prose* (London: Penguin Books, 1970), p. 7.
58. Quoted in *The Critic as Anti-Philosopher*, edited by A. Singh (London: 1982), p. 56.
59. *Method in Theology*, p. 123.
60. T. S. Eliot, *Selected Essays* (London: Faber and Faber, 1951), p. 434.
61. Eliot, *Selected Essays,* p. 431.
62. Lonergan, *A Second Collection*, p. 133.
63. F. E. Crowe, *The Lonergan Enterprise*, (Cowley, 1980), p. 18.
64. Lonergan, "The *Gratia Operans* Dissertation: Preface and Introduction," 1940, published in Vol 1 of *Collected Works of Bernard Lonergan*, ed. Frederick Crowe and Robert Doran, (University of Toronto Press, 2000).

65. Lonergan, *De Verbo Incarnato*, editio altera, ad usum auditorum, (Rome: Gregorian University, p. 440–442).
66. *Method in Theology*, p. 115.
67. Lonergan, *Method*, p. 130; M. Arnold, *St Paul and Protestantism*, p. 16, 70.
68. Lonergan,*Method*, p. 106, 108; Arnold, *St Paul*, p. 25, 31, 46.
69. *Method*, p. 122.
70. *Method*, p. 107.
71. Arnold, *St Paul*, p. 39–40.
72. Lonergan, *A Third Collection*, ed. F. E. Crowe, (London: Darton, Longman and Todd, 1985), p. 106.
73. F. H. Bradley, *Ethical Studies*, 1876, (Oxford University Paperback Edition, 1962), p. 315–318.
74. G. K. Chesterton, *St Francis of Assisi*, (London: Hodder & Stoughton Ltd, 1923), p. 13–14.
75. A. N. Wilson, *The Book of the People: How to Read the Bible*, (London: Atlantic Books, 2015), p. 17, 23.
76. *Method in Theology*, p. 353.
77. Lionel Trilling places Arnold's religious writings in the line of Kant, Ritchl and Schleiermacher but goes on to say that Arnold was influenced more by Spinoza and Coleridge than by the German Kantians or post-Kantians, especially in respect of the notion that morality is God's law written on human nature. See L. Trilling, *Matthew Arnold*, (New York: Meridian Books, 1939), p. 363–365. This is widely acknowledged as the best intellectual biography of Arnold.
78. B. J. F. Lonergan, *Philosophy of God, and Theology* (London: Darton Longman and Todd, 1973), p. 276.
79. Lionel Trilling, op. cit., p. 323–328.

Chapter Five

Reading as Understanding

I have included this chapter because it illustrates the role of the subject in the practical context of reading; it illustrates what the reader gets up to in the process of reading for meaning. This turns out to be more varied and ingenious than might at first be supposed. But "reading as understanding" serves a more general purpose since it can be viewed as a practical exemplification of the various manoeuvres and stratagems taken by all kinds of inquirers—scholars, scientists, detectives, accident investigators, and so forth, as well as readers—when attempting to find the truth by means of close reference to the available evidence. I claim that Frank Smith, the authority on reading I refer to below, has won support from educationists and teachers because he has brought to bear on the topic of reading a theory of comprehension that has more general application. Or, to turn the issue the other way round, I find Smith's theory of comprehension to be very close to Lonergan's theory of cognition, and that his comments on the process of reading for meaning illustrate in a fairly straightforward manner what Lonergan says about cognition in a somewhat more abstruse manner in *Insight*. Smith's style and approach have the virtue of simplifying.

In the authoritative volume, *Extending Beginning Reading*, the authors note that "Definitions of reading are almost as numerous as the many experts who have committed their thoughts to paper."[1] Summing up the recent history of the subject they say, "the main trend in definitions of reading, throughout this (twentieth) century, has been away from the earlier ideas of reading as a mechanistic process towards an acceptance of it as a thoughtful process, requiring the reader not only to understand what the author is endeavouring to communicate but also to contribute his own experiences and thoughts to the problem of understanding."[2]

Today there are three main emphases among reading theorists. There are, first, those who place major emphasis on phonics, on the recognition of the sounds associated with certain letters and letter combinations. Second, there are those who emphasize "whole word" recognition rather than individual letter recognition, the so-called "look and say" school of reading. Third are those who claim that reading is not properly reading unless it is a reconstruction of the author's intended meaning; the ability to "decode" print into sound is not enough. Reading is only successful if it involves the reader in thinking, reasoning, understanding, and acquiring meaning.

In what follows I do not enter into the debate about the best method for the effective teaching of reading. I should perhaps add that while I believe that the work of Frank Smith, whose views I discuss at length, has been of great value to teachers I also agree with a fairly widely held criticism that he fails to distinguish adequately between the needs of fluent readers and the needs of beginners. Beginners would appear to require more instruction in phonics than Smith appears to countenance, so that they have strategies for coping with new words and letter combinations. That, however, is a personal opinion and is not among the issues discussed here.

The emphasis on reading as a process of understanding or acquiring meaning, in which the reader plays an active role, now has many academic champions, foremost among whom must be counted the psycholinguistic school of reading theorists.[3] Psycholinguistics grew out of the intersection of two academic disciplines: psychology and linguistics. Linguistics is the study of language as a system; psychology—or, more precisely, cognitive psychology—is the study of how "humans acquire, interpret, organize, store, retrieve, and employ knowledge."[4]

The most prominent exponent of the psycholinguistic approach to reading is probably Frank Smith, and it is Smith's thinking about reading and reading comprehension that I wish to compare with Lonergan's theory of cognition. The advantages of such a comparison are several. In the first place, it is important that philosophers' theories of knowledge are tested against practical examples of how knowledge is acquired and developed; reading provides such a test. Secondly, the comparison should help to draw out and illuminate certain aspects of Lonergan's theory of inquiry that can easily be overlooked. Finally, the comparison should help to bring out elements of incoherence in Smith's position; more positively, it might indicate how Smith's position could benefit from the rigorous theoretical underpinning which Lonergan's philosophy can provide.

In his revised preface to *Understanding Reading*,[5] Smith explains how his understanding of the reading process has been extended by

> a theoretical liberalization as the behavioural sciences have continued to free themselves from constraints of behaviourism and ventured more into the realm

of mental life, which is surely the area of reading.... There is still a great deal of research that I would consider peripheral to main issues in reading, studies that restrict themselves to eye movement or to letter or isolated word recognition. But there have also been many attempts ... to understand better the notions of meaning and comprehension, and it is these that I feel are contributing most to theoretical and practical issues in reading.[6]

For Smith "reading" and "comprehension" are virtually interchangeable terms. Offering what he terms "a provisional definition of comprehension" he says that it is "relating what we attend to in the world around us—the visual information in the case of reading—to what we already have in our heads. And here is a provisional definition of learning: modifying what we already have in our heads as a consequence of attending to the world around us."[7]

This provides a paradox which Smith loves to play with and impress upon his readers: "the skill in reading actually depends on using the eyes as little as possible.... As we become fluent readers we learn to rely more on what we already know, on what is behind the eyeballs, and less on the print on the page in front of us."[8]

Visual information is, of course, necessary for reading to occur but visual information is not enough. Non-visual information is also necessary. By this Smith means an understanding of the relevant language, familiarity with the subject matter and the ability to read in the sense of decoding signs into sounds.[9] He shows by a number of experiments that what we already know about English reduces our uncertainty about letter or word sequence. We can, for example, predict the letter that will follow Q or fill in the blanks in a well-known phrase. But familiarity with letter or word sequence is not all that is meant by non-visual information. The term also includes the model or theory of the world I carry around with me: "All of the order and complexity that I perceive in the world around me must reflect an order and complexity in my own mind. Anything I cannot relate to the theory of the world in my head will not make sense to me. I shall be bewildered."[10]

This model or theory is the basis of all new learning. It is not a catalogue of facts, nor simply "memories" but "a system, an ... internally consistent model of the world, built up as a result of experience.... If we can learn at all, it is by modifying and elaborating our theory. The theory fills our minds: we have no other resource."[11]

The way in which the knowledge we carry about with us assists learning is related to the guessing and predicting that are basic to learning. Learning is inextricably linked to the activities of hypothesizing and predicting and these rest on our theory of the world. Our theory cuts down the number of possible alternatives, reduces the choices we need to make in order to make sense of the printed words.

> We make predictions about what we are about to read in order to comprehend, and we make hypotheses about what a particular word or passage is likely to be in order to learn. Our predictions and hypotheses come from what we understand about the passage already: and our feedback, the information that tells us whether we were right or wrong, comes from what we go on to read. If we have made a mistake we will probably find out about it and that is the way we will learn.[12]

Against those who would teach reading letter by letter or word by word and thus overburden short-term memory, Smith advocates reliance on the child's natural desire to make sense of things.

> We learn to read by reading, by conducting experiments as we go along. We have built up a sight vocabulary of fifty thousand words—not by someone telling us fifty thousand times what a word is, but by hypothesizing the identity of new words that we meet in print and testing that our hypotheses make sense in the context.... By conducting experiments as we read, we learn not only to recognize new words, but everything else to do with reading. We learn to make use of spelling-to-sound correspondences, not by memorizing the 166 rules and 45 exceptions of formal phonics instruction but by developing implicit procedures for distinguishing one word from another when the number of alternatives is limited to the most likely few.[13]

Guessing or predicting are not blind conjecture, but reasoned hypothesis-testing, "a precise and natural exercise of the human brain."[14]

Questioning is an integral part of predicting, and comprehension is getting our questions answered: "Now at last I can say what I mean by comprehension," Smith announces.[15] Questioning in that sense is predicting. "We do not look out of the window and wonder, 'What shall I see?' we ask, 'Shall I see buses or pedestrians?' and provided that what we are looking at falls within that limited range of alternatives our perception is effortless, efficient and unsurprised."[16]

The question determines what we need to eliminate in order to get an answer; and the answer we get is dependent on the questions we ask. "If we do not know the right kind of question to ask of a maths text or knitting pattern, then obviously we will not be able to read a maths text or knitting pattern."[17]

Questioning is, of course, related to meaning and meaning is the guiding thread in all that Smith wants to say about reading. Another of the paradoxes he likes to impress on his readers is that "it is not in print that the meaning of written language lies."[18] This is paradoxical because it is commonly assumed that we read in order to get meaning from the printed word. Smith overturns this idea by insisting that we bring meaning *to* print rather than get meaning *from* it. To illustrate the point he distinguishes between the "surface structure" of language (the sounds in the air or marks on the page) and the "deep structure" (its meaning). That there is no one-to-one correspondence between surface structure and deep structure is easily demonstrated. Ambiguity is an inescapable feature of words and sentences: "Visiting teachers can be boring," for example. Such ambiguity is endemic in both spoken and written language and is not clarified by an inspection of the surface structure but by attention to context. Again, a single meaning can be expressed in a variety of ways: "the dog chased the cat" or "the cat was chased by the dog." Nor does the order in which words are placed determine their meaning: "man" at the beginning of a sentence may be either a noun or a verb.[19] Against linguists who argue that it is grammar that determines meaning, Smith convincingly argues that we often cannot determine the grammar of a sentence until we have understood its meaning. Is the sentence "Mother was seated by the bishop" active or passive? Only the correct meaning will determine this, as only the correct meaning will determine the grammatical function of "by."[20]

Others have argued that meaning inheres primarily in the spoken word and only derivatively in written language. But Smith shows that there is no one-to-one correspondence between spoken and written language. Many words that sound the same when spoken are in fact written differently (pair, pare, pear); and many printed letters and letter combinations have different pronunciations in different words (for example, ho in house, hose, honey, hour, honest).[21] Written language does not mirror spoken language and so there is no route to meaning simply by decoding print into sound. Besides, we are all familiar with interpreting wordless road signs; we might be able to express their meaning in words but only in so far as we have already interpreted their meaning. Meaning lies as much beyond spoken language as it lies beyond written language.

What is lacking in the views of those who appeal to word order or the rules of grammar or the primacy of spoken language to explain how language means is, Smith contends, the notion of intention. Even the notion that deep structure consists of an underlying transformational grammar that generates meaning by arranging the surface structure of language remains inert without the notion of intention. What puts transformational grammar to work?[22] What comes first for writers and speakers is the intention to express a particular meaning. And they choose their mode of expression because they intend to address a particular audience. Words express meaning because someone has intended their meaning—hence our indignation and surprise when we find our meaning has been misinterpreted or distorted, that it is not as transparent to the audience as it is to ourselves.[23] Audiences and readers for their part are guided by their intention to understand. It is this intention that enables them to predict or anticipate in general what the topic is about and so eliminate the vast area of ambiguity that inheres in decontextualized utterances: unlikely alternatives are ruled out in advance."We do not read a sentence in order to generate a deep structure; we read it *from* a deep structure, seeking to fill gaps, to answer questions, to confirm expectations, and to reduce uncertainties among alternatives."[24]

Children behave like scientists by testing their hypotheses as they read on, Smith says, but then immediately takes exception to the analogy. "The analogy should go the other way. When scientists are conducting their experiments they are behaving like children. . . . The 'scientific method' is the natural way to learn, displayed by all of us in our early years."[25]

Scientific method is only an instance of a much more general method of learning that is natural to children. It is not surprising that Smith is hostile to the behaviourist notion of learning as dependent on reinforcement; he considers learning and the search for meaning to be perfectly natural. The enemies of learning are boredom or situations which children cannot make sense of.[26]

How is Smith able to support his position on reading and comprehension? How does he gain access to the data on which he bases his fairly elaborate interpretation of the reading process? Smith explores these methodological issues in his book on writing. Here he makes the point that thoughts and intentions are not immediately accessible to observation; we cannot point to them or examine them under a microscope.[27] To gain access to thought we should not attempt to look into ourselves but rather should put our thoughts to work and examine the products of our thoughts and intentions. We specify our intentions by analysing our behaviour or intended behaviour, but we cannot examine our intentions directly.[28] This is why language is important, especially written language because of its permanence: Smith believes that thought and language are not the same but goes on to say that "it is only through language or some other manifest product that its (thought's) currents can be perceived."[29]

Smith is unusually insistent on the distinction between thought and language and he also insists on the distinction between thought and visual imagery. "To be meaningful, to make sense, every mental image has to be interpreted. The scenes and events that we conjure up in the mind still have to be dealt with by the elusive processes of thought, just as much as the actual scenes and events that we perceive in the world outside the head."[30]

This at first glance seems to be an area of profound agreement with Lonergan's distinctions between mental acts and expression, and between looking and understanding. It becomes apparent, however, that this is in fact an area where a profound disagreement emerges between Smith and Lonergan. The immediate cause of disagreement is Smith's contention that thoughts, intentions, and actions are somehow "beyond awareness."[31] But this observation in turn is tied to a view of the *mind's relation to the world* (or rather the brain's—Smith uses the terms interchangeably but prefers to talk of "the brain")—a view to which Lonergan's position is radically opposed. But I shall postpone discussion of this until the end of my comparison of Smith and Lonergan, where it fits more naturally.

LONERGAN ON COGNITION

To measure the agreement between Smith and Lonergan I propose to offer a series of propositions, each summarizing a salient feature of Smith's position. Using these as headings I shall then attempt to indicate Lonergan's position under each heading.

Knowledge is Dependent on what we Already Know

Lonergan's philosophy is at odds with those philosophies that entertain any portion of the naive realist's assumption that knowing is like looking and that, as such, there are at least some facts to the establishment of which the knower contributes nothing: she or he simply, as it were, registers them on the retina of the mind. Lonergan's opposition to the theory that knowing is like looking is endemic in his writing. He maintains that knowing proceeds from the invariant pattern of experiencing, understanding, and judging. One implication of this cognitional theory is that there are no non-interpreted facts and no epistemologically privileged facts that act as building blocks for more complex facts.

Furthermore, what we already know orientates us when we address problems or situations that are new to us and for this reason require fresh insights and judgments.

> (P)ast judgments remain with us. They form a habitual orientation, present and operative, but only behind the scenes. They govern the direction of attention, evaluate insights, guide formulations, and influence the acceptance or rejection of new judgments. They facilitate the occurrence of fresh insights, exert their influence on new formulations, provide presuppositions that underlie new judgments. . . . Hence, when a new judgment is made, there is within us a habitual context of insights and other judgments.[32]

Faced with the puzzle of how new knowledge is attainable when such knowledge is not yet acquired, Lonergan finds the answer in what he terms the "heuristic structure." The acquisition of new knowledge need not be a series of wild conjectures. It can be a methodical process achieved by ordering means to an end. Heuristic structure gives method and system to our inquiries. It is very simple: "Name the unknown. Work out its properties. Use the properties to direct, order, guide the inquiry."[33]

These two quotations, taken together, cover the points Smith makes in respect of new knowledge being dependent on what we already know. Applied to reading they suggest (a) that what we already know (about language, life, the area of knowledge being addressed in the passage) informs our reading, and (b) that we use the contextual clues to work out the meaning of words or phrases that are new to us. To take a simple example from algebra:

we are informed that "2x − 4 = 24" and are asked to state the value of 'x.' What we do is use what the equation tells us in order to discover the value of 'x'; and we do that by placing 'x' on one side and everything else on the other. So we add 4 to each side in order to maintain a correct equation, and this gives us "2x = 24 + 4," and hence we know that "x = 14." We use the contextual clues in order to work out what we originally do not know.

We Anticipate Knowledge Claims

In many ways this follows from what has just been said, for inquiry is an anticipatory activity. "(B)y inquiring, intelligence anticipates the act of understanding for which it strives. The context of that anticipated act can be designated heuristically. The properties of the anticipated and designated content constitute the clues intelligence employs to guide itself towards discovery.... Of themselves, heuristic structures are empty. They anticipate a form that is to be filled."[34]

Lonergan at this point is talking about scientific inquiry, but his remarks can be applied to all inquiry and therefore to reading. For reading is a form of inquiry that is truly anticipatory, in which the reader uses available clues (including at times pictures and diagrams) to guide her to an understanding of what she does not yet understand. When Lonergan speaks of "guidance" or "determination" he has in mind much that Smith means when he speaks of the number of choices being reduced by virtue of what we already know and what we anticipate.

We Carry a Model of the World in our Head

Elaborating on the relation of the text's meaning to what the interpreter brings to the text, Lonergan attacks what he calls "the principle of the empty head." This principle

> bids the interpreter forget his own views, look at what is out there, let the author interpret himself. In fact, what is out there? There is just a series of signs. Anything over and above a re-issue of the same signs in the same order will be mediated by the experience, intelligence, and judgment of the interpreter ... the wider the interpreter's experience, the deeper and fuller the development of this understanding, the better balanced his judgment, the greater the likelihood that he will discover just what the author meant.[35]

Smith clearly relishes the paradoxical quality of this claim that we read from a model in our head. This chimes with Lonergan's assertion that the principle of the empty head rests upon a "naive intuitionism." It springs from the belief that objectivity amounts to a "pure receptivity" that excludes "any subjective activity"—the belief of the nineteenth-century empiricists.[36] Lonergan, by contrast, refuses to identify objectivity with the absence of subjectivity. The enemy of objectivity is not the subject's wealth of knowledge but human bias in its various forms.

Another tenet that emerges from this is that

The Sources of Meaning are Immanent in the Interpreter

Although this is Lonergan's formulation, the idea is shared by Smith—for example, when he says that the theory or model of the world "fills our mind: we have no other resource";[37] or when he asks where meaning comes from if all that passes between the writer and the reader is the printed page. "The only possible answer is that readers . . . must provide meaning themselves."[38]

Lonergan makes the point when he repudiates the notion that the truly objective interpreter simply observes the meanings "out there" while the subjective interpreter "reads" his own ideas "into" statements.

> (T)he plain fact is that there is nothing "out there" except spatially ordered marks; to appeal to dictionaries or to grammars, to linguistic and stylistic studies, is to appeal to more marks. The proximate source of the whole experiential component in the meaning of both objective and subjective interpreters lies in their own experience; the proximate source of the whole intellectual component lies in their own insights; the proximate source of the whole reflective process lies in their critical reflection.[39]

It strikes me that there is a broad agreement in these comments of Lonergan with F. R. Leavis's account of how to read a poem. In his reply to the philosopher, Rene Wellek, Leavis gives an account of what is involved in reading a poem:

> By the critic of poetry I understand the complete reader. . . . The critic—the reader of poetry—is indeed concerned with evaluation but to figure him as measuring with a norm which he brings up to the object and applies from the outside is to misrepresent the process. The critic's aim is, first, to realize as sensitively as possible this or that which claims his attention; and a certain valuing is implicit in the realizing. As he matures in his experience of the new thing he asks, explicitly and implicitly, "Where does this come? How does it stand in relation to . . .? How relatively important does it seem?" And the organisation into which it settles as a constituent in becoming "placed" is an organisation of similarly "placed" things that have found their bearings with regard to one another, and not a theoretical system determined by abstract considerations.[40]

Smith, Leavis and Lonergan agree that in respect of reading or interpreting to overlook the contribution of the reader or interpreter is to talk nonsense. This is the cardinal point in the agreement between these authors.

Leavis expresses this view most powerfully, perhaps, because of what he believes is the "fuller responsiveness" required by the reading of poetry, but the essential point remains the same: the primary sources of meaning are immanent in the reader so that the contribution of the reader is essential if understanding is to be achieved; and, what is more, we read by fitting what we read into the "organisation" we already carry about with us in our heads, the effect of which is that over time the man of experience becomes his own criterion. This leads to the hope or expectation that Smith has a coherent and philosophically compatible understanding of the subject or reader. Unfortunately, as we shall see, this hope is not fulfilled.

Predicting and Hypothesizing are Basic to Learning

Once more the proposition follows from and is integral to others that have preceded it. If inquiry is anticipatory and depends on a heuristic structure to be methodical, predicting and hypothesizing will play an important role in the move from ignorance to answer. In Lonergan's cognitional theory understanding precedes knowledge. Understanding by itself is not knowledge but preparatory to knowledge; for understanding to qualify as knowledge, it stands in need of verification. It follows that understanding on its own has the status of a hypothesis that has yet to be verified. "Because the proximate sources of interpretation are immanent in the interpreter, every interpretation is, at first, no more than a hypothesis. Because initially it is no more than a hypothesis, it can become probable or certain only by approximating to the virtually unconditioned or by reaching it."[41]

For Lonergan, verification consists in the fulfilment of the conditions required for the hypothesis to be judged true or probable—that is, in achieving the status of what he calls a "virtually unconditioned." In the context in which the above quotation occurs he is attempting to work out "a general heuristic structure for a methodical hermeneutics" and this requires a "multiply interlocked coherence" as providing the virtually unconditioned that grounds true interpretation. Smith's ambitions are more restricted since he is concerned only with a correct interpretation of the author's intended meaning. His criterion of correctness is the fulfilment of the predictions, etc. we make as we read: if what we go on to read fits or coheres with what we have predicted our hypothesis is to that extent confirmed; if not, we need to revise our hypothesis.[42] For both Smith and Lonergan, speaking in the context of interpretation, coherence provides the principle of verification.

Questions are the Driving Force Behind Comprehension

Smith is insistent on the role of questions in coming to understand a text. Questions direct our reading and it is only by asking the right questions that we can hope to grasp the meanings the text has to offer. On the topic of questions Lonergan is eloquent. It is questions for intelligence that promote us from the experiential to the intellectual level (What? Why? How often? and so on); and it is questions for critical reflection that promote us from the level of understanding to the level of judgment (Is that so or not so? Is it probable or improbable?). Further, our realization that our understanding and knowledge are incomplete commonly generates further questions. The questions identify what we do not know, the "known unknown," and move us to further insights. Insights coalesce into viewpoints and lower viewpoints are raised by further questions and answers to higher view-points.[43] In the area of intellectual development, Lonergan terms the question the "operator," the principle that moves us onwards and upwards. "Thus, unless one asks the further questions, one remains with the insights one has already, and so intelligence does not develop."[44] For the same reason, it is when the stream of questions dries up, when there are no further relevant questions to be asked, that we know we have reached the end of our investigations of a particular situation.[45]

1. There is no One-to-One Correspondence Between Thought and Language or Between Language and Objects
2. Meaning is Not in the Printed Word
3. The Meaning of the Printed Word does not Derive from the Spoken Word

These three tenets of Smith, all of them negative, arise as he attempts to explain whence it is that words are meaningful. Lonergan is in basic agreement with each. Language, he maintains, expresses experience, understanding and judgment. As affirmation or negation, it corresponds with judgment; as meaningful it corresponds with insight or understanding; as instrumental multiplicity it corresponds with experience.[46] There is no identity of expression with knowledge but expression is isomorphic with knowledge. There is discontinuity as well as continuity between expression and knowledge in the sense that deceit remains a possibility and that expression may be less than adequate or shaped to suit the needs of a particular audience.

In a strict sense, words do not mean but people mean. Lonergan distinguishes between principal acts of meaning and instrumental acts of meaning. The former are acts of understanding, judging, deciding, and acting. The latter are expressions of principal acts in gesture, speech, and writing. It follows that words do not mean but people mean through acts of understanding, judging, and acting. In so far as it is in judgment that statements are asserted as true or false, it follows that, strictly speaking, words alone are not true or false. What is true or false is judgment; words are true or false in so far as they express judgments. For that reason, words do not refer directly to things or objects or states of affairs; they refer to these things mediately, through true judgments.

This position takes care of the eighth and ninth of Smith's tenets. For speech and writing are both derivative from principal acts of meaning, and speech is no more the source of meaning than writing is, though there may be other and quite intricate relations between the two. The distinction Smith makes between surface structure and deep structure corresponds to the distinction Lonergan makes between instrumental acts of meaning and principal acts of meaning. As instrumental, words, whether spoken or written, are merely marks on the page or sounds in the air—they are not yet meaningful but simply an experiential source of meaning. The distinction between surface structure and deep structure proves to be of great value to Smith in explaining some interesting features of reading. For example it explains how the same meaning can be expressed in a variety of ways;[47] how we can often make sense of partial, blurred, or even mutilated texts;[48] of how the bridge in translation from one language such as French to another such as English is not direct from French into English but from French into meaning into English idiom.[49]

Meaning is what is Intended

We have seen how Smith makes use of intention as something that is lacking in the Chomskian notion of transformational grammar: without intention the notion of transformational grammar remains mechanistic and, in a profound sense, inhuman. For Chomsky considers speakers to operate like machines.

> We can view the speaker as a machine of the type considered. (This is a machine that switches sequentially from one state to another in producing grammatical sentences.) In producing a sentence the speaker begins in an initial state, produces the first word of the sentence, thereby switching into a second state which limits the choice of the second word etc. Each state through which he passes represents the grammatical restrictions that limit the choice of the next word at this point in the utterance . . .[50]

In his efforts to appear "scientific" Chomsky succeeds in reducing human beings to the condition of a robot, a machine that operates not for a reason or purpose of its own but one that is driven by a succession of mechanistic/mindless events, each triggering or producing another event, which in turn triggers another, and so on down the line till a particular outcome is achieved, rather in the manner of a steam locomotive or a car engine. But human beings are not machines; they operate, say and do things for reasons and for a purpose—in order to achieve particular ends. This kind of teleological explanation is unpopular in modern science and modern philosophy of science but is necessary if we are to understand human beings and their behaviours. I am sure that Chomsky has written his books on language for very good and laudable reasons. If so, he had certain intentions in mind. Actions that are intentional are actions that are directed to achieve a particular end or result. For these reasons, Smith is fully justified in using intention to explain operations like attending, listening, and choosing a particular form of expression. In reading, the intention of the reader helps eliminate the ambiguity that always accompanies decontextualized utterances.

Lonergan penetrates the notion of intention and intentionality more deeply. There is the intentionality peculiar to a wide range of operations such as seeing, hearing, inquiring, understanding, formulating, reflecting, judging, and so on.[51] By virtue of being intentional each of these operations intends its object; by means of them the subject is aware of the object in a particular way. Thus by seeing, the object becomes present to the subject as what is seen; by understanding, it is present as intelligible; by judgment, as what in fact is so; and so on. But underlying these operations is a more basic orientation or intentionality. This is what Lonergan refers to as the pure, disinterested desire to know the truth. It is a fundamental psychic drive or thrust that binds together the various operations required for the real to be reached through true judgments. It takes Lonergan a great many pages to help the reader to grasp what is involved in the dynamic process of coming to know; but intentionality binds this process into one. This basic intentionality relates not just to this or that truth but to all that can be known, to the entire universe of what is, namely being. As such, it is the source of our questioning, taking us beyond the data of sense to the unities and relations that organize the data into a whole; beyond the uncertainties of mere understanding to the affirmation that is done with uncertainties and takes its stand on what is so; beyond each incomplete knowledge claim to further knowledge claims and viewpoints by means of further questions. All human knowing in all fields of inquiry is driven by this basic desire to know, by this *conscious intentionality* of the inquiring subject. For this reason Lonergan took to calling his approach to philosophy "intentionality analysis"—in saying that, he had said it all.

Children do not Behave like Scientists but Scientists Behave like Children

In putting the matter in this provocative way Smith wishes to draw attention to his claim that the pattern of comprehension which he outlines is the natural pattern we follow when we want to learn. Lonergan's way of expressing the same point is to say that the threefold structure of cognition is transcendental, or that it is a meta-method that underpins all other methods or forms of inquiry. That is, it is not an object of choice but a given; it is not the product of cultural development but the necessary condition for the development of culture.[52] The pattern of cognition is normative and the move from one level to another in the pattern is both conscious and spontaneous; as spontaneous it is not something that the inquirer or reader opts to do but is something that occurs naturally and irresistibly. It is constitutive of our humanity and we grow in humanity and as persons the more we conform to its precepts: be attentive, be intelligent, and be reasonable.[53]

This takes us to a final component of Smith's theory of reading and of language.

How do we come to Understand the Process of Reading?

I put it in the form of a question because Smith's analysis at this point is beset by not a little confusion. He claims that it is not possible to observe our thoughts and intentions directly, and with this Lonergan is in agreement if by "observe" is meant looking inside to see what is there. But Smith goes further and claims that thoughts and the theory one holds in the head are "beyond awareness";[54] skills, feelings, and intentions "are not open to direct inspection or immediately accessible to awareness; all are part of the concealed, mysterious, inconceivable realm of the mind's internal processes."[55] Smith is alert to the objections that can be raised against a position that maintains that we are unaware of what we are doing. He says "If we successfully drive our car we have presumably 'attended' to that action . . . but not in the sense that we were consciously aware of what we were doing. If we are engrossed in what we are doing, it is only afterwards that we can remove ourselves from the situation and say what we have done."[56]

He claims that "awareness is retrospective; it always involves reflection."[57] Smith's position here is fairly clear: thinking and doing things are beyond awareness because if we were aware of our thinking and doing at the time they occurred, this would get in the way of our thinking and doing, which would cease; so awareness is always retrospective. But while clear enough this position gives rise to some startling pronouncements: "Most of the time we are not aware of what we write and read (or say and hear)—certainly not while we are writing or reading it—although we can become aware of what we have written and read in retrospect."[58]

This suggests that reading and writing are blind, unconscious activities over which the reader and writer exercise no control—only in retrospect do we become conscious or aware of what we have written or read. But it is difficult to see exactly how one could consciously recollect what one did while in an unconscious state. Is it a matter of stumbling across a piece of one's own writing and saying, "Heavens, that's my handwriting. I must have written that!" Besides, how could one retain what one reads if reading is "beyond awareness"? Smith no doubt would object that such objections do not reflect what he intended. (But how could he know what he intended?)

However, he does lay himself open to criticism in respect of what could possibly count as evidence if what he purports to describe is "beyond awareness."

Smith in fact makes an elementary, if understandable, error that appears to be linked to a further and deeper error which emerges when he speaks of the brain's interaction with the world. When he speaks about awareness Smith makes the erroneous assumption that awareness is an *additional operation* to the operations of thinking or doing something. The subtle point he fails to recognise is that human consciousness is consciousness to the power of two: that whenever I am aware of something I am *simultaneously* aware of myself being aware of it. It is because of this "doubling up" of consciousness that whenever I know something I know that I know it; and this, in turn, means that I can formulate what I know and communicate it to others. It is this feature of human consciousness that stands behind what we call "culture."

Being present to myself is both a necessary condition for conscious activity and a necessary condition for the possibility of retrospective awareness or memory. Such self-presence is not usually the focus of my conscious activity and to that extent is implicit rather than explicit. Even when I make it the object of my explicit attention, I am implicitly aware of myself attending to myself as the explicit object of my attention! At the level of performance, in other words, my self-presence is always implicit. Far from getting in the way of conscious activities like reading or writing or driving a car such implicit self-presence is crucial to them because without it I would be unaware that it was I who was reading or writing or driving the car. And without the "I" there would in turn be no reading or writing or driving at all.

This is what Lonergan is getting at when he says that consciousness is not only cognitive but also constitutive. That is, not only is the "I" needed if consciousness is to take place, but consciousness is needed if the "I" is to exist. "I" am constituted by my consciousness. Because at the level of performance consciousness is implicit rather than explicit it is easily overlooked. And such is the use of the words "conscious" or "aware" in English that they are commonly understood to signify reflective awareness of an object or activity, a deliberate bringing into focus of an object, whether myself or something else. Smith seems to understand awareness in this sense of reflective or explicit awareness and, in consequence, he dismisses it as referring to implicit self-presence, which is in fact necessary for any intentional operation to take place. Smith's position on "awareness" contradicts all that he says on "intentionality." Lonergan's position, by contrast, is that if I am not present to myself—as in a dreamless sleep or a coma—nothing else can be present to me: self-presence is a necessary precondition for anything else being present to me. It is his oversight or misunderstanding of this basic point that causes Smith to commit such howlers as to say that most of the time we are not aware of what we read or write or say or hear!

Smith's obtuseness on the topic of awareness indicates a limitation in his notion of intention. For intention has a subjective pole as well as an objective pole. If seeing is an intentional act it is so by intending the object as seen; but this intention also makes the object present to the subject who sees. Smith misunderstands the subjective pole and this is reflected in his comments on awareness. It comes into the full light of day when he turns to speak about the brain's interaction with the world. Smith writes about the brain lodged in the darkness of the skull. It is a vivid description:

> in prosaic fact the brain leads a life of almost complete isolation in a world without sights or sounds, without even smells or tastes or any kind of tactile sensation. All of these experiences the brain conjures up for itself . . . it is only through a constant barrage of indistinguishable neural impulses . . . that the brain has any contact with the outside world. The brain sits like a technician in a sealed control room at the center of a vast communication network—except that the brain has never been outside. . . . The brain knows nothing at first hand. Everything it pictures as occurring in the world it depicts for itself. . . . Oddly enough, although the brain's only access to the outside world is through neural networks, the incoming neural activity is not anything of which we can ever be directly aware. . . . The brain is aware only of its own products, the images and sensations that it constructs; and we seem destined to remain ignorant of the immediate evidence upon which the brain bases its perceptual decisions.[59]

There is a good deal of this "brain talk" in Smith's work. He speaks of "events" being "superimposed by the brain on a continuous flux of occurrences in the world"; this is "the brain's way of interpreting its interaction with the world," and so on.[60]

What Smith is giving us here is nothing less than a modern version of Cartesian dualism. The brain is the *res cogitans*, with the additional twist that we know that it has no direct contact with the world of bodies "out there"; it is aware only of its own products, the images and sensations it "constructs." The world in turn is an endless stream of occurrences, stretched out in space and time. The brain "freezes" this flow in order to "superimpose" on it distinct "events." Awareness is part of this process of freezing time: it "manufactures" cross sections of the continual flow of time.[61] However, Smith is robust in his resistance to the doubt that afflicted Descartes. Although he speaks as if the constructs of the brain were somewhat artificial and superimposed, he is not disposed to any scepticism in their regard. He has a soothing bedside manner, telling us that we need not allow these theoretical conundrums to confuse us.[62] Well, that is comforting.

CRITICISM OF SMITH

It is not possible to deal here with all the philosophical issues that Smith succeeds in raising. But there is one large philosophical fallacy that should be identified. Throughout one section of his writing Smith talks as if the brain were a person. The brain "depicts," "constructs," "manufactures," "superimposes"; it "interprets," it "knows," is presumed to require "evidence," it makes "perceptual decisions."[63] Throughout this section Smith speaks about "we" (the author and his readers) and "it" (the brain) in a manner that presumes their equivalence. This is, in fact, a version of what has been called the "homunculus fallacy." The brain is conceived as a little man or person in the head, which enjoys all the attributes of persons. But if that is the case does the little person in the head have a brain? And if so, is that brain like a person? And if so, does that person have a brain? And so on, *ad infinitum*. Smith, in short, makes a "category mistake," talking about one thing in a manner suited to another, quite different thing. And this category mistake follows from his radical misunderstanding of the nature of human consciousness.

This is an area of disagreement between Smith and Lonergan and illustrates how scholars specializing in non-philosophical subjects not infrequently come up against philosophical issues and can easily fall prey to philosophical attack which can be used to undermine what is of value in their specialist writing. Further, the disagreement between Smith and Lonergan points to two components of Smith's thinking that sit uneasily alongside each other.

On the one hand, Smith is opposed to a mechanistic account of reading that would reduce reading to the mere translation of marks on the page into sounds. He stresses that reading is a form of comprehension and he has a dynamic understanding of comprehension, one that stresses the role of the subject or the reader: we bring meaning to the text, we ask questions, we anticipate and predict; meaning does not reside primarily in the surface features of language but is what is intended by writers, readers, speakers, and listeners. As Leavis puts it, "Words 'mean' because individual human beings have meant the meaning."[64] Now all of this is about human beings exercising conscious control of their cognitional processes in order to increase their understanding and check that what they understand is the meaning intended by the author. As a conscious and intentional process, cognition is the opposite of processes that are blind, automatic or merely mechanistic.

On the other hand, Smith undermines his position on cognition or comprehension by denying that we are aware of what we say, hear, read, or write while we are engaged in these activities. He takes a further step away from coherence when he proceeds to treat the brain as a person and to confuse the unconscious responses of the brain to incoming neural impulses with conscious thoughts, feelings, and sensations. Smith is in danger, in fact, of reducing the whole edifice of his theory of reading and learning to the automatisms of the brain. He appears to have failed to work out thoroughly the implications of his own theory of reading and learning, which might have led to a more coherent theory of the subject who reads. To do him justice, Smith admits to a good deal of bewilderment in his thinking about the brain/thought interface and, whereas some scientists think that the problems and mysteries will be solved by further research into the brain, he considers that maybe the questions should be framed differently.[65] This hesitation of Smith's hints at the truth: that the analysis of our conscious and intentional operations, such as Lonergan has carried out, should be distinguished clearly from the examination of the neurological events that occur in the brain, which modern scanning devices such as cerebroscopes have made accessible to scientific investigation. Intentionality analysis should not be confused with the examination of the non-conscious functions of the human brain.[66]

CONCLUSION

It would not be wildly speculative to hazard the opinion that those parts of Smith's work that have proved most useful and influential with working teachers happen to fall within the area on which Smith and Lonergan agree. For this reason Smith offers readers of Lonergan the encouraging message that Lonergan's theory of cognition and his comments on learning and interpretation can accommodate a theory of reading that has proved valuable to classroom teachers. Smith also offers a refreshing reminder of the dynamic structure of inquiry within which the triad of knowing is situated. He reminds us forcefully of the subject's role in reading and knowing, and, as such, of the continuing need for intellectual honesty and self-transcendence; and he writes with the pace and raciness of the former journalist that he is.

Lonergan offers a philosophical account of cognition that is a good deal more rounded and extended than Smith's account of comprehension. For example, Smith is not concerned with the problem of relativism that might be seen to emerge from his view that the reader brings meaning to the text. Yet such relativism has become commonplace in literary criticism: the authorial intention is not available as a guarantee that an interpretation is valid; all texts are plural; there is no true reading; interpretations serve ideological interests; and so on. It is to guard against relativism of this kind that Lonergan introduces the notion of the "universal viewpoint."[67] In more general terms, Lonergan's position can offer Smith a rigorous philosophical underpinning that could overcome some of the incoherence in his thinking and protect him from the criticisms that can be ranged against him on philosophical grounds.

NOTES

1. V. Southgate, H. Arnold, and S. Johnson, *Extending Beginning Reading* (London: Heinemann Educational Books for the Schools Council, 1981), p. 22.
2. *Extending Beginning Reading,* p. 22–23.
3. This movement was pioneered in the United States by Kenneth and Yetta Goodman. See K. S. Goodman, "Analysis of Oral Reading Miscues: Applied Psycholinguistics," *Reading Research Quarterly* 1 (1968). An author claimed as a forerunner of psycholinguistics is Edmund Burke Huey who dismissed the notion that reading is mere "word pronouncing" and said it was "thought-getting" in his *The Psychology and Pedagogy of Reading* (New York: The Macmillan Co., 1908).
4. Frank Smith, *Psycholinguistics and Reading* (New York: Holt, Rinehart and Winston, 1973), p. 12.
5. F. Smith, *Understanding Reading* (New York: Holt, Rinehart and Winston, 2nd ed., 1978).
6. Smith, *Understanding Reading,* p. v.
7. Smith, *Understanding Reading,* p. 56.
8. F. Smith, *Reading* (Cambridge: Cambridge University Press, 2nd ed., 1985), p. 8.
9. Smith, *Reading,* p. 13.
10. Smith, *Understanding Reading,* p. 57.
11. Smith, *Reading,* p. 77.
12. Smith, *Reading,* p. 95.
13. Smith, *Reading,* p. 94–95.
14. Smith, *Reading,* p. 94.
15. Smith, *Reading,* p. 83.
16. Smith, *Reading,* p. 83.
17. Smith, *Reading,* p. 104.
18. Smith, *Reading,* p. 49.
19. Smith, *Reading,* p. 70.
20. Smith, *Reading,* p. 71.
21. Smith, *Reading,* p. 55.
22. F. Smith, *Writing and the Writer* (London: Heinemann Educational Books, 1982), p. 56–57.
23. Smith, *Reading,* p. 73.
24. Smith, *Writing,* p. 57.
25. Smith, *Reading,* p. 89.
26. Smith, *Understanding Reading,* p. 220.
27. Smith, *Writing,* p. 29.
28. Smith, *Writing,* p. 38.
29. Smith, *Writing,* p. 39.
30. Smith, *Writing,* p. 40.
31. Smith, *Writing,* p. 31.
32. Lonergan, *Insight,* p. 277.
33. Lonergan, *Insight,* p. 68.
34. Lonergan, *Insight,* p. 126.
35. Lonergan, *Method in Theology,* p. 157.
36. Lonergan, *Method inTheology,* p. 232.
37. Smith, *Reading,* p. 77.
38. Smith, *Reading,* p. 71.
39. Lonergan, *Insight,* p. 582.
40. Scrutiny, Vol 6, p. 60–61.
41. Lonergan, *Insight,* p. 612.
42. Smith, *Understanding Reading,* p. 56.
43. Lonergan, *Insight,* p. 469.
44. Lonergan, *Insight,* p. 495.
45. Lonergan, *Insight,* p. 283–287.

46. Lonergan, *Insight*, p. 553.
47. Smith, *Reading*, p. 70.
48. Smith, *Reading*, p. 74.
49. Smith, *Reading*, p. 74.
50. Noam Chomsky, *Syntactic Structures* (The Hague: Mouton, 1957), p. 20. I am indebted at this point to William Charlton's detailed and illuminating critique of Chomsky's views on language in his book, *Metaphysics and Grammar* (London: Bloomsbury, 2014).
51. This is an abbreviation of a list provided by Lonergan in *Method in Theology*, p. 6.
52. Lonergan, *Method in Theology*, p. 12.
53. Lonergan, *Method in Theology*, p. 18.
54. Smith, *Writing*, p. 32.
55. Smith, *Writing*, p. 38.
56. Smith, *Writing*, p. 43.
57. Smith, *Writing*, p. 44.
58. Smith, *Writing*, p. 42, p. 43.
59. Smith, *Writing*, p. 26.
60. Smith, *Writing*, p. 42.
61. Smith, *Writing*, p. 42.
62. Smith, *Writing*, p. 46.
63. Smith, *Writing*, p. 25–42.
64. Leavis, *The Living Principle*, p. 58.
65. Smith, *Writing*, p. 27.
66. For a glaring illustration of this confusion, see the basic argument put forward by Richard Rorty in *Philosophy and the Mirror of Nature* (Oxford: Basil Blackwell, 1980).
67. Lonergan, *Insight*, p. 564–568 and p. 583. Leavis also speaks of 'the one right total meaning that should control his (the reader's) analysis.' (*Scrutiny*, Vol 9, p. 310).

Chapter Six

Hemingway's Naturalism

In this chapter I shall attempt to place Ernest Hemingway in an intellectual tradition that continues to exert enormous influence on our civilization. The paradox of placing Hemingway, of all people, in an *intellectual* tradition will be dealt with in passing. What I wish to do straightaway is to say what I mean by an intellectual tradition; I shall then sketch the particular tradition I have in mind; the body of the chapter will be devoted to substantiating the claim that Hemingway belongs to this tradition. By way of conclusion I shall say why I believe this kind of thesis, the establishment of which requires a combination of philosophical and literary analysis, is important.

It is not all that easy to say what is meant by an intellectual tradition in the present context. It does not refer to a single, unified philosophical system but rather to a set or series of philosophical systems that hang together naturally because of certain assumptions or methodological principles common to all of them. It is a fairly loose mesh of ideas the various strands of which represent distinct lines of development but nevertheless interconnect and sustain each other in certain important respects. The three main strands of the tradition to which I shall assign Hemingway are empiricism, behaviourism and naturalism. It will be necessary to say briefly what each is or stands for and why they can be considered as amounting jointly to a distinctive pattern of ideas.

Traditional British empiricism received its classical statement from David Hume and it is to Hume that I shall refer in outlining this philosophical option. The importance empiricism places on the senses and on sensations— what Hume calls "impressions"—is vital. The contents of the mind are divided into "impressions" and "ideas," and ideas are said to derive from impressions. This derivation was to be Hume's major critical weapon when considering the merits of his opponents' arguments: "when we entertain, therefore, any suspicion that a philosophical term is employed without any meaning or idea (as is but too frequent), we need but enquire, 'from what impression is that supposed idea derived?' And if it be impossible to assign any, this will serve to confirm our suspicion."[1] By means of this principle, by checking ideas—especially abstract ideas—against the deliverances of the senses, Hume attempted to clear away much metaphysical nonsense and get at the sensible root of all abstractions and generalisations.

Ideas, according to Hume, are either simple or complex; complex ideas are made up of simple ideas, and simple ideas ultimately correspond to simple impressions. Hume was ever faithful to the particular. Believing that knowing was highly analogous to sensing, he concluded that since the senses have as their object only particulars then knowledge too must ultimately be of particulars. Empiricism is the natural enemy of *gestalt* . Further, if ideas derive from sensations, certain ideas such as our idea of causation—of A causing B—are difficult to explain, for most certainly we never see, hear, smell etc. A *causing* B. All that we hear, see, smell is first A and then B. Causation is, in fact, no more than "constant conjunction" and a habit of mind which, by the power of repeated association, when A occurs expects B to happen.

Hume's insistence on the foundational role of sensation was to have profound consequences in the field of ethics. Virtue and vice are not objects of sense. On what grounds then do we consider certain people and actions good or evil? On no other grounds, Hume tells us, than that certain people or actions give rise in us to feelings of pleasure while others give rise to feelings of displeasure—what Hume terms "uneasiness." Morality is delivered over to feeling and the twentieth century version of this ethical theory, as outlined, for example, in AJ Ayer's *Language, Truth and Logic,* is termed "emotivism."

Finally, it should be borne in mind that Hume envisages the knower as an individual on her own. All the individual has to go on are her own, necessarily private, impressions, or sensations, and the corresponding ideas. It is a very lonely situation.

By the twentieth century empiricism had undergone a number of refinements and mutations, while retaining its fundamental insistence that knowledge is not only dependent on sensation but is very closely analogous to sensory experience. One development from empiricism was philosophical behaviourism. This is not immediately evident; it can be argued, for example, that behaviourism diverges radically from empiricism by its exclusion of introspection as a valid means of acquiring knowledge. But a little reflection will, I trust, reveal the strong family resemblance between empiricism and behaviourism.

It is true that Hume, following Descartes, considered the internal more certain than the external, the private prior to the public, thus making the existence of a public world of "bodies" problematic, but latent within his empiricism are the doctrines that were to bring about a reversal of this order. While Hume may have employed introspective analysis to establish his position, his equation of knowledge with "experience and observation" leads logically to the conclusion that only the external (the observable and palpable) is a valid object of knowledge. The way is opened to the reduction of all inner states (feelings, thoughts, desires etc.) to observable bodily behaviour. Moreover, Hume's notion of *association*, which supplies the "cement" binding his world of discrete impressions together, is very similar to the behaviourist account of how stimulus and response are bonded. For example, behaviourism explains that by force of repeated association of stimulus with response, a conditioned reflex is produced in the organism, and this closely resembles Hume's psychological account of causation.

The common root from which empiricism and behaviourism develop is sensation. By taking sensation to be the source of meaning, both empiricism and behaviourism are systematically opposed or indifferent to relationships of *intelligible* dependence or interdependence (other than logical entailment) and so, to explain how things or events are bound together, recourse is had to purely contingent relations between things or events based on spatial and temporal contiguity, and psychological beliefs and habits. In a very real sense, both empiricism and behaviourism are anti-intellectual. The difference between them lies in which side of sensation each opts for, the private or the public. Empiricism traditionally maintains that what *I* see, hear, touch etc. is what is alone indubitable and known; hence the hoary empiricist problems concerning the existence of an external world, the problem of other minds, the problem of knowledge of the past etc. Behaviourism, by contrast, opts for the other side of sensation, that which is the object of my hearing, seeing, touching etc.—the audible, the visible and the strictly observable—such as bodily behaviour. Behaviourism is the public face, empiricism the private face, of one and the same thing; or, to put it another way, behaviourism turns empiricism inside out.

The third strand of the philosophical tradition I am seeking to outline is naturalism. Naturalism in its modern form is allied to the Darwinian theory of evolution which, it argues, provides massive evidence for the age-old assumption that man is nothing other and nothing besides the product of nature.[2] The corollary of this is that to speak of the supernatural, of agents or forces existing beyond the system of nature, is to be guilty of a basic philosophical error. The methodological principle governing philosophical naturalism is that nature is an enclosed system sufficient unto itself, in no need of any external agency to render its operations intelligible. The same methodological principle is operative in Humean empiricism. While empiricism is usually identified with a particular epistemology, it is important to note that behind the advocacy of a theory of knowledge lies a methodological decision—namely, philosophy must be brought into line with science.³ It is for this reason that all supernaturalism (such as miracles) is to be rigidly excluded and the scope of philosophical inquiry restricted to the world of "experience and observation."⁴ Empiricism was developed as a deliberate attempt to import into philosophy the methods of science; evolution, the stronghold of naturalism, appeared to many at the beginning of the twentieth century as the latest and most powerful vindication of the efficacy of those methods.

If, for the reasons I have just given, empiricism can be considered the grandfather of naturalism, behaviourism can claim to be a first cousin. For the central prop of naturalism is evolution which seeks to demonstrate how animals evolve by means of mutations undergone in the process of adapting to the environment in the struggle to survive. Behaviourism describes behaviour precisely as the response of an organism, be it man or animal, to environmental stimuli. From such responses are built up habits, conditioned reflexes, animal characteristics and, in the case of man, human personality. If evolution can be said to provide a framework for a new understanding of the species man, behaviouristic mechanisms can be seen to sit quite comfortably within that framework, indeed to make a notable contribution to the explanation of how the evolutionary system works.

Empiricism, behaviourism, naturalism: what we have here is not a single philosophical position but rather a set of ideas which, for a variety of reasons, are mutually congenial and supportive. It is this set of ideas, I shall argue, that constitute the intellectual universe of Hemingway's art. I put it this way because we should not expect from the artist the same explicit and rigorous exposition of a philosophical system that we demand from a philosopher. Art, we say, does not state its meaning but *enacts* it. To decipher the "meaning" of Hemingway's art we shall have to be attentive not only to its content but also to its form, that is, to the various ways in which his writing not only declares a philosophy but embodies it, becomes a complete concrete realization of his vision.

To sum up, the various features of the empiricist-behaviourist-naturalist intellectual tradition are as follows:

1. Ideas derive from sensation.
2. Complex ideas are made up of an aggregate of simple impressions.
3. Reasoning is tied to experience. By force of this, speculative reason is severely limited and metaphysics excluded.
4. Sensation plus the notion of association constitute the kernel of behaviourism.
5. Behaviourism concentrates exclusively on "outer" phenomena and reduces all inner phenomena such as thoughts and emotions to what is observable.

6. Morality is a matter of feeling.
7. The knower is an individual on her own.
8. In the struggle to survive humans interact with, and adapt to, their environment.
9. Humans are fully explained as an integral part of nature.

Ernest Hemingway's fidelity to the sensations is by now a commonplace of Hemingway criticism. As an apprentice writer in literary Chicago of the early 1920s he would go into the gym where he always received "many strong sensations" and try to identify the various smells. In the evening he would write the sensations down as accurately as he could. Significantly, he did this while the other members of his group sat in the adjacent room discussing artistic creativity.[5] "You've got to see it, feel it, smell it, hear it" was Hemingway's dictum and one to which he remained faithful throughout his literary career. The direct reporting of the physical, be it landscape or action and the careful itemisation of physical phenomena are the hallmarks of his style. A certain anti-intellectualism was the almost natural concomitant of this emphasis on sensation. "I was not made to think," says Frederic Henry in *A Farewell to Arms*.[6] "I was made to eat. My god, yes. Eat and drink and sleep with Catherine." To find in a writer so suspicious of the speculative functions of intelligence an affinity with a broad philosophical movement might seem surprising, but such surprise would be modified by the profoundly anti-speculative bias of the philosophies I have considered.

What is remarkable about Hemingway is not that he deals in sensations and concrete images; most literary art works through the sensible, the concrete and the particular. It is rather the degree to which his writing places the emphasis on the sensible, on what can be observed by the eye or the ear, the way in which his writing is subordinate, as it were, to the principle of *sensation,* which is arresting. It would be silly to pretend that he was a philosopher in any professional sense, who rigorously applied empiricist principles to his art. But the subordination of his writing to a basic belief—"You've got to see it, feel it, smell it, hear it"—led him, it would appear, to the elaboration of a style and of techniques which project the vision of one who was at heart, and despite some regrets, a naturalist (a term I shall from now on understand as inclusive of empiricism and behaviourism).

The emphasis on sensation in Hemingway's work is so all-pervasive as to require no illustration. What is more remarkable, and no one who comes to Hemingway for the first time can fail to be impressed by it, is the frequent itemisation of separate sensations, presented "raw" as the eye, tongue or ear receives them, unaccompanied by commentary or interpretation. A well-known passage from *Fiesta* will serve as an illustration.

> After a while we came out of the mountains, and there were trees along both sides of the road, and a stream and ripe fields of grain, and the road went on, very white and straight ahead, and then lifted to a little rise, and off on the left was a hill with an old castle, with buildings close around it and a field of grain going right up to the walls and shifting in the wind. I was up in front with the driver and I turned around. Robert Cohn was asleep, but Bill looked and nodded his head. Then we crossed a wide plain, and there was a big river off on the right shining in the sun from between the line of trees, and away off you could see the plateau of Pamplona rising out of the plain, and the walls of the city, and the great brown cathedral, and the broken skyline of the churches. In back of the plateau were the mountains, and every way you looked there were other mountains, and ahead the road stretched out white across the plain going toward Pamplona![7]

The technique is a major part of Hemingway's attraction. It inspired Ford Madox Ford's admiration, when he says that Hemingway's words strike us, "each one, as if they were pebbles fresh from a brook. They live and shine, each in its place. . . . The words form a tessellation, each in order beside the other. It is a great quality." All interpretative commentary is excluded; each sensation is fed to us in its purity without the distraction of thought or reflection; we are forced by the technique to savour each fresh sensation in turn; the word "and" operates as a simple conjunction and the writing is unencumbered by "since," "because," "therefore," the weapons of deduction, inference, entailment, ratiocination. The thinking mind is kept at bay and we enjoy the immediacy of sensuous impression. What strikes us as we read is how faithful Hemingway is to each separate sensation: there is an absence of summarising, the whole complex picture is built up from separate units of sensation. There is no discernible pattern or *gestalt,* simply a concatenation of simple impressions.

If this were all we might simply say that Hemingway had devised a new and brilliantly successful technique of painting with words, of communicating the physical aspects of scenery and action with surprising freshness. But this is not all. For interpretation is occurring, but in a uniquely singular fashion. In the passage from *Fiesta* we read that Cohn was asleep, while Bill looks and nods his head. The description is purely external, but enough is said for us to sense the fellow-feeling between Bill Gorton and Jake Barnes, their shared sensitivity and like-mindedness and, by contrast, Robert Cohn's insensitivity, his quality of being "outside" the norms which, in this book, Jake represents. Interpretation is buried in physical description; the internal is rendered in terms of the external. This is a common enough device in fiction, particularly in the novel, but Hemingway took it to exceptional lengths. In *Fiesta* and *Farewell* there is virtually no explicit commentary, certainly nothing that is sustained for any length. It is almost as if Hemingway were afraid to move away from the physical description, the world of sensations, of smells, sights, sounds, tastes, which alone are true and real and to be trusted. Theory, abstractions, interpretations, imposed by the intellect on the world of sensations—these are suspect. Abstractions can betray the truth of the senses, as Lieutenant Frederic reflects in *Farewell:* "Abstract words such as glory, honour, courage or hallow were obscene beside the concrete names of villages, the numbers of roads, the names of rivers, the numbers of regiments and dates."[8]

To chronicle is valid; to go beyond chronicle, beyond the place names and the dates, and offer an interpretation of war or events is to move beyond what sense can confirm and verify. Abstract theories are reduced to concrete particulars: "I am for the Republic and the Republic is the bridge," declares Pilar in *For Whom the Bell Tolls.*[9] The senses are the test of all fine words: "If qualities have odours, the odour of courage to me is the smell of smoked leather or the smell of the frozen road, or the smell of the sea when the wind rips the top from a wave," Hemingway informs us in *Death in the Afternoon*.

Like all empiricists Hemingway has trouble with religious and other systems of thought or bodies of doctrine that resist testing by the senses. God cannot be seen or heard and when Jake who is "technically" a Catholic visits the cathedral in *Fiesta* he tries to think of himself as praying, but adds: "I was ashamed and regretted that I was such a rotten Catholic, but realized there was nothing I could do about it, at least for a while, and maybe never, that anyway it was a good religion, and I only wished I felt religious and maybe I would the next time . . ." Frederic Henry is a nonbeliever; Santiago in *The Old Man and the Sea* says that he is not religious; neither does Robert Jordan, the hero in *For Whom the Bell Tolls*, believe and he even goes so far as to reject, not without some hesitation, the notions of divination and extrasensory perception. Where sensation only is to be trusted any speculative or metaphysical belief is difficult to entertain. Speculation has to be broken down to action. Jake says in *Fiesta:* "Perhaps as you went along you did learn something. I did not care what it was all about. All I wanted to know was how to live in it. Maybe if you found how to live in it you learned from that what it was all about." Refusing credence to anything other than the physically palpable leads Jake and Henry to a form of Nihilism, the latter spending his leave from the war among "the smoke ·of cafes and nights, when the room whirled and you needed to look at the wall to make it stop, nights in bed, drunk, when you knew that was all there was, and the strange excitement of waking and not knowing who it was with you, and the world all unreal in the dark and so exciting that you must resume again unknowing and not caring."[10]

Frederic's mood is no doubt brought on in relief from the war and before he has been touched by love for Catherine. But that love merely supplies an interlude. When it is over, we are left with the rain and a mood of blank despair.

In many ways Robert Jordan is the most paradoxical of Hemingway's heroes (in *For Whom the Bell Tolls*). Lieutenant Henry in *Farewell* is also involved in a war, but there is never any explanation of why he is fighting, there is no discernible political commitment. It is one man's war and then one man's flight from the war. There is not even an account of the larger strategy or the general course of events. There is simply news of defeats and the focus is kept permanently at the level of individual observation: guns and trucks moving, men wading through mud, deserters being shot. Where Tolstoy in *War and Peace* interrupts the narrative dealing with particular characters to engage in a dissertation on high-level planning or the lack of it and at the same time explains his theory of history, Hemingway in *Fare well* avoids this. In *For Whom the Bell Tolls* the theme of commitment to a cause that transcends the individual is not so easily avoided. The Spanish Civil War was one which generated a great deal of intellectual ferment: in many ways, so far as volunteers from abroad were concerned, it was the war of the intelligentsia, involving two great and opposing political creeds and historical forces, Fascism and Communism. Robert Jordan fights on behalf of Communism, a political creed which subordinates the individual to the ultimate goal of the classless society and sees the individual's role as a mere surface detail in the dialectical progression towards that goal. But even here Hemingway's focus is on the particular and short-term, the "now" of intense sensation, and one man's preoccupation with his immediate military objective, the blowing up of a bridge. Certainly, *For Whom the Bell Tolls* marks a movement away from Hemingway's extreme individualism, the individual cut off from his fellows, towards the notion of human solidarity. But what is important to grasp is that this notion of solidarity has nothing to do with communistic beliefs about the priority of society to the individual, but is justified in terms of an individualist philosophy, reminiscent of J. S. Mill's essay *On Liberty*.

"All people should be left alone and you should interfere with no one," Robert Jordan reflects. "So he believed that, did he? Yes, he believed that." Accordingly, he has to justify his own interference in Spanish affairs and he does so on purely utilitarian grounds: "So that, eventually, there should be no more danger and so that the country should be a good place to live in." Communism is reduced to its short-term utility: it offers "the best discipline and the soundest and sanest for the prosecution of the war." Marxist dialectics get short shrift: "You have to know them in order not to be a sucker. You have to put many things in abeyance to win a war . . . afterwards you discard what you do not believe in." Robert Jordan confesses to having no politics himself and is described by Karkov, the Russian general, as "a young American of slight political development."

There had been a time when Jordan was in danger of becoming "as bigoted and hidebound about his politics as a hard-shelled Baptist" but this was dissipated by the experience of sleeping with Maria: "Continence is the foe of heresy." (This is an interesting instance of Hemingway's combination of empiricism and behaviourism. (a) It is suggested that the life of the senses is the only surety in a world of conflicting ideologies; (b) and it is implied that, in matters of ideology, a modification of sensory input results in a modification of one's thought). When he is dying Robert Jordan is not comforted by the thought of sacrificing himself for a higher cause or political creed. His emphasis as he parts with Maria is on the fact that wherever she goes, he goes with her: individual influence is paramount. Even his dying on behalf of others and his "consecration to the oppressed" are motivated by feelings of sympathy rather than by allegiance to a body of doctrine or political theory. Jordan's purpose is utilitarian, his motivation sympathy. The resemblance to traditional empiricist thinking on justice is striking, for Hume's position is exactly similar: "public utility is the sole origin of justice," but "a sympathy with public interest is the source of the moral approbation which attends that virtue."[11] Like Hume's, Hemingway's position stems from, a fundamental individualism which he has not radically altered. *For Whom the Bell Tolls* might mark a movement away from the near-nihilism of *Fiesta* and *A Farewell to Arms* to a sense of fulfilment by means of human solidarity, but that solidarity is established in purely individualist terms and, in the final analysis, it is what the individual achieves that counts.

Hemingway's presentation of values shares the fundamental empiricist contention that values derive from feelings. There is nowhere any justification on rational grounds of a body of values against which his various characters can be judged. Right and wrong are matters of feeling. "He's one of us, though," Brett observes of the Greek count. "Oh, quite. No doubt. One can always tell." Jake too responds to people according to mood: "Under the wine I lost the disgusted feeling and was happy. It seemed they were all such nice people." But it is not quite a matter of *arbitrary* feelings. In *Fiesta* Jake is the embodiment of those norms by which everyone is judged, and Cohn is judged wanting; he does not quite "belong." At first this appears merely to be more a matter of style than of anything he does that is wrong: his style violates the ethos of the group, of Jake, Brett, Bill and Mike. Cohn behaves differently, follows a different "code" and so he is disapproved of. In particular he is slavish in his dog-like pursuit of Brett whereas Romero retains a manly distance, not even looking up during the bullfight ("he did not do it for her at any loss to himself"); and he breaks down and cries. It is this lack of proper emotional restraint which more than anything reveals Cohn as the outsider. Frederic Henry has it:

"Oh, darling," she (Catherine) said. "You will be good to me, won't you?" "What the hell, I thought."[12]

Catherine Berkeley has it: "I'm awfully tired. . . . And I hurt like hell. Are you all right, darling?"[13]

Robert Jordan has it in abundance. Lying dying, he savours each sensation in turn, forcing himself to register each moment sharply and clearly. Emotional blurring is the companion of panic, the contradiction of grace under pressure, of "clarity, distinctness and edge" on which Hemingway places such importance.[14] It is this control under pressure which makes the bullfight an apt metaphor for living.

> Romero never made any contortions, always it was straight and pure and natural in line. The others twisted themselves like corkscrews, their elbows raised, and leaned against the flanks of the bull after his horns had passed, to give a faked look of danger. Afterwards, all that was faked turned bad and gave an unpleasant feeling. Romero's bullfighting gave real emotion, because he kept the absolute purity of line in his movements and always quietly and calmly let the horns pass him close each time. . . . Romero had the old thing, the holding of his purity of line through the maximum of exposure, while he dominated the bull by making him realize he was unattainable, while he prepared him for the killing.[15]

Here we have the most explicit "statement" of Hemingway's ethical code: grace under pressure gives a good feeling and so it is good. (Why it gives a good feeling is a question I shall raise later). Its opposite, the breakdown of control, or worse, blind panic, such as Francis Macomber manifests when he runs away from the lion, is scorned. It humiliates and causes the woman to turn against the man. Later, when Macomber has proved himself against the buffalo, Wilson, the English hunter, reflects, "Fear gone like an operation. Something else grew in its place. Main thing a man had. Made him into a man. Women knew it too. No bloody fear."[16]

There is then in Hemingway a sort of code. Typically it is far from being abstract and is not justified by appeal to first principles or by intellectual reasoning: it consists of physical and emotional control in testing conditions. It is individualistic, the response of the individual to a threatening environment, and has nothing to do with ends, motives or the larger movements of history. Its justification is emotive. "So far about morals," Hemingway tells us in *Death in the Afternoon,* "I know only that what is moral is what you feel good after, and what is immoral is what you feel bad after. . . ."[17] The emotive theory of ethics has rarely been stated so bluntly.

It has often been said of Hemingway that he brought a new tone to American fiction after the long sentences and structural intricacies of Melville, Hawthorn and James. In particular, he is frequently praised for his direct statement of emotions in brief, spare, economical prose. While it is true that his prose is usually spare, it is not true that he represents emotion directly. There is, in fact, no direct access to human emotion. Where D. H. Lawrence, another author who likes to stress the natural in human nature, adapts his style in *The Rainbow* in order to delineate the psychic landscape of his various couples, revealing their emotions from the inside, Hemingway works almost entirely from the outside in. His revelation of feelings is peculiarly oblique, feeling being rendered exclusively in terms of behaviour or bodily states. In *For Whom the Bell Tolls* fear is several times registered by sweating; even the individual concerned seems to read his own emotions by observing his physiological reaction to a situation, as if normal introspection were not to be trusted: "He felt the sweat that came under his armpits and slid down between his arms and his side and he said to himself, So you are scared, eh?"[18] It is by means of such empirical tests that Hemingway achieves his famed objectivity. In the same novel Fernando's pain is suggested by the fact that the fly's tickling cannot penetrate it. This behaviouristic technique is not simply a stylistic device. It is so all-pervasive as to be accountable only as part of Hemingway's basic perspective. Biology takes precedence over thought. Santiago was not born to think about matters such as sin; he was born to be a fisherman as the fish is born to be a fish. Likewise Manuel, the veteran bullfighter in *The Undefeated,* appears to be little more than a constellation of habits and conditioned reflexes acquired in plying his trade, whose thinking is dependent on bullfight slang: "He thought in bullfight terms. Sometimes he had a thought and the particular piece of slang would not come into his mind and he could not realize the thought."[19]

In moments of greatest danger or greatest happiness the senses are at their most acute and each sensuous item, each detail of the environmental scene, is vividly caught. Meals in such conditions are described with minute precision, with meticulous attention to temperature, taste and manner of eating as well as to the incidental details that catch the participant's eye. The outer description acts as an accurate index of emotional heightening or possibly, it *is* the emotional heightening. When sexual climax is reached between Robert Jordan and Maria it is stated that "he felt the earth move out and away from under them"—the emotion is externalised. In a moment of great danger, when Frederic Henry escapes from the carabinieri, there is no explicit reference to fear, anxiety or despair. The whole effect is conveyed in terms of physical sensations, by means of the rhythm of the prose and with minute physical description.

> I ducked down, pushed between two men, and ran for the river, my head down. I tripped at the edge and went in with a splash. The water was very cold and I stayed under until I thought I could never come up. The minute I came up I took a breath and went down again. It was easy to stay under with so much clothing and my boots. When I came up the second time I saw a piece of timber ahead of me and reached it and held on with one hand. I kept my head behind it and did not even look over it. I did not want to see the bank. There were shots when I ran and shots when I came up the first time. I heard them when I was almost above water. There were no shots now.[20]

The tone throughout is unemphatic, but the reader's response (I once tried it out on a group of students) is one of strong empathy. In this respect, Hemingway meets the criteria set by Leavis by means of which the quality of an author's artistry is to be judged: there is no "dead set" at an emotional effect, but rather the reader's emotional response is directed by the author's detailed and concrete realization of an event. Hemingway evokes a response in his reader by the same technique he uses to reveal his character's psychology: by restricting attention almost exclusively to environmental features. He recalls what the eye saw or the palate tasted or the body felt at the precise moment the emotion was experienced and he describes that. The reader's response follows from that. There is avoidance of deliberately evocative words like "terrific," "amazing," "frightening," "painful" etc. There is no overt appeal to emotion; the tone remains flat, unforced, unhurried, but the itemisation of sensory detail obtains the desired response. But while the artistry is superb the theme of the passage is the familiar Hemingway one of physical courage, emotional control and survival.

Hemingway is ever faithful to the senses: only what the senses record is true, is real. To project emotional or psychological states directly, without pinning them to sensations, would be to enter the forbidden zone of speculation, where things can get out of hand, where the mind takes off on its own and fake mystery mongering occurs. In *The Old Man and the Sea*, the old fisherman struggles to resist the onset of such thinking, forcing himself to concentrate on the practical problems confronting him. At one point in *For Whom the Bell Tolls* it looks as if Hemingway is rising above chronicling into large scale interpretation of the course of history. After a grand sweep across the major events of Spain's history and her major personalities Robert Jordan concludes, "This was the only country that the reformation never reached. They were paying for the Inquisition now, all right." But any feeling that this is meant to be taken seriously is quickly extinguished. "Well, it was something to think about. Something to keep your mind from worrying about your work."[21] Practical intelligence is fine; strong interpretation or speculation is a mere luxury, at best distracting, at worst positively dangerous. It is also, it is suggested, probably false and dangerous because it is false. In one of his most revealing short stories, *A Clean, Well - lighted Place,* Hemingway gives us a glimpse of what lies beyond the reach of the senses: *nada.* The old waiter describes the darkness that lies beyond the clean, well-lighted cafe where he works, the darkness into which the old man who wishes to commit suicide will soon return, as "a nothing that he knew too well. It was all a nothing and a man was a nothing too. It was that and light was all it needed and a certain cleanness and order." Later he parodies the Our Father and Hail Mary, the two most common prayers in Catholic countries: "Our nada who art in nada, nada be thy name. . . . Hail nothing full of nothing, nothing is with thee."[22]

The kingdom of God is nada, the Lord is nada, grace is nothing. Beyond this life there is nothing, the promises of religion amount to nothing, he seems to be saying. Within the all-engulfing darkness of existence there is one and only one space that is not in darkness, the space occupied by the five senses of the individual human animal. To extinguish the senses is to extinguish all, to "put out the light" in Othello's phrase. To master life is to master our senses, to keep them alert, ordered and controlled. "Clear up, head," old Santiago continually admonishes. "Clear up."

To live life at its fullest intensity is the most we can achieve. But, significantly, as Jake Barnes observes, "Nobody ever lives their life all the way up except bullfighters."[23] The reason for this comment and for Hemingway's obsession with the bullfight which he says gives him "feelings of life and death and mortality and immortality" is precisely because of the bullfight's function as a paradigm in microcosm of all human existence. It is, literally, an encounter with death, as Hemingway makes clear in *Death in the Afternoon*. The bull represents the very imminent possibility of leaving for ever the well-lighted place and returning to the darkness. The encounter can, of course, be faked and then the feelings it produces are also fake because it has lost its value as a metaphor for life. Life's intensity derives from the inevitability of death. Survival in life, like survival in the bull ring, depends upon the exercise of the utmost control, psychological, emotional, physical. Only in this way can the bull be mastered: only in this way can life be mastered. Emotional restraint in Hemingway is more than a mere matter of style. It touches on man's capacity to live life in the only way that is worthwhile; in terms of Hemingway's ultimate vision, it is such control and its corollary, the intensification of sensation, which confers on life its only validity. Hence the "short, happy life of Francis Macomber" and hence Robert Jordan's consoling reflection as he is about to die: "You've had as good a life as anyone because of these last days." Hemingway's emotivism is tied to a vision of man.

The Hemingway hero, like the knowing subject in empiricist philosophy, is a loner. This is true of Nick Adams, Jake Barnes, Frederic Henry, Robert Jordan and Santiago. Whatever relationships they form with others are essentially transient. This is surely one of Hemingway's weaknesses which derives from his chosen technique. The empiricist-behaviourist model has frequently been accused of being just too inadequate to explain the complexity of human behaviour. By virtually restricting attention to the life of the senses and the observable, Hemingway cuts himself off from large areas of the inner life of his characters. Such inner processes as thinking, reasoning, intending, hoping, trusting, being motivated, being frustrated, the ebb and flow of the feelings—human psychic complexity—all lie outside his range. His instruments are not designed to record, express or analyse such things. Consequently, his man-woman relationships are, at heart, limited, slight, rather playful affairs, in which the man is the object of the woman's uncritical adulation. As such they can hardly be expected to endure, and none does. The technique is superbly equipped to record the transience of human experience: the sensation occurs and is gone. The favourite conjunction, "and," which gives the style its primitive, biblical quality, also conveys the fleetingness of all experience. It is this surely which explains the mood of nostalgia, of glorious things that have been but will be no more, that hangs over all his stories. Time is always short; annihilation, in the form of death or defeat, awaits us.

The same technique is inadequate to deal with the larger stirrings of history. These cannot be rendered in terms exclusively of the concrete and the particular. In *The Grapes of Wrath* Steinbeck, Hemingway's contemporary, tells the story of the Joad family, but does so in such a way that they are seen as but one example among thousands of the human waste enforced by an impersonal economic system, which is analysed in considerable detail. Such analysis is beyond Hemingway. His style and his vision which are ultimately one cannot admit anything other than the world of sensory impressions. For all that his stories are set amidst some of the greatest upheavals in twentieth century western history—the First World War, the 1920s, and the Spanish Civil War—social content other than the superficialities of dress, idiom and current celebrities is virtually absent. The Hemingway code remains the same whether the hero is shooting fascists in Spain or shooting buffaloes in Africa. The Hemingway code that emerges from these considerations fully justifies F. R. Leavis's judgment that Hemingway manifests a "bent towards a simplifying reduction of life"—Hemingway fails the Leavisian standard of "life."

In describing Hemingway as an empiricist and behaviourist I have perhaps overdrawn the picture. It is worth noting, for example, that occasionally, though very infrequently, he does relate the inner emotional condition of his characters directly, more in his later than his earlier writing. And it is highly unlikely that he would subscribe rigorously to every tenet of these philosophies or that he applied certain academic findings to his writing. What is more plausible is that Hemingway, who had a knack of being in touch with the *zeitgeist,* wrote as a man of his time *(In Our Time* was a very early success) during a period in which, in the English speaking world, the empiricist-behaviourist-naturalist nexus was in the ascendancy. This explanation involves the highly complex manner in which politics, economics, philosophy and the higher arts of painting, sculpture, literature and music all interact on each other within the space of a few decades. Yet another part of the explanation may be found in the problems which philosophers and literary artists have in common: the problem of how the individual relates to reality; of what constitutes reality for him; of how he validates his opinions, beliefs and actions. This leads us to seek an explanation in Hemingway's first principle as an author to be faithful to *sensation* . He was a craftsman intent on being honest who thought long and hard about his craft, a term he preferred to art. A craftsman of such seriousness must know his medium intimately. But we would not hope to find in Hemingway any explicit exposition of the principles which govern his style: he confesses to writing "on the principle of the iceberg. There is seven-eighths of it underwater for every part that shows."[24] Hemingway was an artist and the principles he arrived at by remaining faithful to sensation are to be found buried in his art. But his vision reveals its roots.

This vision is given its most explicit statement in his final work, *The Old Man and the Sea* . Santiago, the hero, is a sort of pagan saint *(Sant*iago*)* in total communion with nature (which explains why he is a saint). Addressing a small, tired warbler, he says, "Take a good rest, small bird. Then go in and take your chance like any man or bird or fish."[25] Man, bird, fish: all are part of nature and of the natural processes of living and dying, of preying and being preyed upon. To live one must struggle, as Santiago struggles, sometimes against tremendous odds, but to struggle and endure each has its natural endowment of wit or wisdom or practical intelligence, what Santiago calls his "tricks." To struggle and endure it is necessary to retain control of one's wits and one's emotions, to show grace under pressure. Even if one fails in the worldly sense—the carcase of Santiago's Marlin is devoured by sharks—if one suffers and endures one remains "undefeated" and this, for Hemingway, is the ultimate achievement of man or bird or fish.

The Old Man and the Sea aroused conflicting opinions among the critics. This is significant, for it raises the question of whether Hemingway changed, over-reaching in his later work the style made famous by the earlier work. Philip Toynbee's reaction was extremely adverse: "The book is doctor-bait and professor-bait. And the modem critic of Hemingway should read this nonsense carefully and then re-read *The Killers* or *The Undefeated*. . . . This is one of the genuine literary tragedies of our time."[26] The reference to The *Killers* and *The Undefeated,* two much anthologised short stories, implies what is a common opinion: what Hemingway is *good* at, this opinion goes, is the direct rendering of brutal, violent action. What such critics refuse to condone is the metaphysical Hemingway, the Hemingway of a profound naturalistic vision of man and his place in the scheme of things. What they overlook is that the same Hemingway is present in the early stories, from *In Our Time* onwards, where Nick heals the wounds of the war by immersing himself in nature, and that to fail to see this is to fail in appreciation of such short stories as *The Undefeated* where the theme of struggle and endurance is treated within a more limited compass. All Hemingway did in *The Old Man and the Sea* was to expose some more of the usually submerged section of the iceberg. But it was always there.

The value of concentrating on the empiricism and behaviourism latent in Hemingway's naturalism, as I explained earlier, is that they help to reveal that in its main outline his vision remained constant, albeit some metaphysical doubts concerning Christian religion, divination or extrasensory perception obtrude from time to time. Behaviourism borrows from empiricism and is the ally of the naturalistic philosophy founded on the Darwinian theory of evolution which, using the empirical methods of science, sees man as a particular kind of animal, whose thinking and feeling are an integral part of the biological process of interacting with his environment in the struggle to survive.[27] It is this struggle which Hemingway explores in his art. Empiricism and behaviourism are the hidden framework which shapes at once his style and his vision.

To see Hemingway in this light is to see him as an artist worthy of serious critical consideration because, namely, he is not a mere "teller of good yarns" but has an important representative function, because he is a vehicle by or through which an intellectual tradition, which has at its centre a particular vision of man, is conveyed with the power unique to art. As Terry Eagleton has remarked, quoting Matisse, "All art bears the imprint of its historical epoch, but . . . great art is that in which the imprint is most deeply marked."[28]

NOTES

1. David Hume, *Enquiry concerning Human Understanding*, ed. L. A. Selby-Bigge, (Oxford: Oxford University Press, 1975), p. 22.
2. John Passmore, *One Hundred Years of Philosophy* (Penguin, 1968), chapter 2.
3. David Hume, *A Treatise of Human Nature*, ed. L. A. Selby-Bigge (London: Clarendon Press, 1888), p. xv–xvi.
4. Hume, *A Treatise of Human Nature*, p. xvi.
5. Charles A. Fenton, *The Apprenticeship of Ernest Hemingway*, (New York, 1954), p. 88.
6. *A Farewell to Arms*, published in 1929, was the book that helped make the young Hemingway famous. Other novels referred to in this chapter are: *The Sun Also Rises*, also known as *Fiesta*, published 1926; *For Whom the Bell Tolls*, 1940; *The Old Man and the Sea*, 1951. Reference is also made to two collections of short stories, *In Our Time*, 1925, and *Men Without Women*, 1929. A non-fiction work, *Death in the Afternoon*, dealing mainly with bullfighting, was published in 1932.
7. *Fiesta (The Sun Also Rises)*, (London: Pan book edition), p. 76–7.
8. *A Farewell to Arms*, (London: Penguin Books edition), p. 144.
9. *For Whom the Bell Tolls*, (Penguin), p. 54.
10. *A Farewell to Arms*, p. 14.
11. *A Treatise of Human Nature*, p. 499–500.
12. *Farewell*, p. 25.
13. *Farewell*, p. 251.
14. Tony Tanner, *The Reign of Wonder* has a fine chapter on Hemingway.
15. *Fiesta*, p. 139.
16. *The Short Happy Life of Francis Macomber*, first published in 1936 in *Cosmopolitan* magazine; this quotation is from Penguin edition, p. 39.
17. *Death in the Afternoon*, (London: Penguin), p. 8.
18. *For Whom the Bell Tolls*, (London: Penguin), p. 304.
19. "The Undefeated" in *Men Without Women*, (London: Penguin), p. 36.

20. *Farewell*, p. 176.
21. *For Whom the Bell Tolls*, p. 313.
22. "A Clean Well-lighted Place" in *The Short Happy Life of Francis Macomber*, p. 72.
23. *Fiesta*, p. 10.
24. In an interview printed in *Writers at Work*, (London: Penguin), p. 193.
25. *The Old Man and the Sea*, p. 46.
26. Review of *The Old Man and the Sea* by P. Toynbee, reprinted in *Twentieth Century Interpretations*, (London: Prentice Hall), p. 112.
27. This is the contention of Chomsky, for example, on the question of language acquisition.
28. Terry Eagleton, *Marxism and Literary Criticism*, p. 3.

Chapter Seven

Conversion in *Anna Karenina*

To the best of my knowledge the theme of religious conversion has not been much explored in serious English fiction. Moral change and development and even moral conversion have been explored in depth in the best work in the British tradition—indeed this is such a commonplace that to cite particular authors would be misleading. But when one searches for examples of the fictional treatment of specifically religious conversion one is hard pressed to find one novel that answers to the object of the search. The novels of authors as disparate as D. H. Lawrence, Iris Murdoch and Graham Greene arise for consideration only to be discounted. Even Conrad's profound investigations of human identity lack the religious dimension that alone would justify the inclusion of his novels on any index of world literature dealing with religious conversion.

This is perhaps more surprising than at first may appear when one considers that novels—serious novels at least—frequently chart their protagonists' search for meaning in life and that for many important historical personages such a search has culminated in religious conversion. Think for a moment of the impact of religious conversion on the lives of such influential personalities, within the perspective of Western European history, as Paul of Tarsus, Augustine of Hippo, Martin Luther, Ignatius Loyola, Soren Kierkegaard and Leo Tolstoy. The list could be added to, and doubtless the reader can think of other, perhaps less exalted, personalities who have undergone some form of profound spiritual transformation. But even as it stands this list of famous "converts" is sufficient to suggest something of the complex character of conversion: a personal upheaval that is at the same time the attainment of a settled vantage point; the achievement of a spiritual and psychological integration that also marks a profound change in one's outlook and in the direction of one's life.

If moral seriousness is the hallmark of the "great tradition" among English novelists,[1] the tradition of the Russian novel has been of a more religious and metaphysical temper. And it is in one of the greatest of Russian novels, *Anna Karenina*, that we find an imaginative exploration of the theme of religious conversion that stands comparison with such a "locus classicus" in the religious literature on the subject as Saint Augustine's *Confessions*. *Anna Karenina* is particularly worthy of study because it records not one but three examples of religious conversion; study of these three distinct episodes shall, I feel, throw light on both authentic and inauthentic conversion and what it is that distinguishes them.

Anna Karenina is, in starkest outline, the story of two contrasting journeys: on the one side is Anna's journey towards suicide following the breakdown of her marriage to Karenin under the impact of her love affair with Vronsky, a captain in the army; on the other side is the uncertain journey of Levin, a landowner alive to the issues and events of the day, towards achieved happiness in marriage to Kitty and, even more uncertainly, towards fulfilment in religious faith. Much, however, happens on the way. The range of experiences covered in the novel is immense: marriage, love, seduction, childbirth and death; aristocratic society disporting itself at the opera, at balls, at the races; there is the delightful rendering of strenuous physical exertion such as skating, mowing, hunting or horse riding; finally, the novel covers a wide range of the ideas hotly debated in contemporary Russian society, but the ideas are less obtrusive than in *War and Peace* where they tend at times to supplant the art. *Anna Karenina* is not a novel of ideas but a novel in which ideas play a part. Indeed, so tumultuous is the life of this epic novel that we can sympathise with the early English assessment of it as an unartistic, sprawling "piece of life," the verdict of Matthew Arnold;[2] a kind of "fluid pudding" defiant of "economy and architecture," which was the perception of Henry James.[3] Neither of these distinguished critics grasped what a finely constructed, symmetrically balanced work of art *Anna Karenina* is, because they failed to detect Tolstoy's method of operation. The method of Tolstoy's art in this novel is accurately described by the author in a letter to his friend Strakhov:

> In everything, almost everything, that I have written what guided me was the need to gather together (i.e., establish the links between) thoughts that were interconnected; each idea, expressed in words on its own, loses its meaning, is terribly impoverished by being taken out of the "linking" in which it is found. The linking itself is achieved not, I think, by ideas but by something else, and to convey the nature of this linking in words is impossible; it can only be done indirectly, by words describing images, actions, situations.[4]

In *Anna Karenina* "relatedness is all"; as Greenwood puts it, "Every incident in this book tells upon some other incident."[5] The significance of the novel rests on the comparisons and contrasts, similarities and dissimilarities that subtly weave the book into a unit both at the level of scenes and episodes and at the level of characterisation. There are, for instance, subtle "family resemblances" between Anna and her brother Stiva, Kitty and her sister Dolly, Levin and his brother Nikolai, yet, as is the way in families, each member of these three pairs of characters is strikingly different from the other. The novel is Tolstoy's most mature artistic achievement, free from the pamphleteering that mars its immediate predecessor, *War and Peace*, and not yet hamstrung by the heavy didacticism that limits his later works.

In selecting any one theme from this novel for close examination there is real danger of mutilating or distorting what is a delicate and intricate artistic unit. Nevertheless the literary critic is condemned to select; having said that, he or she would be well advised to bear Tolstoy's words in mind and to point to the links by means of which the book is organised. This can, I believe, be usefully done in respect of religious conversion, which occurs in *Anna Karenina* on three specific occasions. First, there is the conversion of Kitty; then there is the conversion of Karenin, which has certain similarities to Kitty's but also some important differences; finally there is one of the novel's great climactic moments, the conversion of Levin. There is, of course, a fourth conversion, that of Levin's brother Nikolai as he lies dying, but for reasons I shall explain, I shall treat this as being more helpfully considered as a dimension or aspect of the climactic conversion of Levin.

Kitty's conversion has an adolescent quality, it marks a stage in her personal development. It occurs while she is on the rebound from a personally suffered disaster. When abroad recovering from illness brought on by the shame and humiliation of her disappointed love for Vronsky, Kitty comes under the influence of the religious Madam Stahl and her adopted daughter, Varenka. It is Varenka's goodness and simplicity that first attract her. And then

> Kitty made the acquaintance of Madam Stahl, too, and this acquaintance, together with her friendship with Varenka, not only had a great influence on her, it was also a comfort in her mental distress. She found this comfort through a completely new world being opened to her by means of this acquaintance, a world that had nothing in common with her past, an exalted, noble world, from the heights of which she could contemplate her past calmly. It was revealed to her that besides the instinctive life to which she had given herself up hitherto there was a spiritual life. This life was disclosed in religion, but a religion having nothing in common with the religion Kitty had known since childhood.... This was a lofty, mysterious religion connected with a whole series of noble thoughts and feelings, a religion one could do more than merely believe in because one was told to—it was a religion one could love.[6]

Kitty begins to copy Varenka's good deeds to such an extent that her mother, Princess Shcherbatsky, notices that she also copies Varenka's "manner of walking, of talking, of blinking her eyes" (p. 244). But the charm of Kitty's new life is poisoned by life's little complications, by the intractable quality of human experience. When the sick artist, Petrov, forms an emotional attachment to Kitty (his "sister-of-mercy"), his wife becomes jealous. Then a few down to earth words about Madame Stahl from Kitty's father have the power to change Kitty's naive perception of that lady's worth. "All that was left was a woman with short legs, who lay on couches because she had a bad figure, and who martyrized poor patient Varenka for not arranging her rug to her liking. And by no effort of imagination could Kitty bring back the former Madame Stahl." (p. 251)

Taking stock, Kitty realizes the artificiality of her newly adopted practices. Rounding on Varenka, she calls in question her own motives—"To appear better to people, to myself, to God, to deceive everyone. No, I won't descend to that again! I'll be bad; but at any rate not a liar, a humbug! I can't act except from the heart, but you act from principle." (p. 255).

While retaining her affection for Varenka, Kitty, though "she did not give up everything she had learned, . . . realized that she had deceived herself in supposing she could be what she wanted to be. Her eyes were opened, as it were; she felt without hypocrisy or boastfulness all the difficulty of maintaining herself on the pinnacle to which she had wished to rise." (p. 256)

Tolstoy's presentment of this immature conversion is confident and convincing. There is Kitty's vulnerable condition and readiness to be impressed; there is the sheer idealised loftiness of Madame Stahl's religious position (no one knows whether she is Catholic, Protestant or Orthodox), which sets it *above* the common concerns and everyday toil of humanity; and there is the character of Varenka. In her other-worldliness Varenka is not quite human. She sings beautifully but is quite unmoved by the praise this evokes. "She seemed only to be asking: 'Am I to sing again, or is that enough?'"(p. 239). It is a quality of remoteness from normal human affection and spontaneity that is shared by Koznyshev, Levin's half brother, and, significantly, both share a sense of relief when, later in the novel, Koznyshev fails to make the marriage proposal to Varenka that for some time had appeared foreordained and inevitable. (The contrasting scene with this set piece is Levin's famous proposal to Kitty.)

But Kitty's conversion, immature as it is and impossible to sustain in the rarefied atmosphere of Madame Stahl's entourage, is not simply a passing mood. It is true that Kitty has never lost her religious faith, unlike Levin, but her conversion is of the order of a psychological and spiritual adjustment, a necessary corrective and purgative to restore her psychological and spiritual equilibrium which the shame of her frustrated love for Vronsky had upset. It marks a return to inner resources, a reassessment of the importance of spiritual values in recoil from Count Vronsky who had little to commend him save her mother's high estimation of his social station and great wealth. Once she is restored to the sanity and normality of family life, Kitty can put the experience into perspective, overcome her dependency on Varenka and dispose of external props; once she is happily married to Levin Kitty gets on with the everyday responsibility of running a household and the hothouse atmosphere of her conversion is left behind. But the experience has left its mark; like Levin, Kitty has to struggle to achieve the level of maturity which will allow her to realize the calling that befits her character.

Karenin's conversion is like Kitty's in that it occurs when he is attempting to come to terms with deeply felt hurt and shame—in this case the revelation of his wife's love affair with Vronsky. Karenin's initial response to the realization that his wife might be forming an attachment to another man is self-regarding and legalistic.

> "And the worst of it all," he thought, "is that now, just as my work is nearing completion (he was thinking of the project he was bringing forward at the time), when I need peace of mind and all my energies, this idiotic anxiety has to fall on me.... The question of her feelings, of what has taken place or may take place in her heart, is not my affair but the affair of her conscience, and comes under the heading of religion," he said to himself, feeling relieved at having found the category of regulating principles to which the newly-arisen situation rightly belonged. (p. 160)

When the incident at the horse-race forces the affair out into the open between them, Karenin's advice to his wife is that she "conform outwardly to propriety until such time ... as I take measures to secure my honour" (p. 232). Throughout the episode of Anna's break with Karenin the latter's first thought is invariably for his name, reputation and social position. (Vronsky, by contrast, is willing to sacrifice his career for Anna.) Religion, when it enters into the argument, initially does so only as an afterthought that lends weight to his embittered and legalistic desire that Anna should be punished. Religion is used merely as an endorsement of his desires and his instinct for self-preservation.

But the break between Anna and Karenin is not swift and clean cut. There are many moments of "wobbling"; for a long time the characters oscillate between contrasting possible outcomes, a typically Tolstoyan situation that sustains the dramatic tension at a high pitch. (Also Tolstoyan is the juxtaposition of the scenes depicting the instability of the Anna-Vronsky-Karenin relationship with those portraying Levin's and Kitty's achievement of the stability of marriage and Kitty's forgiveness of Levin's "immoral" past). Chancing to meet Vronsky at what both men suppose to be Anna's deathbed, Karenin follows the spontaneous impulse of his heart on the moment, forgives Anna and, at her fevered request, shakes hands with Vronsky. Matthew Arnold sees the impulse to forgive as an instance of grace at work.

> Hard at first, formal, cruel, thinking only of himself, Karenine who, as I have said, has a conscience, is touched by grace at the moment when Anna's troubles reach their height. He returns to her to find her with a child just born to her and Wronsky, the lover in the house and Anna apparently dying. Karenine has words of kindness and forgiveness only. The noble and victorious effort transfigures him, and all that her husband gains in the eyes of Anna, her lover Wronsky loses.[7]

But this account of the matter is oversimple. F. R. Leavis sees more acutely the complexity of feeling present in this strange scene, which in its combination of profound psychological insight with the unexpected is surely one of the most subtly brilliant in the whole of literature.

> The way we take the scene (says Leavis), its moral and human significance for us, is conditioned by all that goes before, and this has established what Karenin is, what Anna is, and what, inexorably, the relations between them must be. We know him as, in the pejorative Laurentian sense, a purely "social" being, ego-bound, self-important. . . . Karenin's inability to bear the spectacle of acute distress and suffering (especially, we have been told, in a woman) doesn't impress us as an unequivocal escape from the ego: that disconcerting fact is what, added to Vronsky's repellent and horribly convincing humiliation, makes the scene so atrociously unpleasant.[8]

Leavis's commentary is closer to the mark, but is in danger of overstating the confidence of the reader's expectation that a final, irreparable break between Anna and Karenin has been accomplished; it is to reduce the subtlety of Tolstoy's art to suggest that we are allowed to adopt a settled viewpoint at this stage. What is certain is that throughout this protracted episode the actions of both of the men in Anna's life are fraught with ironical ambiguity; the nobler sentiments and gestures of each somehow fail to evoke a fully sympathetic response; to each is attached a sufficient modicum of the bogus to make their deeds and words ring just less than true. This is the case with Vronsky's attempt at suicide by shooting himself. It also undercuts the pathos of, for instance, Karenin's self-denying concession to Oblonsky on the question of a divorce (which he later retracts): "It was bitter, there was shame in his heart, but with this bitterness and shame he experienced a sense of joy and emotion at the depth of his own humility." (p. 457–8)

It is when Karenin is most isolated, with Anna recovered and gone abroad to live with Vronsky, that the Countess Lydia Ivanovna presents herself to Karenin (who had quite forgotten her by this time), offering to take charge of his household and proffering the consolations of her new, ecstatic and exclusive religion. Tolstoy's treatment of Karenin, as always, is not without sympathy. He is bereft of friends and, though he is not yet aware of it, his professional advancement has come to an end; socially vulnerable, he is the mocked cuckold, upon whom even the footman appears to smile with derision. It is quite understandable that he should succumb to the wiles of the Countess. "For him she was the one islet not of kindly feeling only but of affection in the ocean of hostility and ridicule that surrounded him" (p. 545). Nevertheless, his conversion is the very contrary of an act of self-transcendence; rather it is thoroughly self-accommodating, intended to shore up his ego and social position at a point of crisis.

"But for Karenin it was a necessity to think thus: it was so essential to him in his humiliation to have some elevated standpoint, however imaginary, from which, looked down upon by all, he could look down on others, that he clung to this delusion of salvation as if it were the real thing." (p. 539)

As Greenwood observes, one of Tolstoy's deftest artistic touches is to present the false religiosity of the Countess Lydia's menage through the eyes of Oblonsky.[9] It is not the abrasive Levin but the worldly, indulgent, but essentially honest Stiva who "places" for the reader the religious atmosphere of Lydia Ivanovna: it is too easy, too comfortable. Perhaps Tolstoy's most damning comment on Karenin's conversion is the simple understatement, "Karenin did not find the conversion difficult." (p. 539)

Levin's conversion near the end of the novel is an altogether more momentous event than either Kitty's or Karenin's and its difference from these is instructive. One of the novel's great dramatic climaxes, it is presented as *the* point of contrast with Anna's suicide. All the preceding sections of the book are a preparation for these two events. From the outset Levin's quest for significance in life, for what it is that makes life worth living, is a thread running through the novel and binding it together, establishing it as an artistic unit. This serious quest for meaning and purpose, and not unrelated to this, Levin's and Kitty's joint attainment of marital happiness, are assigned a certain normative status in the novel; it is by being held against them that the other characters and the other man-woman relationships are placed and, implicitly, judged.

The sheer inconvenience of Levin's single-minded quest for significance, and for the consistency between his personal and his public life such significance demands, is clear from the outset. From his first introduction his self-consciousness and relative detachment from conventional social mores are manifest in the mixture of timidity and irritability that besets him in society. Compared with Oblonsky, charming and worldly, and Vronsky, aloof and obviously "superior," Levin is at once prickly and gauche, prey to fits of blushing and the clumsy asker of unwelcome questions. Oblonsky enlivens social gatherings; as a social mixer and good fellow he is spontaneously adept, and he has the genial tolerance towards the faults of others his marital infidelities and easygoing ways render convenient. Early on he points to the difference between himself and Levin (whom he is addressing):

> There, you see, you're very much all of a piece. It's both your strong point and your failing. You are all of a piece and you want the whole of life to be consistent too—but it never is. You scorn public service because you want reality to correspond all the time to the aim—and that's not how it is. You want man's work, too, always to have a definite purpose, and love and family life to be indivisible. But that does not happen either. All the variety, all the charm, all the beauty of life are made up of light and shade. (pp. 55–56)

Levin's quest entails his involvement in the social questions of the day. A life of self-indulgence which his great wealth could make possible is totally repellent: he cannot buy livery for his footman or enjoy a lavish meal in Moscow without converting the cost into the man-hours worked by a peasant in the field. Much of the book is devoted to his search for a new way of life, a life of common toil with the peasantry, for a new relationship between landowner and peasant, for new methods of husbanding and developing the natural resources of the Russian countryside. "The entire condition of farming and, above all, the condition of the people as a whole must be completely transformed. In the place of poverty we must have universal prosperity and contentment; instead of hostility—harmony and unity of interests. In short, a bloodless revolution, but a mighty revolution, beginning in the little circle of our district, then reaching the province, Russia, the whole world!" (p. 369)

Whatever our view of the Levin-Tolstoy proposal for a new social order, the point I wish to stress here is that Levin's quest entails engagement in the greatest practical detail with issues of social justice and environmental concern, and those critics who object to the disproportionate amount of space Tolstoy devotes to "farming methods" are guilty of a critical oversight. Contrasting with Levin's concern is Oblonsky's amusingly honest (and the amusement stems from the self-evident limitations of the honesty) summing up of his stance: "It comes to this, my dear boy: one must do one of the two things—either accept the existing social order as a just one, and then stick up for your rights; or acknowledge that you are enjoying unfair privileges, as I do, and get all the pleasure out of them you can." (p. 620)

Needless to say, Levin is not satisfied with this: "No, if one had no right to them one could not enjoy these advantages—at least I could not. The great thing for me is not to feel that I am in the wrong." But while rejecting Oblonsky's sybaritic pragmatism, Levin is troubled by the retort that he, Levin, acts justly only in a negative sense.

Levin's journey through the book is propelled by the ceaseless stream of questions that he raises about himself, his honesty, his sincerity, his relationship with the peasants, his relationship with aristocratic Russian society, about marriage, Communism, death, the meaning of life. He attempts to meet each question with an almost abrasive honesty that challenges any temptation to complacency either with regard to his own situation or the conventional wisdom of his social peers. The result is that the identity he achieves by the end of the novel is something he has worked out and made for himself. With Vronsky it is quite other. He takes his values and his code of conduct from the institution with which he identifies—the army. If there is always something suspect about Vronsky's lavish gestures—his gift of two hundred roubles to the widow of the killed railway guard, his attempted suicide, his founding of a hospital, the recruitment of his own private regiment to fight in the Crimea, his public mourning (with the "broad-brimmed black hat")—it is because of the unmistakable feeling (there is nothing over-explicit in Tolstoy's narrative) that, however laudable in themselves, they are performed with an eye to society's approval. Vronsky's identity is, largely, conferred on him; it comes from without, from the institution he belongs to—the army.

> Vronsky's life was particularly happy in that he had a code of principles, which defined with unfailing certitude what should and should not be done. This code of principles covered only a very small circle of contingencies, but in return the principles were never obscure, and Vronsky, as he never went outside that circle, had never had a moment's hesitation about doing what he ought to do. This code categorically ordained that gambling debts must be paid, the tailor need not be. . . . These principles might be irrational and not good, but they were absolute and in complying with them Vronsky felt at ease and could hold his head high. Only quite lately, in regard to his relations with Anna, Vronsky had begun to feel that his code did not quite meet all circumstances and that the future presented doubts and difficulties for which he could find no guiding thread. (p. 327)

The habit of questioning is absent in Vronsky and this is not unconnected with the fact that his attempts at painting are nothing more than "a gift for copying." His praise for the paintings of a true artist, Mihailov,—"There's technique for you"—gives him away and significantly draws Mihailov's angry scowl: the true artist does not simply learn a technique and then apply it; the notion of artistic vision is foreign to Vronsky.

It is the death of his brother, Nikolai, dissolute and disagreeable but beloved as a brother and fired, like himself, with the serious desire to transform society, that forces Levin to face the larger question of life's meaning. Despite his silly arrogance and dissipation, Nikolai is a man of genuine feeling and in many ways Levin's *alter ego* (the point of contrast here is the half-brother, Koznyshev). The brothers understand each other's deepest thoughts and feelings even when no words are spoken, and it is this unavoidable and painful psychological affinity which makes Nicolai's death such a decisive event in Levin's life. The "conversion" his brother experiences on his death bed is, in terms of the novel's overall orchestration, part of the movement that culminates in the conversion of Levin: it is like a prelude or overture, introducing the theme without working it through or bringing it to a resolution. In the end we are left hanging, cut off, unsure of Nikolai's state of mind at the moment of death.

As he advances towards death Nikolai's mood oscillates wildly—as it had in life—between bouts of fervent piety and contemptuous rejection of religion. Having received the sacrament at Kitty's bidding and experienced a temporary remission, he suffers a relapse and, clutching his bottle of medicine, addresses Levin once Kitty has left the room."'I went through that farce for her sake. She is so sweet; but you and I can't deceive ourselves. This is what I pin my faith to,' he said and, squeezing the bottle in his hand, he began breathing over it." (p. 527)

Like Levin's, Nikolai's faith had been shaken by modern science, but his over-stated rationalism is penetrated by Kitty's unqualified, matter-of-fact love, as without fuss or fanfare she nurses him and tends to his needs. Levin is struck by the fact that the enigma of death, which in common with other "great and virile minds" he had long pondered without reaching any satisfactory conclusions, is something that Kitty and Agatha Mihalovna, the old housekeeper, understand intuitively—like "millions of other people" (p. 523).

While Levin is "involuntarily meditating" with the dying Nikolai he becomes aware

> that something was becoming clearer and clearer to the dying man which for Levin remained as obscure as ever.
>
> "Yes, yes, that is so!" slowly murmured the dying man, pausing between words.
>
> "Wait a moment." Again he was silent.
>
> "Right!" he suddenly said in a slow tone of relief, as if all had become clear to him.
>
> "Oh God!" he muttered with a heavy sigh. (p. 528)

The exact nature of the "revelation" experienced by Nikolai is not clear to Levin or the reader, but "It seemed to him (Levin) that he was already lagging far behind his dying brother." (p. 529)

After Nikolai's death Levin does not leave his social concerns behind but his thinking moves on to a higher plane as, painfully, he drags his life round to encounter the issues raised by the fact of death. An unbeliever, he had found the business of confession prior to marriage hypocritical and objectionable. But the death of Nikolai and the birth of his son almost a year later begin to break down his rational objections.

> He only knew and felt that what was happening was similar to what had happened a year ago at the deathbed in a provincial hotel of his brother Niko-

lai. Only that had been sorrow and this was joy. But that sorrow and this joy was equally beyond the usual plane of existence: they were like openings through which something sublime became visible. And what was being accomplished now, as in that other moment, was accomplished harshly and painfully; and in contemplation of this sublime something the soul soared to heights it had never attained before, while reason lagged behind, unable to keep up. (p. 746)

From the time of his wife's confinement Levin's tussle with Christianity begins in earnest. Without being able to say how it happened, he finds that between the ages of twenty and thirty-four he had substituted science for religion.

The organism, its decay, the indestructibility of matter, the law of the conservation of energy, evolution, were the terms that had superseded those of his early faith. These terms and the theories associated with them were very useful for intellectual purposes. But they gave no guidance for life, and Levin suddenly felt like a person who has exchanged his warm fur coat for a muslin garment, and out in the frost for the first time is immediately convinced, not by arguments but with his whole being that he is as good as naked and must inevitably perish miserably. (p. 820)

But doubts never leave him and, while he is attracted to the Church, the disunity of the Churches disillusions him. Things get to such a pitch, and indeed so great is his demand for an answer to his deepest yearnings, that although happily married and in good health Levin has to hide the rope and refrain from going out with a gun for fear of hanging or shooting himself. The temptation to suicide is commensurate with the seriousness of his metaphysical quest.

Leaving off questioning himself for the time being, busying himself in his other concerns, it is when the old peasant Fiodr speaks that Levin reaches out for the truth:

"Oh well, of course, folks are different. One man lives for his own wants and nothing else—take Nityuka, who thinks of stuffing his belly—but Fohanick is an upright old man. He thinks of his soul. He does not forget God."

"Not forget God? and how does he live for his soul?" Levin almost shouted.

"Why, that's plain enough: it's living rightly, in God's way. Folks are all different, you see . . ." (p. 829)

Levin is overwhelmed by the banality of a truth he instantaneously recognises. He has been living rightly, he concludes, but thinking wrongly. The state of faith he finds himself in is not, he feels, the product of reasoning but something "given to me, revealed to me, and I know it with my heart." At this moment he remembers the Church and all the doctrines it professes and asks, "in order to test himself and bring up everything that could destroy his present sense of security," whether he can believe in them. He finds that there is not "a single article of faith which could disturb the main thing—belief in God, in goodness, as the one goal of man's destiny."

> At the back of every article of faith of the Church could be put belief in serving truth rather than one's personal needs. And each of these dogmas not only did not violate that creed but was essential for the fulfilment of the greatest of miracles, continually manifest upon earth—the miracle that made it possible for the world with its millions of individual human beings, sages and simpletons ... to comprehend with certainty one and the same truth and live that life of the spirit, the only life that is worth living and which alone we prize.
>
> Lying on his back, he was now gazing high up into the cloudless sky . . . (p. 834)

Images of light, of light replacing or illuminating the darkness, are repeatedly associated with Levin (and Kitty) in the book's closing scenes. There is an insistent emphasis on the vault of the sky, cloudless and blue or lit up with lightning or picked out with stars, as the symbolic expression of Levin's overwhelming sensation of expansive life. This is deliberately contrasted with the world of Anna, which at the close is diminished to the guttering candle casting its grotesque and distorting shadows on the walls and ceiling of her bedroom. That the contrast between the enlarged world of Levin and the shrunken world of Anna is intentional can be seen from Tolstoy's deliberate selection of the rare word *svecha* (candle), a diminutive of the Russian word for "light" (*svet*) which also means "world" or "society."[10] Levin and Anna are approximately equal forces in the book moving in pointedly opposite directions with a fatality based on the iron laws of morality. That surely is the significance of Anna's recurring dream of a little old man or peasant leaning over iron rails or hammering against iron and muttering, "Il faut le battre, le fer; le broyer, le petrir. . . ."; this sinister image (Vronsky has the same dream and is filled with terror when Anna recounts her experience) portends the disaster; the harsh, violent words represent Anna's wish fulfilment that the iron laws can be remoulded, bent, changed, but the wish is futile and Anna, significantly, meets death on the iron rails.

Tolstoy realizes Anna as a beautiful, sensitive woman, responsive to art and at once vigorous and delicate in her deportment, but his portrayal has the unsentimental detachment of art and at the end she has become an "impossible woman," for whom the stream of ordinary life has become repulsive, the light of whose life has gone out (Vronsky in an early scene shut out the light from the flickering lamp outside), overtaken by a deadening nihilism. Levin like Anna was tempted to suicide but finds the solution to his search in faith and instead of suicide experiences an expansion of life, his horizon now illumined and enlarged, reaching out to infinity but enclosing also his ongoing social concerns.

Anna Karenina is far from being a simple-minded endorsement of religion or faith or conversion as such. The do-gooding of Madame Stahl is amusingly exposed; Kitty's "conversion" is more akin to a reassessment of her values and outlook; the influence of the pious Countess Lydia Ivanovna is ugly and insidious; while Karenin's conversion is a convenient prop and solace for wounded pride. Some forms of religious transformation are clearly judged to be odious, in particular those that result in the converted being deemed to be above or beyond the mass of the people. The religious conversion vindicated in the novel is Levin's because it is the fruit of a serious quest for meaning, the outcome of continuous questioning and searching for full and satisfactory answers; it remains in touch with ordinary life; the impulse behind it is not to set apart the saved or the chosen but to unite and draw men together. Not every kind of religious conversion is considered authentic, but only conversion that is genuinely self-transcending, free of self-gratification and narrow self-accommodation. Tolstoy's artistic presentment of Levin "feeling outwards and inwards" (to borrow Leavis's phrase) in response to the over-riding drive for fulfilment is profoundly convincing.

Leavis, however, draws our attention to the limitations of Levin-Tolstoy's "solution" at the end of the book.

> His (Levin's) sense of problems to be solved focuses on the one hand (in terms of social responsibility) on the peasants, and on the other on his own need for religious belief. Or can we say that the peasants have become, at the close of the book, something like a comprehensive focus? . . . the problems seem merging into one. The solution is to live with the peasants, to be a peasant among peasants. His problem of "belief" he sees as to be solved by his achieving the naive "belief" of the peasants. And this, in a curiously simple way, he identifies with being "good."[11]

Leavis is right to draw attention to the simple-minded quality of the solutions offered in the book to both the problem of belief and the problem of what might constitute a correct social order. The simplicity of the peasant always held a fascination for Tolstoy and the peasant's supposed good sense becomes a final court of appeal in almost all the polemical and prophetic writings which were to occupy him so much during the last thirty years of his long life. The dangers intimated in Levin's "peasant solution" find formulation in his dictum that he had been "living rightly and thinking wrongly." Up to a point this is quite acceptable. But there is no consequent attempt, or intimation of an attempt, to reform and adjust the thinking, to fill it out and complete it, to construct a more durable intellectual framework. The thrust in the novel's closing chapters is distinctly anti-intellectual. The conflict Levin sees between science and religion is not to be overcome by means of a larger synthesis but rather science and religion, thinking and living are to be set at odds with each other. As many critics have noted, we can detect in the closing pages of *Anna Karenina* the seeds of the "old Leo" who came to found his own religion which was in essence a prescription for human behaviour founded on a Christianity shorn of dogmas and mysticism; who was excommunicated by the Russian Orthodox Church; and who denounced his own greatest artistic achievements, including *Anna Karenina*. To explore the development of Tolstoy's life and thinking after *Anna Karenina* would require separate treatment; this chapter must confine itself to what the novel itself gives us. Nevertheless, the question must be asked if the unsatisfactory quality of Levin's proposed solution to his problems at the close of *Anna Karenina* invalidates or undermines Tolstoy's account of Levin's religious conversion.

I think not. Lonergan makes an important distinction, particularly helpful in the present context, between conversion and the faith it gives rise to, on the one hand, and belief, on the other. True conversion is the fruit of self-transcendence, a falling in love with God. Faith is the knowledge born of religious love, an orientation to mystery, a recognition of God as the originating value so that the human good is absorbed in an all-embracing good. Belief, on the other hand, is the interpretation of that orientation to mystery. It consists in accepting and subscribing to particular judgments of fact and value, particular teachings and doctrines.[12] This distinction helps us to grasp how it is that Levin-Tolstoy could hold onto faith but dispense with the traditional doctrines of the Christian Church.

At this point we would do well to recall that Tolstoy had read Matthew Arnold's religious writings, and had been drawn to Arnold's account of Christianity as being, at heart, about right conduct, about the quest for righteousness, about behaviour. The traditional beliefs and doctrines of Christianity were consigned by Arnold to the realm of "aberglaube" or "extra-beliefs," fairy-tales that could be dropped or treasured simply as "poetry" without harm being done to what Christianity essentially stood for. When he had read Arnold's *Literature and Dogma* (1873), Tolstoy remarked that "Half of M. Arnold's thoughts are my own. I rejoice to read him."[13] It would be true to say that Arnold's reductive approach has failed to gain the support of most Christian scholars or theologians, who have found that it does not measure up to what we actually find in the bible or the New Testament. The same might be said of Tolstoy's somewhat Arnoldian stance towards Jesus and Christianity.[14]

However, the distinction between faith and belief drawn by Lonergan allows us, I think, to share Leavis's profound misgivings about the quality of Levin's proposed "peasant solution" while accepting that Tolstoy has, in the case of Levin, faithfully depicted the texture and structure of authentic religious conversion. The reductionism implicit in Levin's formulation of his new found faith ("At the back of every article of faith of the Church could be put . . .") is suggestive of how Tolstoy was to interpret his own conversion; but the formulation can legitimately be distinguished from the experience of conversion itself. As far as Levin's conversion is concerned ("'Not forget God? and how does he live for his soul?' Levin almost shouted . . .")—bearing in mind the propelling force and the motives behind the question—*Anna Karenina* presents us with the real thing.

NOTES

1. When asked, shortly before his death, what the drive was behind his writing, D. H. Lawrence said, "One writes out of one's moral sense; for the race, as it were." Quoted by F. R. Leavis in *Anna Karenina and Other Essays* (London: Chatto and Windus, 1973), p. 12.Leavis goes on to define "moral" as "the distinctive preoccupation with ultimate questions."

2. Matthew Arnold, "Count Leo Tolstoi" in *Essays in Criticism*, Second Series, first published 1897 , (London: Macmillan & Co., 1921), p. 260.

3. Quoted in F. R. Leavis, *Anna Karenina' and other Essays* (Chatto and Windus, 1973), p. 9–10.

4. Letter to N. N. Strakhov in *Tolstoy's Letters*, Vol. 1, edited by R. F. Christian (London: 1978), p. 296–7.

5. E. B. Greenwood, *Tolstoy: the Comprehensive Vision* (London: Routledge, 1975), p. 105.

6. Leo Tolstoy, *Anna Karenina*, translated by Rosemary Edmonds, (London: Penguin edition, 1954), p. 242. All quotations from the novel are from this edition.

7. Matthew Arnold, "Count Leo Tolstoi" in op. cit., p. 271. Arnold appears to have read the French edition of *Anna Karenina*.

8. F. R. Leavis*, Anna Karenina and Other Essays*, p. 17–18.

9. E. B. Greenwood, op. cit., p. 106.

10. Barbara Hardy, *The Appropriate Form*, (first published 1964, London: Bloomsbury edition 2013) p. 212f.

11. F. R. Leavis, op. cit., p. 27–28.

12. Lonergan, *Method in Theology*, p. 115–119.

13. Henry Gifford, *Tolstoy,* (Oxford: Oxford University Press, 1982), p. 46.

14. Where Arnold and Tolstoy differ is in their proposed solutions to the problems they diagnose in their respective societies. Arnold sympathises with "the workers" but does not believe that, as things stand, they are fit or ready for government. Tolstoy, by contrast, threw in his lot—including his intellect—with the peasantry. The two men, Tolstoy and Arnold, had actually met, in March 1861, when Tolstoy visited England. At Tolstoy's request, Arnold, as chief inspector of schools, furnished him with a letter of introduction to seven state schools in London, which Tolstoy was keen to visit in an effort to understand how public education was conducted in England. See A. N. Wilson, *Tolstoy*, (London: Penguin books, 1989), p. 161.

Conclusion

I chose to conclude this book with the two essays on, respectively, the novels of Hemingway and *the great* novel of Tolstoy because I wished to offer the reader practical examples of how literary criticism works, how it builds up a case slowly by attending to a variety of specific incidents or features and how it is that a judgment eventually emerges. In this way I wanted the reader to appropriate and make her own the critical method or method of inquiry of both Leavis and Lonergan—for each emphasizes the fact that all of us have within us the intellectual and moral resources and capacity to form critical judgments of our own. And, in the context of literary criticism, I have attempted to develop an appreciation of Leavis's criterion of "life." For it is ultimately in relation to this criterion that the reader will be challenged to form an overall judgment of the art of Hemingway and the art of Tolstoy. And it seems to me, based on my detailed analyses in these essays, that Leavis is justified in commenting negatively on Hemingway's "bent towards a simplifying reduction of life." This contrasts markedly with Leavis's exalted valuation of *Anna Karenina*, which he calls "the greatest of novels" and "the great novel of modern—of our—civilization."[1]

The extent of Leavis's admiration for *Anna Karenina* can be measured by his refusal to go along with D. H. Lawrence's comments on the Anna-Vronsky love affair and Lawrence's criticism of Tolstoy's art. Leavis not only admired Lawrence greatly as a novelist but also considered him a "marvellously perceptive critic" whose views on art and writers he frequently quotes with enthusiastic approval. But Lawrence on *Anna Karenina* is an exception. As Leavis sees clearly, Lawrence was inclined to see the Anna-Vronsky affair as analogous to his own love affair with Frieda, and this is a "simplification" that Leavis, with detailed references to the novel, refuses to accept or condone.[2] He sums up his admiration for Tolstoy's art by saying,

"All the book is a feeling out, and a feeling inwards, for an adequate sense of the nature of life and its implicit laws, to break which entails the penalty."[3]

The life in *Anna Karenina* is without question more tumultuous, more varied and more comprehensive and inclusive than the life we find in Hemingway. Where Hemingway's vision pares things down to the gratification of the senses and a consequent tough-minded nihilism, Tolstoy opens up whole realms of meaning and whole dimensions of human experience that Hemingway is blind to. The reason is not hard to find. It is because Tolstoy explores human inwardness, the world of interiority, whereas Hemingway focuses almost exclusively on externals, what the senses see, touch and taste. While Lonergan does not speak of "life" as such, he does, in his philosophical way, talk of human consciousness, which he sees as operating at four different levels: the empirical, the intelligent, the rational and the responsible levels. As far as he can, Hemingway keeps the focus on the empirical level to the extent of undercutting and deliberately minimising the intelligent level whenever it appears—natural human inquiry is deliberately quashed and eliminated as something not to be trusted or entertained. Not so in the great Russian novel which presents a huge variety of people working at all of these levels and, furthermore, pushes hard at those ultimate questions—What for? What ultimately for? What do men live by?—with an urgency and depth of insight that are admirable and, frankly, life-enhancing.

In *Insight* Bernard Lonergan invites the reader to appropriate her own cognitional processes when coming to know something. He asks her to embark on a project of using one's self as a source of data, to embark on a journey of discovery (a journey of self-discovery since to truly understand transcendental method is to understand what a human being essentially is) with Lonergan acting as guide—as guide only since the reader has to make the discovery for herself. From Leavis's comments about how we come to have a poem only by an inner kind of possession and his claim that the poem is "there" only in the reader's re-creative response to the black marks on the page, it would appear that he too is using himself as the source of data—he is recollecting and expressing as clearly as he can his own experience when reading and coming to a judgment about a poem or work of literary art. This comes through also in his reply to Rene Wellek, where he makes it clear that the critic, or reader, does not evaluate a poem by means of some external norm but has to fall back on her own resources and creative response to the various elements the poem or work of literary art has to offer. This is what Leavis means by the "third realm": "a realm that is neither merely private and personal nor public in the sense that it can be brought into the laboratory or pointed to"; but nevertheless it "is something in which minds can meet."[4] This is what he is getting at when he talks about the nature of criticism, "the collaborative-creative process in which the poem comes to be established as something 'out there,' of common access in what is in some sense a public world."[5]

From what I have heard of Leavis's method of teaching, this is also the approach he took in his seminars: he did not see himself as a teacher imparting hard knowledge or information to otherwise ignorant minds; rather he looked on his educational task as one of collaboration, of working on a text with a group of students, dating the text and comparing it with others, and *together* coming to a judgment as to its meaning and value. It was a joint creative process (albeit it often turned into a monologue as the students waited to hear their tutor's analysis and verdict). The root of the agreement I detect between Lonergan and Leavis resides in their shared understanding of how understanding and judgment are arrived at, of how true learning takes place. Both are concerned, deeply concerned, with human inwardness or what Lonergan calls "interiority." Both know that it is what is inside a person—their understanding, knowledge and moral character—that will determine how they perform in the public realm; that without that dimension of inwardness, a human person is just an empty husk. And that is, I believe, what most truly unites them and explains their engagement in education and the affinity in their intellectual and moral outlooks which I have attempted to explore in these pages.

If we review the points of affinity between Lonergan and Leavis, what strikes me as most significant is the way in which both authors consider the intellectual and the moral spheres of human activity to be inseparable. This is seen in the criterion of self-transcendence which both consider to be the criterion of objectivity in both spheres: for it is self-transcendence that requires the intellectual inquirer to put aside any merely personal preferences or prejudices and submit to the evidence, and the same criterion operates when a person is faced with a moral choice or a value judgment as to the merits of a literary work of art. In the latter case, as Leavis describes it, the critic must attend to the issue of how well a particular episode or event is artistically realized; it is this that must be allowed to direct and guide the reader's response and evaluation of a poem or novel. In so far as the reader's response is guided by the artistic realisation of an episode or event, the work of art can be said to be enacting its meaning and its value judgments. Again, as both of our authors maintain, the reader's judgment is an intellectual and moral commitment, and as such the reader cannot take over someone else's judgment. It is in being true to the criterion of self-transcendence—a notion Leavis seeks to explore and share by reference to such features as impersonality, disinterestedness, maturity, life, and so forth—that there occurs the morally beneficial outcome of the disciplined study of English literature. As I have said, it is in the personal commitment of the reader at the point of judgment that there occurs the process of moral and intellectual conversion that Leavis sets such store by—what he calls "stocktaking of a peculiarly valuable kind." Both of our authors keep the spotlight on inwardness, on interiority, on intellectual development and moral maturation. This is of vital importance to both. For Lonergan, objectivity in both the intellectual and the moral spheres is simply the consequence of authentic subjectivity; and for Leavis, artistically realised objectivity fosters authentic subjectivity.

To fashion a philosophical position in which self-transcendence or authentic subjectivity is the criterion of intellectual and moral objectivity, both Lonergan and Leavis had to get rid of the obstacles that stood in the way of such a project. For Lonergan this required what has been called "the turn to the subject": the abandonment of the objective notion of "being" as the starting point in one's philosophy and the replacement of such a starting point with a theory of cognition, in which the role of the inquiring subject was paramount. In the case of Leavis, it meant "liberation from prosody," the so-called "science of metrication and versification," so that the focus fell firmly on the honest response of the individual reader. For both of our authors, the sources of meaning are immanent in the inquirer or reader—there is no other norm or criterion "out there" that the inquirer or reader can fall back on to guide their understanding or response. At the same time, neither falls into the Cartesian trap of privileging the private over the communal or public. Neither subscribes to the notion of the reader or inquirer as an isolated disembodied centre of consciousness looking out at the world and passing judgment upon it. For both what begins as a personal response can be shared with others, and indeed requires such sharing if a response is to be tested and verified and can ultimately become a public possession. Neither subscribes to Cartesian mind-body dualism. To that extent both are in agreement with Wittgenstein but it is worth noting that each of them developed his opposition to such dualism in a manner that differed from Wittgenstein: for whereas Wittgenstein developed his position by illustrating the absurdity of considering the meaningfulness of language to be primarily private and only derivatively public, Lonergan and Leavis developed their respective positions by exploring how what begins as a private response or insight is capable of being shared and communicated and, in this way, of becoming public. This approach enables them to explain how language changes and develops over time, something that Wittgensteinian analysis is not capable of doing since it works by studying how words are actually used in the language game which is their "original home" (P.I. 116).

The profound agreement I detect between Lonergan and Leavis lies in the way in which Leavis's approach to literary criticism shares the same *structure* as Lonergan's cognitional theory or transcendental method. The point of contrast here is Kant's use of the unconditioned in his theory of knowledge and Susanne Langer's development of a Kantian understanding of aesthetic judgment. The Kantian view is monistic—there is no distinction between understanding and judgment, no dualism of the data of sense and the understanding of the data, that is then overcome in judgment when the data and the understanding are posited as a unity—the data-as-carrying-this-meaning. It is the ability to test the explanation or interpretation against the data that makes Lonergan's epistemology *critical*; it is the ability to gauge or measure the validity of the emotional response manifested in a work of literature by comparing this with the artistic realisation of a justifying episode or event that provides Leavis with a genuine criterion of objectivity in the case of aesthetic judgment. In Kantian philosophy the intuitions of sense and the *a priori* operations of the understanding and reason simply complement each other and neither can function without the other, and for this reason a comparison or testing of one *against* the other, leading to verification, is not possible either in the case of knowledge claims or aesthetic judgments. Confronted with the question, How do we know that a particular work of art is truly symbolic of human feelings?, Susanne Langer can only point us to "intuition"; the validity of such intuition cannot be tested or verified, and it is difficult to see how intuition would allow us to compare one artist with another. For both Lonergan and Leavis, some form of verification or justification is required and it is the shape or structure taken by such verification or justification that enables the reader not only to form a judgment but actually to *measure artistic excellence* and, in this way, to be able to compare the merits of different literary artists, something Leavis did again and again throughout his life, something he clearly believed it was the duty or task of the literary critic to perform. It is this agreement regarding the structure of judgment—intellectual, moral or aesthetic—that allows me to claim that Lonergan's "transcendental method" underwrites Leavis's critical method, while Leavis's critical method vindicates Lonergan's "transcendental method" in the area of literary art.

Finally, Lonergan translates the four levels of transcendental method into the eight functional specialities that make up the tasks of theology, eight functional specialities that can also be seen to apply to literary criticism. As I have said, I have found that exploration of the functional specialities throws light on the central focus of Leavis's work as a critic and an educationist. For what the functional specialities do is provide the scholar with a method for investigating the past in order to bring it into a living and significant relationship with the present and the future. And this is what Leavis is about—the interpretation of poems, plays and novels in their given historical periods and, with his eye on the central criterion of self-transcendence, bringing the best that was known and said in the past into a living relationship with the present, since "it is only in the present that the past lives." As he got older, Leavis became more and more impatient with the term "academic" to the extent of saying, close to the end of his Richmond lecture, "I will only say that the academic is the enemy and that the academic *can* be beaten, as we who ran *Scrutiny* for twenty years proved."[6] These comments were made in the context of Leavis's advocacy of the English School in the university whose function would be to assist the university to be more than "a collocation of specialist departments—to make it a centre of human consciousness: perception, knowledge, judgment and responsibility."[7] What Leavis (and his fellow Scrutineers) were protesting against was any attempt to reduce English as a university discipline by holding up the ideal of textual editing, or narrow specialist studies of Anglo-Saxon or Renaissance literature, as one of the main tasks—perhaps *the* main task—performed by the English School. Instead, Leavis, driven by his earnest conviction, saw the main task of the English School as fostering in his students the pursuit of true judgment, collaboratively arrived at, based on their creative responses to poems, plays and novels; and this, in time, would help them "place" their judgments in relation to other judgments in the map of English literature. In short, Leavis saw the main tasks of an English school as corresponding to what Lonergan refers to as Dialectics (collaboration), Foundations (earnest conviction), Doctrines (established judgments), Systematics (placing or mapping) and, of course, Communications (discussing, sharing and publishing in "the common pursuit of true judgment")—the functional specialities that bring the past into a living relationship with the present and the future. Lonergan's functional specialities help to bring clarity to the whole field of endeavour; help us to see the various tasks in their relation to each other and how, together, they add up to a "form of knowledge" deserving of its place in the university curriculum, and one that can make valid claims to unique educational benefits.

These are all areas of profound agreement between our two authors. The main disagreement, I have to say, relates to their differing attitudes to religious belief. Lonergan was a man of profound religious faith whereas Leavis, as we noted earlier, remained an agnostic till his death, describing himself as "a Puritan without religion." Michael Tanner refers to the fact that in his seminars Leavis made no attempt to disguise his dislike of Christianity, despite the fact that his seminars frequently attracted Anglican and Catholic priests, and quotes him as saying, "However hard they try, they won't succeed in assimilating me to Christianity or The Anscombe." (The Catholic Wittgensteinian philosopher at Cambridge with whom Leavis worked at one point).[8] Now I have no wish to pass judgment on Leavis's espoused position here—in matters of religion a man, and certainly a man with Leavis's independence of mind, must be allowed to make his own decisions. But I do feel that certain features of Leavis's behaviour and conversations towards the end of his life might possibly betray a certain conflict at the heart of his own thinking that might explain aspects of his conversations and behaviour in his late years. L. C. Knights is quoted by Leavis as saying of him at this period in his life that he was "miserable," something Leavis attempted to deny.[9] But Tanner, who visited the Leavises frequently in Leavis's final years, says of

Leavis at this time "his monologues became longer, more soul-searching and more painful," and the picture that emerges is of someone who was deeply unhappy in some part of his psyche. Tanner goes on to say of Leavis during his final illness, "he was sunk in unapproachable and terrifying gloom. I can't imagine seeing anyone looking so desperate."[10]

I cannot help wondering if this deep despondency in Leavis at the end of his life might be associated with the cooling of his admiration for T. S. Eliot following Eliot's conversion to Anglican Christianity or to what Eliot preferred to call the "Catholic Church in England." For many years Leavis had taken a deserved pride in the fact that he was one of the few literary critics to recognise the poetic genius of *The Waste Land*, and that his critical appreciation of Eliot as a major poetic talent had helped to establish Eliot's reputation.[11] But in his relative old age Leavis turned against Eliot and his critical treatment of *Four Quartets* in a long essay in his penultimate book, *The Living Principle*, is devastating: although he continues to admire Eliot as a major poet whose technical virtuosity amounts to genius, he expresses a revulsion for Eliot's vision or message, which he attributes to a "variety of Christianity." His conclusion is that Eliot exhibits a "fear of life and contempt (which includes self-contempt) for humanity"[12] and describes him as "a divided man," someone whose "dividedness remains irremediable."[13] It is as if Leavis at this late stage in his life, experienced Eliot's conversion as a personal betrayal, despite the fact that Eliot was baptised and confirmed in 1927. This repugnance felt by Leavis in respect of Eliot's Christian faith is all the more startling when compared with his earlier exalted opinion of *Four Quartets* when it first appeared. Sebastian Moore writes that shortly after the appearance of "Little Gidding," Leavis said to him: "The only poetic development comparable to that of Eliot from *The Waste Land* to 'Little Gidding' is Shakepeare's."[14] Leavis held fast to the position he had set out in *New Bearings*, that "poetry matters because of the kind of poet who is more alive than other people, more alive in his own age. He is, as it were, at the most conscious point of the race in his time. . . . The potentialities of human experience in any age are realized only by a tiny minority, and the important poet is important because he belongs to this (and has, of course, the power of communication)."[15] In the same volume that he made these claims on behalf of poetry and poets, Leavis made it clear that the poet who had departed most radically from the ideal of the "poetical" entertained in the nineteenth century, the one who had taken the lead in forging a new form of consciousness, a consciousness attuned to the age in which he lived, was T. S. Eliot. It would seem not too speculative to associate Leavis's state of mind at the end of his life with the fact that on the ultimate question of "the meaning of life"—"What for? What ultimately for? What do men live by?"—he and the finest poet of the age, someone he referred to as "genius," were at odds with one another.

This is even more puzzling given Eliot's concern, shared by Leavis, with the quality of modern civilization. Not unlike Leavis, Eliot attacked a world system organised on the principle of private profit, which was leading to a form and scale of industrialisation which would damage the world of nature and for which future generations would have to pay the price.[16] This is a view widely held today on the basis of an abundance of evidence, but it was not commonly held or anticipated in the late 1930s. The difference between Leavis and Eliot was that Eliot's outlook was informed by his Christian faith, a point he made very clear in his prose works, in radio broadcasts, in his plays as well as in poems like *Ash Wednesday* and *Four Quartets*. He was deeply concerned with a society that disregarded traditional Christianity and pursued purely materialistic goals. He concluded his essay, *Thoughts after Lambeth*, by urging Christians to be patient so as to preserve the Faith in the dark ages to come and save the world from suicide.[17] In the same essay, Eliot remarks that the experiment of trying to form a civilization without Christianity at its heart would fail. This was a view that clashed fundamentally with Leavis's outlook and endeavours and would appear to have contributed to Leavis's rejection of Eliot's religious outlook, which he chose to express after Eliot's death.

Three of those who contributed to the same volume of reminiscences as Michael Tanner express grave reservations about Leavis's attitude to Eliot in his later writings. L. C. Knights, one of the founders of *Scrutiny* who had worked with Leavis over many years, suggests that Leavis was driven by "some force with a built-in guarantee of disappointment," and doubts whether even an English faculty "well stocked with men and women he had taught would have come anywhere near his ideal English school."[18] He concludes his memoir by observing that Leavis's later writings on Eliot's *Four Quartets* make "sad reading" because they betray "an animus against a man who in his greatest poem—and certainly with no less courage than Leavis's own—refused to simplify his sense either of what life can offer or of what we can do with what creative potential as we have."[19] In his essay, Knights links this trait in the older Leavis with his refusal "to accept much less than total endorsement."[20]

David Holbrook, another contributor to the volume of reminiscences, who became, like Leavis, Director of English Studies at Downing College, pays tribute to Leavis's influence in making English an important and serious discipline before turning his attention to the quality of Leavis's argument in his essay on Eliot's *Four Quartets*. He points out that Leavis's critical comments about Eliot's vision owe little to literary criticism and rest upon several philosophical positions which are not so much argued for or explored but rather assumed as being somehow unassailable. Leavis affirms that time is process and that life is process and, therefore, life cannot be conceived outside of time; time is essential to the reality of life as we know it. To yearn for a spiritual reality outside of time is vacuous, is to yearn for a "nullity." By way of support for his assertions about time, Leavis invokes R. G. Collingwood who affirmed that time is process. But, of course, Collingwood was an historian and a philosopher of history and what he was asserting concerned time as it is understood by the historian, time as we experience it on this earth. To move from that to a dismissal in the most strident terms of the notion of a reality and a life outside of time is not to provide proof or demonstration but simply to make assertions. And from there Leavis moves to assert that "The great drive behind his (Eliot's) creativity is desperation," the need he feels to "escape from transience." Holbrook's conclusion is that Leavis's negative critical judgment of *Four Quartets* was based on "philosophical and psychological principles which simply do not hold water"; and that these principles are not offered in an "open" manner for scrutiny or argument, but simply "as unquestionable axioms."[21]

Speaking personally, I have noticed the tendency in Leavis to relate a religious orientation to "a need"—in his comments on *Anna Karenina*, he refers to Tolstoy's "need for religious belief"—and in the case of Eliot Leavis was not above suggesting that the need was born of sexual inadequacy. That is why in his later lectures, following Eliot's death, he used to say that "Tom" Eliot's poetry was too much "up there"—pointing upwards—and not enough "down here"—pointing to the ground, or possibly to his crotch; and speaking of Eliot to the publisher, Michael Black, Leavis said, "There was something wrong with him down here," striking himself "well below the belt."[22]

Sebastian Moore is the third contributor to take issue with Leavis's treatment of *Four Quartets*. Moore shares L. C. Knights's judgment on the courage behind Eliot's religious conversion, noting that "Eliot said 'Yes'—at, I believe, deep personal cost; it did cost him 'not less than everything.'"[23] Moore suggests that Leavis might have projected onto Eliot his own dividedness; as he approached his own demise, it is possible that Leavis did wonder if he had always remained faithful to the central criterion of self-transcendence. In the volume of reminiscences, John Harvey refers to the fact that Leavis was troubled by his own formidable ego, and comments that "his victory over ego was at best an equivocal one."[24] And in the same volume Muriel Bradbrook remarks of the Leavises that "while hostile reviews . . . were taken as an affront, their own abrasive attacks were considered disinterested blows in a righteous cause."[25]

At a more philosophical level, a case can be made that, in his hostility to Christianity, Leavis experienced the sense of an inconsistency in his own philosophical outlook, an inconsistency that attacked his own fundamental criterion of excellence and purity of motive. For, as Lonergan and Matthew Arnold were aware, the criterion of self-transcendence—invoked time and again in Leavis's writings when judging character, authenticity and the quality of a poem or novel—would seem to have religious connotations: there is a sense in which the imperious quality of the demands made by the drive for truth and the desire for what is right points beyond itself and beyond mere human nature. As Arnold says of the pursuit of righteousness, "we feel we did not make it, that it discovered us, that it is what it is whether we will or no."[26] Leavis would appear to have shared Arnold's belief that "righteousness tendeth to life." But Arnold did not stop there. He saw in the notion and experience of *ratio recta*—which equates with self-transcendence—evidence of "the Eternal," "the enduring power, not ourselves, that makes for righteousness,"[27] just as he saw those who lived by and promoted *ratio recta* as "pliant organs of the infinite will."[28] These quotations reveal the Arnoldian understanding of God and his belief that *ratio recta* is that in human nature that is continuous with the divine nature itself; and this would explain how it is that our experience of self-transcendence moves us as it does, takes us out of ourselves and is experienced as of something that lies beyond ourselves. Arnold clearly believed that the human nisus or drive for righteousness, *ratio recta*, required some explanation. Leavis would appear to have agreed with his Victorian mentor up to a point, but despite the fact that "he associated literature with the hunger for ultimate meaning without which we would not be human,"[29] he appeared to feel the need to stop short of any declaration of theism.

Yet, despite his avowed agnosticism, Leavis is capable of describing the experience of tragedy as residing in "the willing adhesion of the individual self to something other than itself"[30], and he clearly endorsed the depiction of Tom Brangwen in *The Rainbow* where Lawrence says of Tom that "He knew he did not belong to himself."[31] As we saw in chapter four, Arnold's advocacy of "right reason" is a prominent feature both of his religious writings and of his comments on society and culture. The comments of Leavis quoted above can be explained within the religious framework of Matthew Arnold and T. S. Eliot; but are difficult to explain within the "this-worldly" agnostic framework Leavis formally espoused. They bear out the observation made by John Harvey that "What is both idiosyncratic and profound in Leavis's own best writing is the presence of a religious impulse which in another age might have been directed to God, but is here directed to civilization."[32]

Lonergan also finds that the "question of God" arises, not when we investigate the physical universe, but when we question our questioning, our drive for truth—a drive that, considered strictly as a drive, is unrestricted and seeks to know everything about everything. Lonergan faces up to the issue of how it is possible that our questioning can lead to full and satisfactory answers, whether they be questions about factual realities or questions about values and moral behaviour.[33] He too feels the need to account for the success of our questioning, the fact that we not only seek the truth but can know the truth: that there must be a source for the universe's intelligibility if its intelligibility is to be intelligible. As noted earlier, Lonergan's position is that "the intellectual, the moral and the religious are three phases in the single thrust to self-transcendence."[34]

Sebastian Moore, a monk who devoted many years to pondering the religious quest, makes a distinction that Leavis was quite blind to. Moore writes, "It has often been observed that there are two types of mystic: one whose sense for the transcendent is born of emotional wounding or deprivation . . . another for whom it is born of emotional fulfilment."[35] What Moore is suggesting here is that what Leavis takes to be Eliot's negative attitude to human life was not an expression of "a nullity" but a driving force towards "a sense for the transcendent" that provided the answer to the questions that challenged him. As Moore observes, Leavis appears to have felt that "creativity . . . has no place in it for surrender to another and altogether higher power," and quotes Leavis as saying that where Eliot said "Yes" to the ultimate question about life's meaning, Leavis said "'No' to Eliot."[36] What is surprising in Leavis's comment here is its personal nature, the focus on Eliot himself. Instead of saying, as we might have expected, that he said "No" to religion or "No" to Christianity, Leavis affirmed that he said "'No' to Eliot." It is this manner of expressing his standpoint that makes one ask if Leavis regarded Eliot's conversion as an act of betrayal; as if Eliot had somehow failed to acknowledge the debt he owed to Leavis! And certainly Leavis, and the Leavises, were not immune to feelings of having been betrayed where relationships with colleagues, former students and others were concerned.[37]

At the philosophical level the question remains: in saying "No" to Eliot, and in the manner that he did, was Leavis failing to account for, and be true to, the central criterion, that of self-transcendence, by means of which he passed judgment on literature and on life itself? Several commentators who knew him well commented on Leavis's religious sensibility or temperament—but it was a religious sensibility without religious belief. Could this be the explanation of his "final despair"?[38] Was it Leavis, and not Eliot, who was deeply conflicted and divided?

NOTES

1. *Anna Karenina and Other Essays*, p. 9 and p. 32.
2. *Anna Karenina and Other Essays*, p. 21–24.
3. *Anna Karenina and Other Essays*, p. 27.
4. These points occur in several places in Leavis's writings but are neatly summarised in his reply to Snow; see FRL, p. 74–75.
5. FRL, p. 75.
6. FRL, p. 75–6.
7. FRL, p. 75.
8. Michael Tanner, "Some recollections of the Leavises," op. cit., p. 133.

9. Tanner, "Some recollections," p. 136. Denys Thompson in the same volume says (p. 51) of Leavis in his old age that he looked "not so much old or ill as miserable and harassed."
10. Tanner, "Some recollections," p. 139.
11. See *New Bearings*, op. cit., chapter 3.
12. *The Living Principle*, p. 205.
13. *The Leavises*, op. cit., p. 207.
14. *The Leavises*, p. 64.
15. *New Bearings*, op. cit., p. 16.
16. See the reference to Eliot's *The Idea of a Christian Society*, published in 1939, in Geoffrey Elborn's article, "A Poet in search of the good life," The Tablet, 13 April 2019.
17. Eliot, "Thoughts after Lambeth" in *Selected Essays*, (London: Faber & Faber, 1951) p. 387.
18. L.C. Knights, "'Scrutiny' and F. R. L.," in *The Leavises*, op. cit., p. 80.
19. *The Leavises*, p. 81.
20. *The Leavises*, p. 81.
21. *The Leavises*, David Holbrook, "F. R. Leavis and the sources of hope," p. 159.
22. *The Leavises*, Michael Black, "The Long Pursuit," p. 97.
23. *The Leavises*, Sebastian Moore, "F. R. Leavis: a memoir," p. 66.
24. *The Leavises*, John Harvey, "Leavis: an appreciation," p. 181.
25. *The Leavises*, M. C. Bradbrook, "'Nor Shall My Sword': the Leavises' mythology," p. 34.
26. Arnold, *Literature and Dogma*, p. 37.
27. Arnold, *Literature and Dogma*, p. 46.
28. Arnold, *Culture and Anarchy*, p. 210.
29. Sebastian Moore, *The Leavises*, p. 60.
30. Leavis, *The Common Pursuit*, p. 131–2.
31. FRL, p. 69.
32. John Harvey, *The Leavises*, p. 181.
33. *Method*, p. 101–103. Lonergan writes, "In the measure that we advert to our own questioning and proceed to question it, there arises the question of God."
34. *Method*, p. 127.
35. *The Leavises*, p. 65.
36. *The Leavises*, p. 64, 66.
37. *The Leavises*: see the comments in this volume by D. W. Harding, p. 192–93, and by John Harvey, p. 182.
38. *The Leavises*: the phrase used by David Holbrook, p. 168.

Bibliography

Arnold, Matthew. *Culture and Anarchy*. Published 1869. Cambridge: Cambridge University Press, 1950.
———. *Essays in Criticism*. Published 1897. London, Macmillan and Co., 1921.
———. *Essays Literary and Critical*. London, Everyman, 1906.
———. *Essays Literary and Philosophical*. Ed. G. K. Chesterton. London,1907.
———. 'General Report for the Year 1876' in *Reports on Elementary Education 152–1882*. London: HMSO: 1908.
———. *God and the Bible*. London, 1875.
———. *Last Essays on Church and Religion*. London, 1877.
———. *Literature and Dogma*. London, 1873.
———. *St Paul and Protestantism*. London, 1873.
Ayer, A. J. *Language, Truth and Logic*. Published 1936. London, Victor Gollancz, 1967.
Bradley, F. H. *Ethical Studies*. Oxford: Oxford University Press paper back edition, 1962.
Burke Huey, Edmond. *The Psychology and Pedagogy of Reading*. New York: Macmillan and Co., 1908.
Casey, John. *The Language of Criticism*. London: Methuen and Co Ltd, 1966.
Charlton, W. *Metaphysics and Grammar*. London: Bloomsbury, 2014.
Chesterton, G. K. *St Francis of Assisi*. London: Hodder and Stoughton Ltd, 1923.
Chomsky, Noam. *Syntactic Structures*. The Hague: Monton, 1957.
Coleridge, S. T. *Constitution of Church and State*. London, 1839.
Crowe, F. E. *The Lonergan Enterprise*. Cowley: Cambridge Massachusets, 1980.
Eagleton, Terry. *Marxism and Literary Criticism*. London: Routledge Classics, 2002.
Eliot, T. S. *Selected Essays*. London: Faber and Faber Ltd., 1952.
———. 'Little Gidding' in *Four Quartets*. London: Faber and Faber, 1942.
Fenton, Charles A. *The Apprenticeship of Ernest Hemingway*. New York, 1954.
Fitzpatrick, Joseph. *Philosophical Encounters*: *Lonergan and the Analytical Tradition.* Toronto: University of Toronto Press, 2005.
Gifford, Henry. *Tolstoy*. Oxford: Oxford University Press, 1982.
Greenwod, E. B. *Tolstoy: The Comprehensive Vision*. London: Routledge, 1975.
Greene, Marjorie. *The Knower and the Known*. Basic Books, 1966.
Hardy, Barbara. *The Appropriate Form*. London: Bloomsbury, 2013.
Hemingway, Ernest. *In Our Time*. Boni and Liveright, 1925.
———. *The Sun Also Rises*. Scribner's, 1926. Published as *Fiesta.* London: Jonathan Cape, 1927.
———. *A Farewell to Arms*. Scribner's, 1929.
———. *Men Without Women*, Scribner's, 1929.

———. *Death in the Afternoon*. Published 1932.
———. *For Whom the Bell Tolls*. Charles Scribner's Sons, 1940.
———. *The Old Man and* the *Sea*. Charles Scribner's Sons, 1952.
Hick, John. Ed. *The Existence of God*. London: 1964.
Hume, David. *Enquiry Concerning Human Understanding*. Ed. L. A. Selby-Bigge. Oxford: Oxford University Press, 1975.
———. *Treatise of Human Nature*. Ed. L. A. Selby-Bigge. London: Clarendon Press, 1888.
Kenny, Anthony. *Aquinas*. Oxford: Oxford University Press, 1980.
———, ed. *The Oxford History of Philosophy*. London: QPD, 1994.
Keating, P. J. *Matthew Arnold: Selected Prose*. London: 1970.
Korner, S. *Kant*. London: Pelican Books, 1955.
Langer, S. K. *Philosophy in a New Key*. Harvard: Harvard University Press, 1942.
———. *Feeling and Form*. New York, 1953.
Lawrence, Fred. Ed. *Lonergan Workshop 16*. Boston: Boston College, 2000.
Leavis, F. R. *New Bearings in English Poetry*. London: Chatto and Windus, 1932; London: Penguin edition, 1982.
———. *Education and the University*. London: Chatto and Windus, 1943.
———. *The Great Tradition*. London: Chatto and Windus, 1948; London: Peregrine Books edition, 1966.
———. *The Common Pursuit*. London: Chatto and Windus, 1952; London: Hogarth Press, 1984.
———, ed. *Scrutiny*: A *Quarterly Review*. Reprinted in 20 volumes by Cambridge: Cambridge University Press.
———. *D. H. Lawrence: Novelist*. London: Chatto and Windus, 1955.
———. *Anna Karenina and Other Essays*. London: Chatto and Windus, 1973.
———. *The Living Principle: English as a Discipline of Thought*. London: Chatto and Windus, 1975.
———. *English Literature in Our Time and the University*. The Clark Lectures of 1967. Cambridge: Cambridge University Press, 1979.
———, ed. Singh, A. *The Critic as Anti-Philosopher*. London, 1982.
———. *Two Cultures?: The Significance of C. P. Snow*. Ed. Collini, S. Cambridge: Cambridge University Press, 2003.
Lonergan, Bernard. *Insight: A Study of Human Understanding*. 2nd ed. London: Longman, Green and Co., 1958; Volume 3 of Collected Works of Bernard Lonergan. Toronto: University of Toronto Press, 1992.
———, ed. Crowe, F. E. *Collection: Papers by Bernard Lonergan*. London: Darton, Longman and Todd, 1967. Reprinted as Vol. 4 of Collected Works of Bernard Lonergan, ed. F. E. Crowe and R. M. Doran. Toronto: University of Toronto Press, 1993.
———, ed. Burrell, David. *Verbum: Word and Idea in Aquinas*. London: Darton, Longman and Todd, 1968. Volume 2 of Collected Works of Bernard Lonergan. Totonto: University of Toronto Press, 1997.
———. *Method in Theology*. London: Darton, Longman and Todd, 1972. Volume 14 of Collected Works of Bernard Lonergan. Toronto: University of Toronto Press, 2017.
———. *Philosophy of God and Theology*. London: Darton, Longman and Todd, 1973.
———. Ed. Ryan, W. F. J. and Tyrrell, Bernard J., *A Second Collection*. London: Darton, Longman and Todd, 1974. Volume 13 of Collected Works of Bernard Lonergan. Toronto: University of Toronto Press, 2017.
———, ed. Crowe, F. E. *A Third Collection*. London: Geoffrey Chapman, 1985. Volume 16 of Collected Works of Bernard Lonergan. Totonto: University of Toronto Press, 2017.
McCarthy, Patrick J. *Matthew Arnold and the Three Classes*. New York and London, 1964.
McShane, Philip. *Foundations of Theology*. Dublin: Gill and Macmillan, 1971.
———. *Language, Truth and Meaning*. London: Gill and Macmillan, 1972.
Passmore, John. *One Hundred Years of Philosophy*. London: Penguin, 1968.
Polanyi, Michael. *Personal Knowledge*. London: Routledge and Kegan Paul, 1958.
Richards, I. A. *Principles of Literary Criticism*. Published 1924. London: Routledge and Kegan Paul, 1963.

Rorty, Richard. *Philosophy and the Mirror of Nature*. Oxford: Basil Blackwell, 1980.
Snedden, Elizabeth J. *The Eros of the Human Spirit: The Writings of Bernard Lonergan SJ*. New York: Paulist Press, 2017.
Snow, C. P. *The Two Cultures*. First published 1959. Ed. Collini, S. Cambridge: Cambridge University Press, 1998.
Smith, Frank. *Psycholinguistics and Reading*. New York: Holt, Reinhart and Winston, 1973.
———. *Understanding Reading*. New York: Holt, Reinhart and Winston, 1978.
———. *Reading*. Cambridge: Cambridge University Press, 1985.
———. *Writing and the Writer*. London: Heinemann Educational Books, 1982.
Southgate, V., Arnold, H., Johnson, S. *Extending Beginning Reading*. London: Heinemann Educational Books for the Schools Council, 1981.
Storer, R., MacKillop, I. Eds. *F. R. Leavis: Routledge Critical Thinkers* edition. London: Routledge, 2009.
Super, R. H. *The Complete Prose Works of Matthew Arnold*. Ann Arbor, 1962.
Tanner, Tony. *The Reign of Wonder*. Cambridge: Cambridge University Press, 1965.
Thompson, Denys. Ed. *The Leavises: Recollections and Impressions*. Cambridge: Cambridge University Press, 1984.
Tolstoy, Leo. *Anna Karenina*. Translated by Edmonds, R. London: Penguin, 1954.
Trilling, Lionel. *Matthew Arnold*. New York: Meridian Books, 1939.
Varden, Erik. The *Shattering of Loneliness: On Christian Remembrance*. London: Bloomsbury, 2018.
Vygotsky, L. S. *Thought and Language*. Massachusets: Massachusets Institute of Technology Press, 1962.
Walsh, William. *F. R. Leavis*. Chatto and Windus, 1980.
Willey, B. *Nineteenth Century Studies: Coleridge to Matthew Arnold*. London: Chatto and Windus, 1949. Penguin, 1973.
Wilson, A. N. *Tolstoy*. London: Penguin, 1989.
Wittgenstein, L. *Tractatus Logico-Philosophicus*. First published 1922. Trans. Pears, D. F and McGuinness, B. F. London: Routledge, 1974.
———. *Philosophical Investigations*. Trans. Anscombe, G.E.M. Oxford: Basil Blackwell, 1953.
———. *On Certainty*. Trans. Paul, D. and Anscombe, G.E.M. Oxford: Basil Blackwell, 1979.

Index

Anscombe, G.E.M., 36n5, 196
Aquinas, Thomas, 10, 15, 36n2
aristocracy, 101–102, 106
Aristotle, 10, 15
Arnold, Matthew, 3, 33, 48, 188, 199;
    Chapter 4 *passim*
authenticity,. *See* self-transcendence 78
Ayer, A.J., 68

behaviourism, 158–159
Bradley, F.H., 128
bullfight, 166, 169
Byrne, Patrick, 6n7

Casey, John, 82, 96n28
Charlton, W., 156n50
Chesterton, G.K., 129, 133n2
Chomsky, N., 148, 156n50
class divisions, 106
classicism, 50, 51–52
Collingwood, R.G., 3, 198
conceptualist, 10
conversion, 5, 10, 59, 60, 126, 127; chapter
    7 *passim*
consciousness, 21–22, 71, 151, 192; levels
    of, 12, 71–72
critical realism, 26, 27
Crowe, Frederick, 64, 125
culture, 73, 100–101, 102, 104

data, 8; of sense, 8; of consciousness, 10

decline, 111
democracy, 101–102, 102–103
Descartes, R., 13–14; cartesian dualism,
    14–15

Eagleton, Terry, 61–62, 172
earnest conviction, 60
Eliot, George, 83, 91
Eliot, T.S., 73, 197, 198–199, 200, 201
emotivism, 22, 166
empiricism, 20–21, 68, 69, 157–158
English school, department, 44

feelings: nature of, 63, 71
functional speciality: eight in number, 29,
    63, 71, 195

Hemingway, Ernest, 4, 5, 191, 192; chapter
    6 *passim*
Holbrook, David 198
heuristic structure, 143
Hume, David, 18, 21, 22, 157–158, 165

idea: notion of, 14
idealism, 26–27
intellectualist, 10
intention, intentionality, 141, 148–149, 192
inwardness, interiority, 87, 95, 112–113,
    132, 192, 193

Kant, Immanuel, 24–26

Knights, L.C., 196, 198
knowledge, 8, 9, 69, 138

Langer, S.K., 3, 80–82, 194
language: essentially public, 17–19; and meaning, 140–141, 147; linguistic change, 18, 19, 20
Lawrence, D.H., 56, 91, 166, 175, 200
Leavis, F.R., 1–5, 16, 19, 39–40, 41, 42–45, 180, 187, 191–199, 200–201; critical method, 53–54, 56, 57, 58, 75, 77, 78, 83
logical positivism, 1, 57, 158
Lonergan, Bernard, 1–5, 40, 45, 188, 192–196, 199, 200; chapter 1 *passim*; cognitional theory, 8–10; transcendental method, 11–12, 25, 29–31, 87; and Wittgenstein, 16–18; and Hume, 21–22; and Kant, 24–26

marxism, 57, 61, 62, 164
Moore, Sebastian, 5, 201

naturalism, 27, 159–160, 161

objectivity,. *See also* subjectivity 10–11, 56, 83

poetry,: reading of, 54, 75–76, 77

Polanyi, Michael, 16, 41
progress, 109, 111

religion, 60, 94, 103, 112, 163, 200, 201; Matthew Arnold on, 114–127, 199
right reason, ratio recta, 105, 106, 107, 113, 194

self-transcendence, 10, 55–56, 61, 78, 94, 112, 201
Snow, C.P. 73; controversy with Leavis, 83–95
Steinbeck, John, 170
subject, subjectivity, 10, 28, 51, 56

Tolstoy, Leo, 164, 189n14, 191; chapter 7 *passim*
tragedy, dramatic, 55, 94, 200
Trilling, L., 90, 135n77

university, 44. *See also* controversy with Leavis

Vico, G., 69
Vygotsky, S., 69

Wellek, R., 75
Wittgenstein, Ludwig, 10–16, 19–20, 36n4, 194

About the Author

Joseph Fitzpatrick is a philosophy and theology graduate of the Gregorian University, Rome, where Lonergan was a professor; he also graduated in English Literature at Cambridge University, where Leavis worked and taught for most of his life. He taught English literature at high school and college and was for many years a member of Her Majesty's Inspectorate of Schools. He lives in West Yorkshire, England. His two previous books are *Philosophical Encounters: Lonergan and the Analytical Tradition* (2005) and *The Fall and the Ascent of Man: How Genesis Supports Darwin* (2012).

Printed in Great Britain
by Amazon